Legalines

Editorial Advisors:
Gloria A. Aluise
Attorney at Law
David H. Barber
Attorney at Law
Jonathan Neville
Attorney at Law
Robert A. Wyler
Attorney at Law

Authors:
Gloria A. Aluise
Attorney at Law
David H. Barber
Attorney at Law
Daniel O. Bernstine
Professor of Law
D. Steven Brewster
C.P.A.
Roy L. Brooks
Professor of Law
Scott M. Burbank
C.P.A.
Jonathan C. Carlson
Professor of Law
Charles N. Carnes
Professor of Law
Paul S. Dempsey
Professor of Law
Ronald W. Eades
Professor of Law
Jerome A. Hoffman
Professor of Law
Mark R. Lee
Professor of Law
Jonathan Neville
Attorney at Law
Laurence C. Nolan
Professor of Law
Arpiar Saunders
Professor of Law
Lynn D. Wardle
Professor of Law
Robert A. Wyler
Attorney at Law

CRIMINAL LAW

Adaptable to Sixth Edition of Kadish Casebook

By Frank L. Bruno
and
Gloria A. Aluise
Attorneys at Law

A COMPLETE PUBLICATIONS CATALOG IS
FEATURED AT THE BACK OF THIS BOOK.

HARCOURT BRACE LEGAL AND PROFESSIONAL PUBLICATIONS, INC.
EDITORIAL OFFICES: 176 W. Adams, Suite 2100, Chicago, IL 60603

Legalines

REGIONAL OFFICES: New York, Chicago, Los Angeles, Washington, D.C.
Distributed by: **Harcourt Brace & Company** 6277 Sea Harbor Drive, Orlando, FL 32887 (800)787-8717

SERIES EDITOR
Astrid E. Ellis, J.D.
Attorney at Law

PRODUCTION COORDINATOR
Sanetta Hister

SHORT SUMMARY OF CONTENTS

TABLE OF CONTENTS AND SHORT REVIEW OUTLINE

VII. GROUP CRIMINALITY

I. THE PROCESS OF ESTABLISHING GUILT

A. SUBSTANCE AND PROCEDURE

The study of criminal law includes examination of specific crimes and defenses as well as the procedures followed to apply sanctions against those who commit the crimes. The two areas of criminal law are normally studied separately in law school. As the cases studied in substantive courses all involve some procedural considerations, a brief overview of the criminal justice system is critical even in a course on substantive criminal law. Largely due to the overriding mandates of the United States Constitution, the procedural rules of each state and the federal government are similar; still, important variations exist which should not be forgotten even if beyond the scope of this brief overview.

B. TYPICAL STATE PROCEDURE

1. **Offense.** The criminal justice system reacts to criminal conduct. The process begins when an offense is reported to the police. Investigators gather evidence, testimonial, tangible, or otherwise, with the objective of determining who perpetrated the crime. One significant procedural issue that frequently arises at this stage involves searches and seizures.

2. **Arrest.** Once sufficient evidence is gathered to constitute probable cause that an identified person committed the crime, the suspect may be arrested with or without a warrant, depending on the circumstances. The arresting officer takes the suspect into custody and brings him to the police station.

3. **The Charge.** The police ask the district attorney to make out a formal charge and an affidavit, which is a written complaint charging the accused with a specified crime or crimes. A complaint is prepared in advance when a person is arrested under a warrant because it is used to obtain the warrant.

4. **Proceedings Before a Magistrate.** After arrest, the accused is taken before the committing magistrate, a municipal court judge for example, who advises the accused of her rights and sends her back to jail or allows her to post bond. If the charge is a misdemeanor, the accused is immediately arraigned and must plead to the charge. If the charge is a felony, the accused normally does not have to plead; instead, a date is set for a preliminary hearing.

5. **Preliminary Hearing.** When a felony is charged, the accused is entitled to a preliminary hearing to determine whether there are sufficient grounds to bind the accused over for a trial.

    a. **Sufficient evidence.** The committing magistrate rules on the evidence. If the critical evidence is suppressed for some reason at this point, then the accused may be set free and the charge dismissed. The accused has a chance to cross-examine the prosecution's evidence, which is an important discovery technique.

    b. **Decision.** If the committing magistrate finds that the evidence is sufficient, the accused is committed.

    c.   **Writ of prohibition.** If the magistrate finds sufficient evidence, the accused may bring a writ of prohibition to appeal the magistrate's findings.

6.   **Indictment.** As an alternative to a preliminary hearing, the prosecution may seek an indictment. The prosecuting attorney presents a written accusation to an investigatory body, such as a grand jury. An indictment is simply a finding made by the grand jury that there is sufficient evidence to warrant a conviction of the crime. A grand jury indictment may either precede or follow arrest. The prosecution may choose the indictment procedure when it wants to keep its information confidential, because in most states the accused does not have the opportunity to appear or to challenge the prosecution's evidence.

7.   **Accusatory Pleading.** The prosecution of the case commences once the government files either an indictment or an information. An information is simply the written charge on which the accused will be tried.

8.   **Arraignment.** Once the pleading is filed, the accused is brought before the court and informed of the charges. The accused then pleads to the charge.

9.   **Motions and Pleas.** The accused is normally permitted to make certain motions of one of several different pleas.

    a.   **Motions.** The accused may file a demurrer, or a challenge to the legal sufficiency of the accusatory pleading, such as that the court lacks jurisdiction or that no crime is alleged. Other motions include ones to quash or set aside the indictment or information, to dismiss, to change venue to another court, to obtain discovery, or to suppress certain evidence.

    b.   **Pleas.** If the charges hold up after consideration of the motions, the accused may plead guilty, not guilty, or nolo contendere, which is the same as pleading guilty except that the conviction cannot be used in subsequent civil proceedings.

10.   **Discovery.** Normally, both sides continue the fact-finding process to prepare for trial. The parties use the discovery process to find out as much as possible about the opposition's case.

11.   **Extraordinary Writs.** The accused may file certain extraordinary writs before trial begins. The writ of prohibition is an appeal to a higher court to terminate the judicial process, normally on the basis of a lack of proper jurisdiction in the lower court. The other writ in common use is that of habeas corpus ("bring forth the body"), which tests any restraint that is contrary to "fundamental law," *e.g.,* to the state constitution.

12.   **Trial.** Numerous procedural issues arise during the trial process, including the following:

    a.   The competency of the accused to stand trial, as well as the sanity of the accused at the time of the offense.

    b.   The accused's right to counsel.

    c.   The right to trial by jury and the selection of jurors.

d. The right to a fair trial.

e. The accused's and the witnesses' privilege against self-incrimination, including the accused's right not to testify as a witness at all.

f. The right to compulsory process to obtain witnesses.

g. The right to confront accusers and cross-examine witnesses.

h. Issues relating to trial of two or more accused persons in the same trial; to more than one trial of the same accused for the same criminal act; and to the trial of the same accused for more than one crime arising from the same act.

i. Evidence questions relating to the introduction or order of evidence, the burden of proof, motions, jury instructions, etc.

j. The verdict, the sentence, and the entry of judgment by the court.

13. **Sentencing.** Ordinarily the judge has substantial discretion in determining the appropriate sentence. However, modern statutes sometimes set a minimum sentence as well as a maximum sentence for a particular offense.

14. **Post-trial Motions.** Typically, the accused who has been convicted may assert several post-trial motions, including a motion to vacate because the judgment was based on erroneous facts or was obtained by fraud or deceit, and a motion for a new trial.

15. **Appeal.** Most states grant a first appeal from a criminal conviction as a matter of right. Other appeals may also be available.

16. **Habeas Corpus.** The writ of habeas corpus is available at any stage of the criminal process.

C. FEDERAL PROCEDURE

1. **Similarities to State Procedure.** In many respects, federal criminal procedure resembles state procedure. In fact, the Federal Rules of Evidence and Federal Rules of Criminal Procedure have served as models for state procedure. A few of the significant rules are discussed below. (Remember that only federal crimes are prosecuted in the federal system.)

2. **Arrest.** A warrant may be issued on presentation of a complaint by the United States Attorney, identifying the crime and the accused. [Fed. R. Crim. P. 4(a)] A valid arrest may also be made without a warrant where there is probable cause.

3. **Appearance Before a Magistrate.** If the accused was arrested without a warrant, then a complaint is prepared. If a warrant was used, the complaint was previously prepared. The accused is next brought before a magistrate. This must be done without unnecessary delay. [Fed. R. Crim. P. 5(a)]

4. **Preliminary Examination.** Preliminary examinations are also held before a magistrate. [Fed. R. Crim. P. 5(c)]

5. **Grand Jury Indictment.** If a grand jury has returned an indictment against the accused, he is not entitled to a preliminary examination, except that Fed. R. Crim. P. 5(c) provides that if a person is taken into custody before the indictment is given, he is entitled to a preliminary examination. This avoids the problem of a lengthy holding of a defendant waiting for a grand jury.

6. **Arraignment.** The accused is arraigned in federal district court.

7. **Motions and Pleas.** Under Fed. R. Crim. P. 12, the motion to dismiss is used in place of all other motions discussed above under state procedure. This motion attacks all possible defects.

D.   HOW A CASE IS PROVED

1. **Presenting Evidence.**

   a. **Introduction.** Rules governing the admissibility of evidence are fairly complex, and a complete discussion is beyond the scope of this outline. However, a fundamental rule is that evidence which is not relevant is not admissible. To be relevant, evidence must be both material and probative, meaning that the proposition to be proved affects the outcome of the case and that the evidence tends to establish the proposition. Even relevant evidence may be inadmissible if its prejudicial effect outweighs its probative value, or if the evidence is privileged information, or if it is prohibited because of the exclusionary rule.

People v.
Zackowitz

   b. **Character evidence--People v. Zackowitz,** 254 N.Y. 192, 172 N.E. 466 (1930).

      1) **Facts.** Zackowitz (D) admitted killing Coppola, who had insulted D's wife by propositioning her on the street. D warned Coppola to leave the street when he learned of the insult, then accompanied his wife to their apartment, where she told D exactly what Coppola had said. D was enraged again and returned to the street, which Coppola had not left. D began fighting Coppola and shot him. D claimed he acted in self-defense. He had been drinking that night. D told the police that he had armed himself with a pistol at the apartment, but at trial he claimed he had carried the pistol in his pocket all evening. In order to show that D had a criminal inclination, the state introduced evidence that D kept three pistols and a tear-gas gun in his apartment. Under state law a killing provoked in the fury of the fleeting moment was first degree manslaughter as opposed to first degree murder, which required a deliberate and premeditated murder. D was convicted of first degree murder and appeals, claiming the introduction of character evidence was prejudicial error.

2) **Issue.** May the state by itself make character an issue in a criminal prosecution?

3) **Held.** No. Judgment reversed and a new trial ordered.

   a) The basic rule is that character is not an issue in a criminal prosecution unless brought into issue by the defendant. The purpose is to avoid the danger to the innocent that would result from making character probative of crime. A defendant may not be proved guilty by proof of character.

   b) Here, D admitted killing the victim and the only question was his state of mind. Ownership of weapons left at home does not indicate a murderous disposition, especially in light of D's explanation that he was a collector. The likelihood that the jury would condemn such possession regardless of D's guilt of the crime charged is a sufficient ground for reversal for prejudicial error.

4) **Dissent.** The evidence was admissible to show that D may have formed a murderous intent before he left the apartment (*i.e.,* he chose a particular weapon before leaving). If possession is a separate crime, that does not render the evidence inadmissible.

2. Standard of Proof.

a. **Introduction.** Generally, the fact finder in a civil trial may base its findings on a preponderance of the evidence. In criminal trials, however, the defendant is presumed innocent. To convict, therefore, a jury must find the defendant guilty beyond a reasonable doubt. The conviction must be based on proof beyond a reasonable doubt of every fact required to make up the crime charged. This high standard of proof reflects the serious consequences of a criminal conviction, which should not attach to a person when there is a reasonable doubt about guilt.

b. **Allocating the burden of proof--Patterson v. New York,** 432 U.S. 197 (1977).

1) **Facts.** Patterson (D) was charged with second degree murder and at trial raised the affirmative defense of extreme emotional disturbance which, if successful, would result in a verdict of manslaughter. Consistent with New York law, the trial court instructed the jury that D had the burden of proving his affirmative defense by a preponderance of the evidence. The jury found D guilty of murder and the appellate division affirmed. D appealed on the basis that requiring D to prove his affirmative defense is an improper shifting of the burden of persuasion from the prosecutor to the defendant and is therefore a violation of due process.

2) **Issue.** Is it unconstitutional under the Fourteenth Amendment's Due Process Clause for a state to require a criminal defendant to prove an affirmative defense which does not serve to negate any facts of the crime which the state is to prove in order to convict?

3) **Held.** No. Judgment affirmed.

    a) To recognize a mitigating circumstance does not thereby require the state to prove its nonexistence in each case in which the fact is put in issue, if in the state's judgment this would be too cumbersome, too expensive, and too inaccurate.

    b) However, the state may not shift the burden of persuasion with respect to a fact which the state deems so important that it must be either proved or presumed in order to convict a defendant of the crime.

4) **Dissent** (Powell, Brennan, Marshall, JJ.).

    a) The state may not shift the burden of proof to the defendant if the following two factors exist: (i) the factor at issue makes a substantial difference in punishment and stigma; (ii) the factor in question historically has been held to be of great importance in the Anglo-American legal tradition.

    b) To avoid this two-step test by leaving a factor out of the statutory elements of a crime is to undermine the presumption of innocence and to establish form over substance.

c. **Use of presumptions.** Presumptions may allow a fact finder to infer a fact not proved from a fact actually proved. This evidentiary sense of the term is distinct from the term when used, for example, in the phrase, "presumed innocent until proven guilty." The latter usage merely is a way to state that the prosecution must prove guilt. The evidentiary presumptions, however, may allow the prosecution to prove guilt without actually proving every critical fact, when permissible inferences may be drawn from the facts proved.

3. The Jury's Responsibility.

a. **Introduction.** The jury has the responsibility of hearing all the evidence, receiving instructions from the judge about the law, and then applying the law in finding facts and making the ultimate decision of guilt or innocence.

    1) **Constitutional provisions.**

        a) **Article III, section 2.** "The trial of all Crimes, except in Cases of Impeachment, shall be by jury . . . ."

        b) **Sixth Amendment.** "In all criminal prosecutions, the accused shall enjoy the right to speedy and public trial, by an impartial jury of the State and district wherein the crime shall have been committed."

    2) **Effect.** By virtue of Article III, section 2 and the Sixth Amendment, a defendant charged in a federal court with any serious offense (as distinguished from a "petty" offense under the common law) is entitled to trial by jury.

3) **Serious vs. petty offenses.** Because the Sixth Amendment guarantees a jury trial only where a serious offense is charged, it becomes necessary to distinguish between "serious" and "petty" offenses. The court looks to the nature of the offense and the maximum potential sentence.

4) **Number of jurors.** The number of jurors in federal criminal trials is 12, but this is by statute [Fed. R. Crim. P. 23] and is not constitutionally required. State rules allowing use of fewer than 12 jurors (in noncapital cases) have been upheld. [Williams v. Florida, 399 U.S. 78 (1970)]

b. **Application to the states--Duncan v. Louisiana,** 391 U.S. 145 (1968).

1) **Facts.** Duncan (D), a black youth, was accused of battery on a white youth, but he claimed that all he had done was touch the white person on the elbow. Louisiana state law provided a jury trial guarantee only for capital punishment or where imprisonment at hard labor could be imposed. Battery was punishable by only up to two years in prison and a $300 fine; D's request for a jury trial was denied. D was convicted and appealed, claiming that his denial of a jury trial denied him due process of law.

2) **Issue.** May a state deny a jury trial in a criminal prosecution if D would receive a jury trial had the trial been in a federal court?

3) **Held.** No. Reversed.

a) D is entitled to a jury trial. The Sixth Amendment right to a jury trial in all criminal cases was applicable to the states in all situations where, if the trial were to have been brought in federal courts, such a jury trial would have been given. This was a "fundamental right," but also was within the scope of the Bill of Rights.

4) **Dissent** (Harlan, Stewart, JJ.). The opportunity was taken by the court in this case to act as a laboratory. This Court is available to correct any experiments in criminal procedure that prove fundamentally unfair to defendants.

c. **The jury's inherent prerogative to acquit--United States v. Dougherty,** 473 F.2d 1113 (D.C. Cir. 1972).

1) **Facts.** Dougherty and others (Ds) entered offices of Dow Chemical Co. and destroyed property in protest of the Vietnam War. Ds were charged with malicious destruction. At their trial, Ds requested an instruction that the jury could disregard the court's instructions even as to matters of law. The judge refused to give Ds' requested instruction, and Ds were convicted. Ds appeal.

2) **Issue.** Does a defendant have a right to have the jury instructed that it may acquit regardless of the law and the evidence?

3) **Held.** No. Judgment affirmed.

a) A jury has the prerogative to bring in a general verdict of not guilty in a criminal case, regardless of the law and the evidence. The court may not reverse such an action. The prerogative is allowed so that juries may refuse to convict a person who is guilty when the criminal law violated is unjust or otherwise unacceptable.

    b) However, the jury may not be specifically instructed about this prerogative. Otherwise the prerogative could be overused and result in anarchy. The prerogative remains as a last resort which will be used only in extreme circumstances.

    4)   **Dissent in part.** If the jury has this prerogative, which it does, it should be properly informed to use it.

4. Counsel's Responsibility.

    a.   **Competence.** Although the Supreme Court has held that defendants have a right to "effective and substantial aid" from counsel, development of a usable standard is difficult. Generally, the early test of "gross incompetence" has been replaced by a "reasonably effective" test, but defendant must also show that the adversarial process was so undermined by counsel's conduct that the trial produced an unjust result.

    b.   **Ethical duties.** The Code of Professional Responsibility requires a lawyer to represent the client zealously within the bounds of the law. This prohibits the use of fraudulent, false, or perjured testimony or evidence. At the same time, defense counsel must obtain the confidence of defendants and not disclose information provided in the attorney-client relationship. Difficult problems arise when defendants insist on testifying with the intent to lie under oath and counsel knows about the lie.

Nix v.
Whiteside

    c.   **Counsel's refusal to let the client commit perjury--Nix v. Whiteside,** 475 U.S. 157 (1986).

    1)   **Facts.** During preparations for his murder trial, Whiteside (P) told Robinson, his defense attorney, that he was convinced the victim had a gun, although P had not actually seen it. No gun was found and no other witness saw a gun. Then just before trial, P told Robinson that he had seen "something metallic" in the victim's hand, and that, if he didn't say he saw a gun, he'd be "dead." Robinson refused to allow P to commit perjury and told P he would withdraw from the case if P did so and would advise the court about his reason for withdrawing. P testified that he did not actually see a gun. P was convicted. After state appeals failed, P sought federal habeas corpus relief for lack of effective assistance of counsel. The district court denied relief, the court of appeals reversed, and the Supreme Court granted certiorari.

    2)   **Issue.** Does a defense attorney's successful effort to prevent his client from committing perjury provide a basis for a claim of ineffective assistance of counsel?

    3)   **Held.** No. Judgment reversed.

    a) Mere breach of an ethical standard does not necessarily constitute a denial of the Sixth Amendment guarantee of assistance of counsel. Standards of professional conduct are established by the states, not the Constitution. However, virtually all such standards include a specific exception from the attorney-client privilege for disclosure of a client's perjury. The attorney is required, not just permitted, to disclose such perjury. Thus, Robinson's conduct did not constitute serious attorney error under *Strickland*.

b) P also asserted a due process claim. The only thing that P was deprived of in this case was his contemplated perjury. But there is no constitutional right to testify falsely. [*See* Harris v. New York, 401 U.S. 222 (1971)] Robinson's conduct did not force P into an impermissible choice between the right to counsel and the right to testify because P had no permissible choice to testify falsely. Even if the jury might have believed P's perjury, he was not prejudiced by his inability to try to deceive them.

4) **Concurrence** (Brennan, J.). The only issue is whether Robinson's conduct deprived P of a fair trial. The knowledge that P refrained from giving false testimony does not undermine the Court's confidence in the outcome of P's trial. Hence, P was not deprived of a fair trial and has suffered no prejudice. Indeed, if the jury or judge had seen him lie, and known he was lying, his fate could have been worse.

II. CRIMINAL PUNISHMENT

A. PURPOSES OF PUNISHMENT

1. **Introduction.** Criminal laws are enacted in recognition of the fact that certain types of conduct have the effect of disrupting social order and infringe on the rights of others. Some form of punishment is affixed to violations of the criminal laws, but the justification for such punishment is not always apparent.

Regina v.
Dudley and
Stephens

    a. **Application--Regina v. Dudley and Stephens,** 14 Q.B.D. 273 (1884).

        1) **Facts.** Four shipwreck survivors in a lifeboat went days without food and water. Dudley and Stephens suggested killing the youngest member; the third person on board refused; finally Dudley and Stephens killed the 17-year-old boy, who was too weak to resist or assent. The three fed off of the dead body. The jury found that the three survivors, who were picked up four days later, would not have survived otherwise. The legal effect of the fact finding was left to the court.

        2) **Issue.** Does the extreme necessity of saving one person's life justify taking another's?

        3) **Held.** No. Hunger is not an excuse for taking the life of another person.

           a) The argument is only successful when protecting oneself against an offending party. Here, the victim was innocent of any wrongdoing toward his murderers.

        4) **Comment.** Although sentenced to die, the three were pardoned by the Queen.

        5) **Query.** What is the purpose of punishment in this type of situation? Will it deter such events in the future? Is the purpose restraint? Rehabilitation? Or is it simply retribution for a "wrong"?

2. **Retribution.** The retribution theory of punishment states that a criminal must be punished for the "wrong he has committed." This theory of punishment looks to the past and not to the future, and rests solely upon the foundation of vindictive justice.

3. **Deterrence.**

    a. **Introduction.** Punishment serves many functions for society. One belief of penologists is that by punishing those who commit acts condemned by society, others will be deterred from committing similar acts for fear of the punishment which will result from their acts.

b. **Value structure.** Society's demand that certain acts be punished expresses its collective belief in the wrongfulness of some acts. Failure to punish these wicked acts has the effect of endorsing acts that are contrary to society's value structure of what is right and what is wrong.

c. **Forms of deterrence.** There are many possible forms. Social embarrassment is one (antitrust violators suffer social disgrace, for example); in other words, the sentence means little but the conviction means a lot. And, in murder cases, an indictment alone is often as much of a stigma as would be a conviction in some other crimes.

d. **Summary comments on deterrence.** Deterrence theories furnish the most widely accepted rationale of the practice of punishment. According to these theories, punishment should not be designed to exact retribution upon convicted offenders but to deter the commission of future offenses. However, most studies indicate that severity of punishment has only a slight effect in deterring crime. For example, white-collar business crimes and drug trafficking are two types of crimes for which there is no evidence that fear of lengthy incarceration affects any significant number of criminal decisions. More important in deterring crime is increased certainty of arrest, conviction, and imprisonment. Certainty and severity of punishment together operate as the most effective deterrents of crime. Either one alone is ineffective.

4. **Rehabilitation.**

a. **Introduction.** Punishment has purposes in addition to retribution and/or crime deterrence. Penology also seeks to reform the criminal to become a useful member of society.

b. **Conflicting purposes.** Penology is in constant tension between the purposes or ends it seeks to serve. Should deterrence be given supremacy? Should rehabilitation? Should retribution? It would be a paradox if the main purpose of providing punishment for murder was to reform the murderer, not to prevent the murder. Yet, rehabilitation is an important, though elusive, goal.

5. **Segregation.** An additional goal of the criminal law is to protect society by segregating the criminal offender from general society, thereby limiting the number of people against whom he can commit further crimes.

6. **Summary.** The purpose of the criminal law is to protect the public interest by preventing certain undesirable conduct. There are differing theories of punishment. Retribution focuses primarily on the nature of the offense and its condemnation by society. Retribution has little support today, while rehabilitation, at least in theory, has become the chief goal of penology.

B. **DETERMINING AN APPROPRIATE PUNISHMENT**

1. **Introduction.** The philosophical debate over the purpose of punishment provides at best broad, generalized guidelines for determining an appropri-

ate punishment in a particular case. Until recently, most of the sentencing responsibility rested with the trial judges. Modern trends disperse the sentencing authority through specific sentencing statutes, administrative sentencing guidelines, etc.

United States
v. Bergman

2.   Deterrence--United States v. Bergman, 416 F. Supp. 496 (S.D.N.Y. 1976).

a.   **Facts.** Bergman (D) was a prominent clergyman who owned and operated rest homes. He was indicted for defrauding the federal government by submitting falsified medicare claims. As part of a complicated plea bargain, he agreed to plead guilty to two counts of an 11-count indictment. The case was the subject of much public interest and attention by the press, and D submitted material to argue against a prison sentence. D was 64 years old and was in somewhat ill health.

b.   **Issue.** In setting a sentence, may a court consider such social policies as deterring other *potential* lawbreakers and not deprecating the seriousness of the criminal's crime?

c.   **Held.** Yes. Prison sentence of four months is imposed.

1)   Rehabilitation is rarely served through imprisonment, but is now generally attempted through other means alternative to or parallel with imprisonment.

2)   It is appropriate to imprison a lawbreaker to deter others from committing the same offense, since they have broken the law by their free choice and are not merely punished as examples for others.

3)   The seriousness of the offense would be reduced both in the minds of the public and the offender if penalties were not imposed.

4)   Alternative charitable service cannot be substituted for imprisonment in this case because to do so would be to grant deferential treatment to D because of his prestige and social prominence.

5)   D's harsh treatment in the press cannot serve as punishment, since the treatment resulted mainly in a loss of the high esteem that the press now felt had been wrongly conferred because of ignorance of D's transgressions.

6)   The term was set at four months because of the health and age of D as well as the fact that a violation of the law in the future was highly unlikely.

d.   **Comment.** In *Browder v. United States*, 398 F. Supp. 1042 (D. Or. 1975), D was convicted of a white-collar offense involving $500,000 in stolen securities. D was sentenced to 25 years' imprisonment. He petitioned the federal court to set aside the sentence as cruel and unusual because most white-collar criminals are fined rather than imprisoned. The court upheld the sentence and expressed dismay that sophisticated white-collar criminals were not generally sentenced in proportion to the societal costs of their crimes.

3. **Insignificant Sentence Fails to Fulfill Purpose of Punishment--State v. Chaney**, 477 P.2d 441 (Alaska 1970).

    a. **Facts**. Chaney (D) was convicted of two counts of forcible rape and one count of robbery. The presentence report included D's version of the offenses, including D's statement that he was not violent and the acts were not forcible or against the victim's will. The report also included a recommendation by the Division of Corrections that parole be denied. The prosecutor recommended concurrent seven-year sentences with two years suspended for the rapes, and a five-year consecutive term for the robbery, all suspended with probation. The judge imposed concurrent one-year sentences and stated that it would be satisfactory for the Parole Board to grant parole as soon as 10 days from the date of sentencing. The State of Alaska (P) appeals, claiming the sentence was too lenient.

    b. **Issue**. Does a sentence of the minimum permissible term, together with comments from the sentencing judge encouraging early parole, fulfill the purposes of criminal punishment?

    c. **Held**. No. Judgment affirmed but disapproved.

        1) An appeal by the prosecution of a criminal sentence cannot result in any increase in the sentence, but it does permit the appellate court to formally approve or disapprove the sentence.

        2) In this state, criminal punishment serves five primary purposes: (i) rehabilitation; (ii) isolation to protect society; (iii) deterrence of the offender personally; (iv) deterrence of other potential offenders; and (v) societal condemnation that reaffirms societal norms of behavior.

        3) In this case, D was convicted of forcibly raping and robbing a female he picked up downtown. Although D otherwise led an exemplary life both prior to and during his service in the Army, he was convicted of very serious crimes. Given that the victim's version of events was found to be correct, the sentence was too lenient.

        4) This sentence does not serve the objective of reformation; D was not remorseful and the sentence suggests he was technically guilty but not really blameworthy. The sentence also fails to reaffirm societal norms. A substantially longer sentence than one year was called for.

4. **Life Sentence Permissible--United States v. Jackson**, 835 F.2d 1195 (7th Cir. 1987).

    a. **Facts.** Thirty minutes after he was released from prison, Jackson (D) robbed a bank while brandishing a revolver. He was sentenced to life without parole. D had been previously convicted of four armed bank robberies and one armed robbery. The statute in effect provides that anyone who possesses a firearm and has three previous felony convictions for robbery or burglary, or both, shall be fined and imprisoned for not less than 15 years without parole. D appeals.

b. **Issue.** May a life sentence be imposed on a defendant who commits armed robbery for the fifth time based on a statute that provides for imprisonment of "not less than 15 years"?

c. **Held.** Yes. Affirmed.

    1) D's argument that the statute permits only a determinate number of years and not a life sentence is silly when one considers D's age (35) and a long prison term, for example, 60 years. The result is the same.

    2) The selection of a sentence within the statutory range is essentially free of appellate review.

d. **Concurrence.** Although the sentence is too harsh, there is no ground on which we are authorized to set it aside.

C. PUNISHABLE CONDUCT

1. **Introduction.** There are numerous means available to induce compliance with preferred social norms of conduct. Criminal sanctions are but one example. Others are civil liability, licensing regulations, private or social pressures, etc. Often there is a great deal of latitude.

United States
v. Johnson

2. **Judicial Discretion in Federal Sentencing--United States v. Johnson,** 964 F.2d 124 (2d Cir. 1992).

a. **Facts.** Johnson (D) and Purvis were convicted of stealing money from a Veterans Administration Hospital by falsely adding raises to other employees' paychecks, and then receiving 50% kickbacks from those workers. The sentencing judge reduced D's offense level by a total of 13 levels, 10 of which were based on "family circumstances." The lowered offense level permitted the court to impose a sentence with no term of incarceration. The government (P) appeals.

b. **Issue.** Do family circumstances justify a downward departure in a defendant's offense level?

c. **Held.** Yes. Judgment affirmed.

    1) While ordinary family circumstances would not justify a downward departure, Congress specifically provided that a district court may adjust an offense level if it finds a circumstance not adequately taken into consideration by the guidelines.

    2) Extraordinary circumstances existed here, since D was solely responsible for the upbringing of four small children, who would have suffered greatly as a result of D's incarceration.

d. **Comment.** It is fair to assume that, had D committed a crime of violence, the court would have been less inclined to exercise its discretion in her favor, regardless of her family circumstances. So, while the departure may be ostensibly based on family circumstances, there is no doubt that the nature of the crime was factored in as well.

3.   **Crime and Sexual Misconduct.**

   a.   **Introduction.** The issue of the legitimacy of criminal enforcement of private morality has been the subject of long-standing debate. The United States Supreme Court has held that there is a "zone of privacy created by several fundamental constitutional guarantees." [Griswold v. Connecticut, 381 U.S. 479 (1965)] What bearing, if any, does this language have upon a state's power to use the law to enforce its moral judgments by prohibiting various forms of sexual practice in which consenting adults might engage?

   b.   **The *Wolfenden Report*.** The *Wolfenden Report* (1957) takes the view that the proper role of the criminal law is not to concern itself with private morals but only to restrict conduct that injuriously affects the rights of other citizens (*i.e.,* public solicitation for immoral purposes).

4.   **Homosexual Acts--Bowers v. Hardwick,** 478 U.S. 186 (1986).

   a.   **Facts.** Hardwick (P) was charged with committing sodomy with another adult male in P's bedroom in violation of a state law forbidding sodomy by any person. The district attorney decided not to pursue the case, but P sued, challenging the constitutionality of the statute as applied to consensual sodomy. The district court dismissed the suit, but the court of appeals reversed. The Supreme Court granted certiorari.

   b.   **Issue.** Does a person have a fundamental constitutional right to engage in consensual homosexual sodomy?

   c.   **Held.** No. Judgment reversed.

      1)   Prior cases have recognized a right of privacy in matters of child rearing and education, family relationships, procreation, contraception and abortion. None of those rights bears any resemblance to the right P claims to engage in homosexual sodomy. The precedent does not recognize a constitutional right to engage in any kind of private sexual conduct between consenting adults.

      2)   Rights that qualify for heightened judicial protection are those fundamental liberties implicit in the concept of ordered liberty, such that neither liberty nor justice would exist without them, and those that are deeply rooted in the country's history and tradition. A right to homosexual sodomy falls within neither category. Sodomy is a common law offense that is still forbidden by 24 states. The Court must be prudent in expanding the substantive reach of the Due Process Clause.

      3)   The fact that an offense takes place in the home does not make it immune from criminal sanction. Adultery, incest, and other sexual crimes may be punishable even when they are committed in a home. The *Stanley* case involved First Amendment freedoms and is distinguishable from this case.

   d.   **Concurrence** (Burger, C.J.). There is no such thing as a fundamental right to commit homosexual sodomy. The act has long been denounced as immoral. The states have legislative authority to forbid such conduct.

e. **Concurrence** (Powell, J.). P may have had an Eighth Amendment issue, since the statute permits a punishment of up to 20 years' imprisonment for a single act of private, consensual sodomy. That issue is not raised, however.

f. **Dissent** (Blackmun, Brennan, Marshall, Stevens, JJ.). P's claim that the statute impinges on his privacy and right of intimate association does not depend on his sexual orientation, because the statute does not apply only to homosexuals. The right of privacy extends to personal decisions such as how a person may define himself through sexual intimacy. There may be many "right" ways of conducting intimate sexual relationships, and much of the richness of a relationship may come from the freedom an individual has to choose the form and nature of the intensely personal bond. Additionally, the right of an individual to conduct intimate relationships in the intimacy of his or her own home is the heart of the Constitution's protection of privacy.

g. **Dissent** (Stevens, Brennan, Marshall, JJ.). The law applies as well to married persons, thereby affecting intimate decisions clearly protected by the Due Process Clause. Thus, the statute is overbroad at least. The state cannot justify selectively applying the law to homosexuals.

III. THE SUBSTANTIVE CRIMINAL LAW: BASIC ELEMENTS IN DEFINING AND GRADING CRIMINAL CONDUCT

A. INTRODUCTION

1. **Definition of a Crime.** A crime is an act or an omission to act which is prohibited by law enacted for the protection of the public and made punishable in a judicial proceeding initiated by the state. It is important to understand that a crime is a "public" wrong, to be distinguished from "private" or "civil" wrongs to an individual.

2. **Classification of Crimes.** There are many ways to classify crimes (*e.g.*, on the basis of the quantum of punishment meted out for violation, on the basis of felony or misdemeanor, etc.).

   a. **Felonies and misdemeanors.** Crimes are divided into these two classes depending on the grievousness of the offense and the severity of the punishment.

      1) **Felonies.**

         a) **Common law.** The common law punished all felonies by total forfeiture of the offender's lands and goods, or alternatively, by death.

         b) **State law.** Felonies are usually defined by statute to be those which are punishable by death or by confinement in the state prison.

         c) **Federal law.** All offenses which are punishable by death or imprisonment for one year or more are felonies.

      2) **Misdemeanors.** All crimes that are not felonies (or treason) are misdemeanors. They are normally crimes which are thought to be less serious in nature. Note also that misdemeanors may be further subdivided into misdemeanors and "petty" offenses (crimes of minor seriousness).

   b. **Crimes mala in se and mala prohibita.** Sometimes crimes are also classified as "mala in se" or "mala prohibita."

      1) **Mala in se.** These crimes are often said to be those acts or omissions to act which are wrong from their very nature (crimes such as murder, robbery, or rape).

      2) **Mala prohibita.** Those crimes that are "mala prohibita" are wrong merely because they are prohibited by statute.

3. **Merger of Crimes.** The very same act may constitute more than one crime. For example, every murder necessarily includes an assault and battery.

   a. **Common law.** At common law if the offenses were not of the same degree (*i.e.*, if one were a felony and the other a misdemeanor) then there was a merger, but only if one of the crimes was necessarily included within the other. Therefore, one tried for a felony could not also or alternatively be convicted of a necessarily included misdemeanor.

    b.   **Modern rule.** Most jurisdictions no longer apply the merger doctrine in this way, so that a person indicted for a higher offense may be convicted of a lesser offense necessarily included therein.

4.   **Corpus Delicti—The Prima Facie Elements of a Crime.**

    a.   **Preliminary elements.** Before the state can attempt to prove that the defendant is the one who committed the alleged crime, it must first prove (i) that there has actually been an occurrence of some injury which constitutes a crime, and (ii) that somebody's criminal act is responsible (as opposed to the happening of a mere accident). Therefore, in a murder case the state would have to show that someone was dead and that somebody's criminal act was the cause of that death.

    b.   **Criminal agent.** After the state has proved the corpus delicti it may then proceed to prove that the defendant is the one who has committed the crime (*i.e.*, that he is the criminal agent or cause).

        1)   **General rule.** As a general rule, the corpus delicti cannot be proved solely by resort to the out-of-court confession or admission of the defendant. Such admission or confessions should not be admitted into evidence until the corpus delicti has been established. However, improper prior admission is not reversible error on appeal.

        2)   **In-court confessions or admissions.** If the defendant takes the stand in court and confesses the crime, this may be used to prove the corpus delicti.

    c.   **Standard of proof.** Only "slight" evidence is needed to prove the corpus delicti (that is, the two requisite elements need not be proved "beyond a reasonable doubt"). Most states hold that circumstantial evidence, for example, is sufficient (*i.e.*, evidence from which the fact to be proven may be inferred).

B.   **CULPABILITY—ACTUS REUS AND MENS REA**

1.   **Introduction.** There are two basic elements of every crime: (i) the actus reus, or the commission (or omission) of some act prohibited by law; and (ii) the mens rea, or some criminal state of mind. To constitute a crime, the act must concur with the intent; *i.e.*, the intent must accompany the doing of the act, and the actus reus must be attributable to the mens rea.

2.   **Actus Reus—The Forbidden Acts.**

    a.   **Definition of an "act."** Some wrongful outward act or manifestation is required. Furthermore, an "act" is any event which is subject to the control of the will (although the will need not actually be exercised since omissions to act are also punishable); thus, to meditate is an act, but to dream is not.

b.   Speaking or verbal acts. Such acts can be the subject of crimes; for example, solicitation.

c.   Involuntary acts.

1)   **Introduction.** The act that is the subject of a crime must be "voluntary." Thus, reflexes, convulsions, and other acts done while sleepwalking or while in the middle of an epileptic fit, etc., are not voluntary acts.

2)   **Epileptic reflexes.** In *People v. Decina,* 138 N.E.2d (N.Y. 1956), Decina (D), aware of his epileptic condition and the likelihood of being rendered unconscious as the result of a seizure, drove his vehicle on a public way. He suffered an attack and the car went up onto the sidewalk, killing four people. He was charged with criminal negligence in the operation of a vehicle. The court found D's actions constituted criminal negligence because D deliberately chose to take a chance by driving alone while he was aware of his vulnerability to seizures and did so in disregard of the results that might follow. Note the necessity of prior knowledge; a disabling attack, without any prior knowledge, would be viewed differently.

3)   **Voluntariness--Martin v. State,** 17 So. 2d 427 (Ala. 1944).

   a)   **Facts.** Martin (D) was arrested at his home and taken onto a public highway, where he used loud and profane language and manifested a drunken condition with other persons present. He was convicted of drunkenness in a public place under a state statute.

   b)   **Issue.** May a person be guilty of a crime where his conduct was not voluntary?

   c)   **Held.** No. Conviction reversed.

      (1)   The statute presupposes that the defendant voluntarily appears in public in a drunken condition. D was brought to the public place involuntarily by the arresting officer.

4)   **Unconsciousness--People v. Newton,** 87 Cal. Rptr. 394 (1970).

   a)   **Facts.** Newton (D), involved in an altercation with a police officer subsequent to his arrest, was shot in the midsection, but then managed to grab the gun and fired several shots at the officer, killing him. D testified that he remembered nothing after being shot (except for a few events at an emergency hospital) until recovering consciousness at a second hospital. Expert testimony established that a shock reaction (producing unconsciousness) could have resulted from the shot and could have lasted up to a half hour. The defense asked for an instruction to the jury on unconsciousness but the trial court refused. D was convicted of voluntary manslaughter. D appeals.

Martin v.
State

People v.
Newton

        b)   **Issue.** Is it error to fail to instruct the jury on the issue of unconsciousness as a defense?

        c)   **Held.** Yes. Judgment reversed.

             (1)   Unconsciousness, where not voluntarily induced, is a complete defense to murder.

             (2)   Unconsciousness includes situations where the defendant can act physically but is not conscious of what he is doing.

             (3)   D is entitled to a jury instruction on the consciousness issue even if the inference that he was unconscious arises from his own testimony. The jury must be allowed to consider whether D was in fact unconscious.

  d.   **Status crimes.** The "act" may involve simply the status or condition of an individual, such as those crimes punishing individuals for vagrancy or habitual drunkenness.

  e.   **Prohibited acts.** In all instances the "act" must be prohibited in order for a crime to exist. A person might intend to commit a crime by performing some act, but if that act is not prohibited, then there is no crime.

  f.   **Negative acts or omissions to act.** A defendant may be criminally liable for an omission or forbearance to act when there is a legal duty for him to so act.

        1)   **Legal duty.** A punishable negative act is a nonoccurrence which involves a breach of defendant's legal duty to take positive action.

Pope v. State   **2)**   **Child neglect--Pope v. State,** 396 A.2d 1054 (Md. 1979).

             a)   **Facts.** Pope (D) took Norris and her three-month-old child into D's home because Norris had no place to go. Norris was mentally ill and occasionally would go into a violent religious frenzy. At D's home, Norris began beating and tearing at the child, believing that Satan was hidden within the child's body. D did not protect the child or seek police or medical assistance. Instead, she went to church with Norris and brought her back home. The child died that night from the beating. D was charged with child abuse and misprision of felony. D was convicted.

             b)   **Issue.** Does a person who charitably assumes partial support of a parent and her child become criminally responsible for child abuse committed by the parent on the child?

             c)   **Held.** No. Judgment reversed.

                (1)   The crime of child abuse consists of a person who is responsible for the supervision of a minor child causing, or being accountable for, whether by commission or omission, abuse to the child, including physical injury. D's failure to prevent the beating of the child and her failure to seek medical assistance constitute omissions that are cruel and inhuman treatment. She

20 - Criminal Law

could therefore be convicted if she was a person "responsible for the supervision" of the child.

  (2) D was not the child's parent, nor was she in loco parentis to the child. The prosecution claimed that D assumed responsibility for the child within the statute once she began to house, feed, and care for the child and Norris. However, Norris was always present. D could not usurp Norris's role as mother. It would be incongruous to impose criminal liability premised solely on acts of hospitality and kindness.

  (3) D may have had a strong moral obligation to assist the child, but she had no legal obligation to do so. Accordingly, D was not in the class of persons that fall within the statute.

  (4) The offense of misprision of felony has become obsolete, and is no longer cognizable by the criminal law of this state.

3) Contractual duty--Jones v. United States, 308 F.2d 307 (D.C. Cir. 1962).

 a) **Facts.** Green and her baby lived for some period of time with Jones (D). The baby died from neglect and malnutrition. D was charged with the death. At trial, conflicting evidence was presented as to whether Green had hired D to care for the baby or whether Green was staying with D and should have been taking care of the baby herself. D wanted an instruction that the jury must find beyond a reasonable doubt that D had a legal duty to care for the baby. The court failed to give the instruction and D was convicted of involuntary manslaughter. D appeals.

 b) **Issue.** When a person is criminally charged with an omission to act, must the government prove there was a legal duty to act?

 c) **Held.** Yes. Judgment reversed.

  (1) Breach of a legal duty may arise in four situations:

   (a) Where a statute imposes the duty of care;

   (b) Where one stands in a certain status relationship to another;

   (c) Where one has assumed a contractual duty to care for another; or

   (d) Where one has voluntarily assumed the care of another and has withdrawn the helpless person from others who could render aid.

  (2) Criminal liability for failure to act must be based on more than just a moral duty to act. The government must prove that D had a legal duty to act. Although the facts would justify a finding that D had such a legal duty, the evidence is conflicting and the issue should have been given to the jury with appropriate instructions.

d) **Comment.** Legal duty and moral duty are *not* synonymous, although the trend is to equate one with the other.

4) **Failure to continue life-support systems--Barber v. Superior Court,** 195 Cal. Rptr. 484 (1983).

 a) **Facts.** Herbert underwent surgery at the hands of Nejdl and Barber (Ps), who were surgeons. After the successful operation, Herbert suffered cardio-respiratory arrest and was placed on life-support equipment. Herbert lapsed into a coma from which he was not expected to recover. The family asked that the equipment be removed and Ps complied with the request. Herbert continued breathing, but had to be fed intravenously. After again consulting with the family, Ps removed the intravenous tubes and Herbert died a short while later. Ps were charged with murder, but the magistrate dismissed the complaint. The Superior Court reinstated the complaint and Ps appeal.

 b) **Issue.** May a doctor be charged with murder for failure to continue to provide life-sustaining treatment?

 c) **Held.** No. Judgment reversed.

  (1) Historically, death consisted of the cessation of heart and respiratory function. By statute, death consists of irreversible cessation of all brain function. By either definition, Herbert was not dead when Ps ceased further treatment.

  (2) Disconnecting mechanical life-support devices, including the IV tubes, is comparable to withholding manually administered injection or medication. Ps could have criminal liability only if they had a legal duty to continue to provide life-sustaining treatment. Under these circumstances, after coordinating with Herbert's wife and children, Ps had no duty to continue treatment.

5) **Other applications.**

 a) In *Airdale NHS Trust v. Bland,* All E.R. 821 (H.L. 1993), an insensate patient, with no hope of recovery, continued to live by means of artificial feeding and antibiotics. The House of Lords held that the treatment could lawfully be withheld even when withholding such treatment meant that the patient would shortly die. The House of Lords distinguished between a doctor's decision not to act, and the decision to actively administer a lethal drug to bring a patient's life to an end. A doctor who switches off a life support machine does not "act" but rather does not struggle to maintain life. This is not a breach of duty, since he is not obligated to continue in a hopeless case. The law does not permit a doctor to prescribe a lethal injection, however, because the law does not authorize euthanasia. *Note:* The court succinctly stated the common fear that "once euthanasia is recognized as lawful in these circumstances, it is difficult to see any logical basis for excluding it in others." However, it is difficult to justify the notion that one may legally withdraw feeding tubes, thus condemning a patient to literally starve to death, but one may not legally hasten that death.

b) In *Commonwealth v. Hall*, 323 Mass. 414 (1948), the defendant left her illegitimate baby in the attic unattended, and it died. The court held that there had been a malicious omission to act where a legal duty existed.

c) In *People v. Beardsley*, 150 Mich. 206 (1907), the court refused to find a legal duty where the defendant failed to summon a physician for his weekend mistress when she took a fatal dose of morphine.

d) But in *Jones v. State*, 220 Ind. 384 (1942), the court found a duty to rescue where the defendant raped a child who then jumped into a creek and drowned (the court emphasizing the fact that the defendant had been the "cause" of the child's actions).

6) **Knowledge.** In general, no criminal act can be found **unless** the defendant is shown to have had knowledge of his legal duty to act.

a) **Exceptions:**

(1) Where the duty to act arises from a statute.

(2) Where negligence results in the imposition of criminal liability in exceptional cases where the potential risk of harm is very great. (For example, a railroad switchman was held criminally liable for failure to throw a switch even though his attention was distracted and he was unaware of danger.)

3. Mens Rea—The Mental State Accompanying the Forbidden Acts.

a. Introduction.

1) **Definition.** Mens rea is a guilty or wrongful purpose; a criminal intent. The intent required is **not** the same for all crimes (for example, negligence may be sufficient in some crimes).

2) **Motive distinguished.** Proof of motive is immaterial in establishing criminal liability. Motives create an intent to act, while intent itself is merely a determination to act in a certain way. An accused's motive may be relevant in proving the probability of his having committed the offense and/or of having had a certain type of intent when an act was committed. But failure to prove motive will not prevent a conviction.

b. Types of intent.

1) **Introduction.** Each crime has its own standard as to the nature and quality of the intent required. At common law there were three types of mens rea: general mens rea, specific mens rea, and criminal negligence.

2) General intent. General intent requires only that the accused meant to do the act he committed (*i.e.*, that the prohibited result was substantially certain to flow from the intentional conduct, even if the result that occurred was not subjectively intended). For example, if A voluntarily fires a gun into the middle of a crowd, even if he does not want to injure someone, and B is killed thereby, A may be held for murder (*i.e.*, he intended to fire the gun into the crowd, and objectively speaking, the killing of a person was substantially certain to follow).

    a) Proof of general intent. Intent is inferred by the results that occur. Therefore, general intent may be proved simply by showing that the prohibited result was caused by a voluntary act of D.

    b) Transferred intent. When a person has the required intent to commit one criminal act, he may be held responsible for results which he did not intend if he inflicts the kind of harm intended and if the injuries sustained do not require a different mens rea.

        (1) Usually the intent from the first crime will only be transferred to the second where the first act was "malum in se." For example, where A attempts to hit B and unintentionally hits and injures C, A is guilty of assault on C.

        (2) The transfer generally occurs only where the unintended result involves the same mens rea requirement as the intended act. Therefore, if A shoots at B, misses, and the bullet strikes an oil lamp, igniting a fire, A is not guilty of arson because arson requires that specific intent to start a fire be shown (specific intent is discussed below), and here A can only be held to have had the intent to do personal injury.

3) Malice.

    a) Introduction. Malice can refer to a specific criminal state of mind where D is subjectively cognizant of the likely harmful results of his actions, yet inexcusably carries out these potentially harmful acts. Malice may also be inferred where D acts recklessly or with wanton disregard for the consequences of his actions. Finally, malice may be used in its dictionary meaning, as in the crime of malicious mischief (defendant acting out of resentment or hatred of the owner of the injured property).

Regina v.
Cunningham

    b) Application--Regina v. Cunningham, 2 Q.B. 396 (1957).

        (1) Facts. Cunningham (D) tore the gas meter from the wall in a house in order to steal the money contained therein. He did not turn off the gas and it leaked into the next house and asphyxiated an elderly lady. D was convicted under a statute for "maliciously causing another to take noxious things." D appeals.

        (2) Issue. May a person be convicted under a statute which requires malicious intent when he did not actually intend to do the harm done and did not foresee the result?

        (3) Held. No. Conviction reversed.

(a) "Maliciously" requires that the defendant act recklessly with foresight of the actual consequence, or it requires actual intent to do the particular harm done. Recklessness is where the defendant foresees that such harm might occur but does the act anyway.

(b) Malice does not require that ill will toward the person injured be shown, nor does it require that the act done in itself be unlawful (as the stealing of the gas meter was here).

(c) The jury instructions by the trial judge were thus erroneous; the jury should have been left to decide whether D foresaw possible injury occurring from his act.

4) **Acting willfully.** This term usually requires only a general mens rea but may be elevated to a standard of specific intent if expressly required by the terms of a statute.

5) **Wanton or reckless conduct.** This type of conduct consists of the intentional failure to take reasonable care when confronting a known risk. Such a failure may be subjective (*i.e.,* the defendant having been actually aware of the probable consequences of his actions) or objective (a reasonable person would have known of the risk).

6) **Criminal negligence.** Criminal negligence is a flagrant and reckless disregard for the safety of others. The test applied, whether it is an act of omission or commission, is what a reasonable person would do under like circumstances.

a) **Degree of negligence required.** The lack of due care required for criminal liability is greater than that required for tort liability. How much greater is not always certain because both are supposedly measured by the same standard.

b) **Negligence standard--Santillanes v. New Mexico, 849 P.2d 358 (N.M. 1993).**

Santillanes v.
New Mexico

(1) **Facts.** Santillanes (D) cut his seven-year-old nephew's neck with a knife and was convicted of child abuse for "negligently" endangering the child's life. The trial court rejected D's request for a jury instruction as to criminal negligence. Instead, the court utilized the lower standard of civil negligence. D appeals.

(2) **Issue.** Does felony punishment require criminal negligence, not ordinary civil negligence?

(3) **Held.** Yes. Judgment affirmed.

(a) At common law, a criminal conviction required proof of intent. Today, the legislature may define certain conduct as criminal without intent.

(b) When a statute is silent as to the element of intent, we will presume intent to be an essential element.

(c) Here, the intent element is included but not defined. Therefore, we hold that absent a lesser standard definition, we will presume that the criminal negligence standard is required. However, we affirm the judgment on the finding that, based on the facts, the error was harmless.

c) **Model Penal Code.** The Model Penal Code distinguishes between "reckless" and "negligent" conduct as follows:

   (1) **Recklessness.** The defendant acted with conscious disregard of a substantial and unjustifiable risk to another.

   (2) **Criminal negligence.** The defendant failed to perceive a substantial and unjustifiable risk to another resulting from his conduct in contravention of the standard of care of the reasonable person.

7) **Deliberate Ignorance--United States v. Jewell,** 532 F.2d 697 (9th Cir. 1976).

   a) **Facts.** Jewell (D) was convicted of knowingly transporting marijuana from Mexico to the United States, concealed in a secret compartment in his car. D testified he did not know that the marijuana was present. The evidence showed that D might have known of the marijuana, or that he might have deliberately avoided such positive knowledge. The court instructed the jury that "knowingly" could mean actual knowledge or deliberate avoidance of actual knowledge. D appeals his conviction.

   b) **Issue.** Are deliberate ignorance and positive knowledge equally culpable?

   c) **Held.** Yes. Conviction affirmed.

      (1) One can "know" facts without being absolutely certain of them. "Knowingly," therefore, can mean an awareness of the high probability of the existence of a fact.

   d) **Dissent.** The majority justifies the "conscious purpose" jury instruction as an application of the "willful blindness" doctrine. But the instruction makes no mention of "high probability" that D knew of the marijuana, nor does it state that "actual belief" could thwart a conviction. The jury instruction also wrongly indicates that ignorance or not actually being aware could still lead to a conviction.

c. **Mistake of fact.**

1) **Introduction.** "Mistake of fact" is an unconscious ignorance of a material fact. It is a common defense challenging the mens rea necessary to convict.

2) **Crimes requiring specific intent—actual belief.** Where the defendant makes an honest and reasonable mistake of fact and his conduct would not be criminal if the facts were as he supposed them to be, then his mistake of

fact is a defense to a crime requiring that *specific* intent be shown. However, mistake of fact is not a defense to a crime requiring only general intent.

3) **Strict liability crimes.** There are crimes where the accused is criminally liable regardless of fault. Mistake of fact cannot serve as a defense to strict liability crimes.

   a) **Rationale.** Mistake of fact in strict liability crimes is not a defense because of the traditional rule that, regardless of the mistake, the accused's conduct is still "morally wrong" and should be punished. Hence, there is no mens rea requirement. There is a minority trend away from strict liability, especially with the more serious offenses.

   b) **Reasonable belief as a defense to strict liability crimes--Regina v. Prince,** 2 Cr. Cas. Res. 154 (1875).

Regina v. Prince

   (1) **Facts.** Prince (D) was convicted of having sexual relations with an unmarried female under 16 in violation of a statute. The girl was 14 but told D she was 18. D appeals.

   (2) **Issue.** Is a reasonable but mistaken belief in a particular fact a defense to a strict liability crime?

   (3) **Held.** No. Judgment affirmed.

   (a) D's belief was reasonable, but it was irrelevant because it did not constitute a defense to a strict liability crime. The statute forbids taking a girl out of the possession of her parents or another having legal charge of her. Whoever does this act does so at the risk of her being under 16. D had the mens rea to do the forbidden act, although he did not know the girl's true age. If D did not know the girl was in someone's possession, or thought he had permission, he would not have had mens rea.

   (4) **Dissent.** Because D would not have committed an offense if the facts had been as he thought, he had no intent to commit an offense and is not guilty.

4) **Good faith belief as to age--People v. Olsen,** 685 P.2d 52 (Cal. 1984).

People v. Olsen

   a) **Facts.** Two months before her fourteenth birthday, Shawn was permitted by her parents to sleep in the family's camper in the driveway. She claimed that after she had locked the door and fallen asleep, she was awakened by Garcia, who was in the trailer and had a knife. Garcia then called to Olsen (D), who entered the trailer as well. Garcia told Shawn to let D have intercourse with her or he would stab her. During the act, Shawn's father came in and grabbed D. Garcia stabbed Shawn's father, and D and Garcia escaped. At D's trial for rape, Shawn admitted that she had told Garcia and D that she was older than 16. Garcia testified that he in fact had had intercourse several times with Shawn the night before the incident, pursuant to Shawn's invitation. Shawn had invited D and Garcia back, and asked to have sex with D first. At his trial, D claimed the defense of good faith belief. After the court rejected the defense of good faith belief, D was convicted of statutory, but not forcible, rape. D appeals.

      b)   **Issue.** Is a good faith belief that the female is over 16 years old a valid defense to a statutory rape charge?

      c)   **Held.** No. Judgment affirmed.

          (1)   In a prior case, this court adopted a defense to statutory rape based on an accused's good faith and reasonable belief that the victim was at least 18 years old. Despite that holding, at least one court of appeal in this state refused to recognize the defense in the context of a charge of offering marijuana to a minor.

          (2)   In the statute defining lewd or lascivious conduct, the legislature provided for probation for accused persons who "honestly and reasonably believed the victim was 14 years old or older." This demonstrates that the legislature did not intend to approve the honest and reasonable belief defense; otherwise, there would be no need to provide for probation, because the person would not be convicted.

          (3)   The legislature has determined that persons under age 14 need special protection. Those who commit sexual offenses with such young persons are punished more severely than those who do so with older persons under age 18. Recognition of the defense in cases involving victims under age 14 would undermine the legislative purpose and cannot be permitted.

      d)   **Concurrence and dissent.** It is unfair for a person to be sentenced to prison when he committed the offending act only because his belief about the facts of the victim's age were incorrect. Strict liability may be applied for regulatory offenses, but traditional crimes should require at least some proof of fault. The legislature could impose a strict standard of what is reasonable, such as reasonable inquiry, but once the belief becomes reasonable as measured by a legitimate standard, there should be no criminal liability.

  d.   **Abandonment of mens rea.**

    1)   **Introduction.** Strict liability criminal statutes have been adopted to deal with particular problems for which the mens rea requirement was ineffective. These statutes have distinct characteristics.

Morissette v.
United States

    2)   **Mens rea requirement in "true crimes"--Morissette v. United States, 342 U.S. 246 (1952).**

      a)   **Facts.** Morissette (D) entered an Air Force bombing area and appropriated some old, rusty bomb casings. He flattened out the metal and sold it as scrap for $84. He was indicted and convicted of violating a federal law which makes it a crime to "knowingly convert" government property. His defense was that he honestly thought the government had abandoned the casings. The trial court took the view that this was no defense because the federal statute does not explicitly require the intent to steal. Thus, the trial court viewed the crime as one of strict liability in which mens rea was unnecessary.

D's conviction was subsequently affirmed. The Supreme Court granted certiorari.

b) **Issue.** Can a person be held criminally responsible on a strict liability basis for a codified crime which at common law required proof of bad intent?

c) **Held.** No. D's conviction is reversed.

(1) There is a difference between true crimes such as conversion of property and public welfare offenses (such as violation of the liquor code). Where the criminal law, as in this case, is entirely statutory and the statute makes no mention of a mens rea requirement, mens rea will be deemed inherent in any offense which is a codification of a common law crime.

(2) At common law all crimes were mala in se. Thus, all crimes required mens rea. Today public welfare offenses dispense with the mens rea requirement. But codifications of common law crimes do require the existence of a bad intent.

d) **Comment.** Where a statute is merely a codification of a common law crime, mens rea usually remains an element whether it is mentioned in the statute or not. However, despite the commitment of traditional Anglo-American law to the mens rea requirement, there have been departures in a number of instances (*e.g.,* the felony-murder and misdemeanor-manslaughter rules, bigamy, and sex offenses with minors).

3) **Mens rea--United States v. Staples,** 114 S. Ct. 1793 (1994).

United States
v. Staples

a) **Facts.** Staples (D) was convicted of violating the National Firearms Act by possessing a weapon capable of automatically firing more than one shot with a single pull of the trigger. The rifle was not manufactured as an automatic weapon, but had been altered to allow automatic firing. D contended he never knew the rifle could fire automatically. D appealed; the court of appeals affirmed. The Supreme Court granted certiorari.

b) **Issue.** Can a defendant be convicted of possession of an automatic weapon without proof that he knew that his rifle could fire automatically?

c) **Held.** No. Reversed and remanded.

(1) The Act is silent concerning a mens rea requirement. Silence, however, does not mean Congress intended to dispense with the element of mens rea.

(2) We require some indication of congressional intent to dispense with mens rea; absent such an indication, it will be presumed to be required.

(3) Our previous analysis in *U.S. v. Freed,* 401 U.S. 601 (1971), was premised on the assumption that the defendant knew he possessed a particularly dangerous item. That assumption is not warranted here.

(4) We will not ease the path to convicting persons whose conduct would not even alert them to the possibility that they were violating the Act.

d) **Concurrence** (Ginsberg, O'Connor, JJ.). Even though the word "knowingly" does not appear in the Act, the general rule is that absent a contrary indication, it will be assumed that Congress intended to retain the mens rea requirement.

State v.
Guminga

4) Limitation on vicarious criminal liability--State v. Guminga, 395 N.W.2d 344 (Minn. 1986).

a) **Facts.** Two undercover officers accompanied a 17-year-old woman into a restaurant owned by Guminga (D). The three ordered alcoholic drinks, and when the waitress brought them, the minor paid. The officers verified that the drinks were alcoholic and then arrested the waitress. D was later charged with violating the law against serving underage persons. The law held employers vicariously liable for violations by employees. D was unaware of the entire incident. D moved to dismiss the charges as denying him due process. The trial court denied the motion, but D appealed. The court of appeals certified the issue to the state supreme court.

b) **Issue.** Is a statute consistent with due process if it imposes vicarious criminal liability on an employer for the acts of his employee in serving alcoholic beverages to underage customers?

c) **Held.** No. The statute deprives D of due process.

(1) The penalty D faced if convicted of the gross misdemeanor included up to one year of imprisonment or payment of a fine of up to $3,000, or both. D could also lose his liquor license. Even though D might not receive these penalties, he still faces a possible gross misdemeanor conviction, which would give him a criminal record.

(2) Due process requires a balancing between the public interests behind a statute and the private interest in liberty. Alternative means to achieving the public purpose must also be evaluated.

(3) The statute in this case assists in deterring violation of the liquor laws, while D has a private interest in liberty, his reputation, and other effects of criminal prosecution, such as a longer sentence if ever convicted in the future. The infringements on private interests are not justified by the public interest in this case. The state could use other alternatives, such as civil fines or license suspension, to accomplish the same ends. The statute does not distinguish between employers who properly train their employees and those who do not; it simply imposes vicarious liability without consideration of the employer's degree of responsibility.

d) **Dissent.** The state has a strong public interest in deterring drinking by minors. The potential criminal sentences are reasonably related to the purpose of enforcing the law. The legislature could rationally conclude that, without criminal sanctions, owners such as D would be less likely to insure that their employees do not violate the law. Most other states have upheld imposition of vicarious liability in this type of case.

5) **Standards for a defense under strict liability--State v. Baker,** 571 P.2d State v. Baker
65 (Kan. 1977).

    a) **Facts.** Baker (D) was convicted of speeding. He had wanted to introduce evidence that the excessive speed was due to the malfunction of his car's cruise control and that he had subsequently had the defective cruise control repaired. The trial court had sustained the State's (P's) motion to suppress D's offered evidence, and D appeals.

    b) **Issue.** Under a strict liability criminal statute, is the malfunction of a nonessential component of an automobile a defense to criminal liability for the consequences of the malfunction?

    c) **Held.** No. Judgment affirmed.

        (1) Even if D had been able to prove that the malfunction caused him to speed, such proof would not constitute a defense to strict liability because he himself activated the cruise control. This is a case of delegation of partial control of the car, which differs significantly from failure of an essential component of a car such as a brake or a throttle.

        (2) To be valid, a defense to strict liability must show that the violation was the result of an unforeseen occurrence or circumstance, not caused by D and not preventable by him.

6) **Absolute liability in Canada.** In *Regina v. City of Sault Ste. Marie,* 85 D.L.R.3d 161 (1978), the Supreme Court of Canada noted that the basic justifications for absolute liability in public welfare offenses—the need for a strong incentive and administrative efficiency—do not override the violation of fundamental principles of penal liability. There is no empirical evidence of the incentive rationale, and it is clear that even if the penalty is relatively small, a significant stigma attaches to a conviction. Administrative convenience is an insufficient justification. Rather than the extremes of defining crimes as requiring either full mens rea or absolute liability, the Court noted the availability of offenses in which mens rea need not be proved, but the accused retains the option of avoiding liability through proof that he took all reasonable care. Such a category of offenses would include public welfare offenses. In 1985, relying on the *Sault Ste. Marie* reasoning, the Supreme Court of Canada held that the doctrine of absolute liability was unconstitutional. Specifically, it held that imprisonment for an absolute liability offense is a deprivation of liberty guaranteed by the Canadian Charter of Rights and Freedoms.

e. **Ignorance or mistake of law.** Ignorance or mistake of law arises in two entirely different contexts: (i) those in which, because of ignorance or mistake as to a collateral law, the defendant lacked the mental state required for a conviction; and (ii) those in which the defendant had the requisite mental state but claims he was unaware that his conduct was proscribed by the criminal law.

    1) **Mistake as to collateral law.** Some crimes involve a particular belief concerning a legal matter. If the defendant was ignorant or mistaken as to that legal matter, he lacked the necessary mens rea. This is a mistake not regarding the criminal statute itself, but a collateral law. For example, if a person mistakenly believes that he owns certain property that he finds, when in fact he does not, he could not be convicted of larceny if he keeps the property.

2) **Mistake as to criminal statute.** Criminal mens rea requires only that the defendant intended to do the prohibited act. Ignorance or mistake of the law is not a defense, on the theory that such a defense would undermine the enforcement of laws. The rule encourages the public to learn the laws. There are exceptions, however.

a) **Statute later held unconstitutional.** A defendant who acted in good faith reliance upon a statute that permitted her conduct may assert this reliance as a defense, even though the statute was later invalidated.

b) **Judicial decision.** If a judicial decision held that the particular conduct was not criminal, a defendant who relied on the decision may assert that reliance as a defense. In most jurisdictions, the decision does not need to be that of the highest state court.

c) **Official interpretation.** Reliance upon an official interpretation of the law by one responsible for administering or enforcing the law may constitute a defense.

d) **Advice of private counsel not a defense.** Unlike the exceptions set forth above, the courts have held that a person who in good faith relies on the advice of private counsel may not assert that reliance as a defense.

People v. Marrero

3) **Irrelevance of mistake when intent is not an element of the offense--People v. Marrero,** 507 N.E.2d 1068 (N.Y. 1987).

a) **Facts.** Marrero (D) was a federal corrections officer. D carried a loaded .38 caliber automatic pistol, but he was not licensed to do so. He was arrested for violating the unlicensed possession law. By its terms, the law did not apply to "peace officers," which was defined to include correction officers of any penal correctional institution. D claimed he was exempt from the law because of his status, but he was charged with the violation. The trial court dismissed the indictment, but the appellate court reversed and reinstated the indictment. At his trial, D requested a jury instruction that would have led to an acquittal if the jury found that D reasonably believed the exemption applied to him. The court refused the instruction, and the appellate court affirmed. D appeals.

b) **Issue.** Is a misinterpretation of a statute a valid defense to a crime that does not require an intent to violate the statute?

c) **Held.** No. Judgment affirmed.

(1) When intent is an element of the crime, a mistake of law may constitute a defense. In a kidnapping, for example, if the defendant believed that he seized the victim with authority of law, he could not have the necessary intent to confine another without authority of law. In this case, however, liability for weapons possession is imposed regardless of the defendant's intent, so a mistake of law is no defense.

(2) The mistake of law defense applies when the defendant has relied on an official statement of the law contained in a statute or an official interpretation of the statute. D claims that his reasonable but mistaken interpretation of the statute should constitute a defense. However, the proper rule is that the defense applies when the defendant relies on an official statement of the law that is thereafter determined to be invalid or incorrect. It applies only when the statute in fact authorizes the conduct, not when a defendant incorrectly reads the law.

(3) The narrow defense of mistake of law is intended to encourage respect for and adherence to the law. D's proposed approach would instead encourage mistakes about the law. Defendants could in many cases come up with reasonable but mistaken interpretations of criminal statutes that would constitute a defense.

d) Dissent. A person should not be convicted for committing an act that is not inherently wrong or immoral, but is a crime solely because of a statute, if the person acted in good faith but mistakenly believed that the act was not an offense because of the wording of the statute. Such a person has not knowingly committed an offense, so there is no rationale for punishment. The common law notion was formed when crimes were acts that by their nature were evil. That approach should not be carried forward to apply to conduct that would be lawful but for a criminal statute. This is the basic difference between acts malum in se and malum prohibitum. In this case, D's interpretation of the statute was certainly reasonable. The more just approach would be to permit a defense based on a defendant's good-faith but mistaken belief based on a well-grounded interpretation of an official statement of the law contained in a statute.

4) Requirement of "willful" violation--Cheek v. United States, 498 U.S. 192 (1991).

Cheek v. United States

a) Facts. Cheek (D) was convicted of "willfully" evading taxes and failing to file a return. D's defense was that he believed that he owed no taxes and that the tax laws were unconstitutional. While deliberating, the jury indicated they were divided as to D's honest and reasonable belief that he owed no taxes. The judge gave further instructions that "an honest but unreasonable belief does not negate willfulness," "[a]dvice or research resulting in the conclusion that wages . . . are not income or that tax laws are unconstitutional is not objectively reasonable," and "[p]ersistent refusal to acknowledge the law does not constitute a good faith misunderstanding of the law." D appealed. The court of appeals affirmed. The Supreme Court granted certiorari.

b) Issue. Was the trial court correct in instructing that only an objectively reasonable misunderstanding of the law negates the requirement of willfulness?

c) Held. No. Remanded for further proceedings.

(1) We have long held that ignorance of the law is no defense, but because of the proliferation of laws, Congress has lessened the burden by requiring specific intent to violate certain tax laws.

Criminal Law - 33

(2) In *United States v. Murdock,* 290 U.S. 389 (1933), the Court held that an accused was entitled to an instruction with respect to whether he acted in good faith based on his actual belief.

(3) As it has evolved, "willful" means the "voluntary, intentional violation of a known legal duty." It requires proof that: (i) the law imposed a duty on D; (ii) D knew of his duty; and (iii) D voluntarily and intentionally violated that duty.

(4) One cannot "know" of a duty if there is a good faith misunderstanding of that duty. However, a good faith misunderstanding is not the same as a researched conclusion which is wrong. Such a taxpayer may not ignore his duty without risking criminal prosecution.

5) **Knowledge of regulation.** In *Liparota v. United States,* 471 U.S. 419 (1985), Liparota (D) owned a sandwich shop that was not authorized to accept food stamps. On three occasions, D purchased food stamps from an undercover agent for less than their face value. This was a violation of food stamp regulations. Federal law provided that anyone who knowingly uses, transfers, acquires, alters, or possesses coupons in any manner not authorized by the regulations is guilty of an offense. D was tried for illegally acquiring and possessing the food stamps. The Court found that in the absence of a contrary purpose in the language or legislative history of a statute forbidding knowing conduct, the government must prove that the defendant knew his conduct to be unauthorized by law. The statute itself requires "knowing" conduct, but does not specify what element that knowledge relates to. Criminal statutes that do not require mens rea generally have a disfavored status. When it is not clear that Congress intended the statute not to require mens rea, the courts will construe the statute to require mens rea. Thus, the government had to prove that D knew his acquisition or possession of food stamps was in a manner unauthorized by statute or regulations. The dissent replied that the most natural reading of the statute is that "knowingly" modifies only the verbs to which it is attached; *i.e.,* uses, transfers, acquires, alters or possesses food stamps. The statute requires only that D be aware of the relevant aspects of his conduct, but not that it was illegal. D's conduct in this case was intentional; he knew what he was doing and did not act through ignorance, mistake, or accident. Whether he knew which regulation he violated is beside the point.

United States v. Albertini

6) **Judicial decisions having ex post facto effect--United States v. Albertini,** 830 F.2d 985 (9th Cir. 1987).

a) **Facts.** Albertini (D) received a "bar letter" from the commander of a naval base that prohibited him from entering the base. Despite the letter, D entered the base to participate in a demonstration. D's entry violated federal law and D was convicted. The court of appeals reversed the conviction on First Amendment grounds. Before the Supreme Court accepted the government's petition for certiorari, D received another bar letter and continued his demonstrations. The Supreme Court subsequently reversed the court of appeals and upheld the first conviction. D was then convicted for his second set of violations. D appeals, claiming that the reversal of the first appeal could not be applied retroactively.

b) **Issue.** May a person be convicted for engaging in conduct that an appellate court has held constitutionally protected if the appellate court's decision is overturned after the person engages in the conduct?

c) **Held.** No. Judgment reversed.

(1) The Ex Post Facto Clause of the Constitution prevents any legislature from making criminal any act done before the law was enacted. This clause applies to the legislatures, not the courts, but the principle is fundamental to constitutional liberty.

(2) When D prevailed on appeal in this court, he received the equivalent of a declaratory judgment that his participation in the demonstrations was lawful. D was justified in relying on that opinion, at least until the Supreme Court granted certiorari.

(3) The government claims that mistake of law is not a defense, but an exception to that principle applies when the defendant reasonably relies on an official statement of the law that is later overruled. D's conduct in reliance on the first opinion of this court, prior to the Supreme Court's granting of certiorari, is therefore justified.

7) **Ignorance of laws imposing a duty to act--Lambert v. California,** 355 U.S. 225 (1957).

a) **Facts.** Lambert (D) was convicted under a Los Angeles ordinance that required convicted felons to register with the police. The ordinance defined "convicted person" as any person who had been convicted of a felony in California, or convicted of any offense in any other state which, if committed in California, would have been punishable as a felony. Another section of the ordinance required any convicted person who stayed more than five days in the city or who had visited the city more than five times in a 30-day period to register with the police. Failure to register was a continuing offense, each day's failure to register being treated as a separate offense. D was arrested on suspicion of another crime and charged with violating the registration ordinance. She appeals her conviction.

b) **Issue.** Does a city ordinance that requires convicted persons to register with the police violate the Due Process Clause when it is applied to a person who had no actual knowledge of her duty to register?

c) **Held.** Yes. Judgment reversed and remanded.

(1) It is a general maxim of criminal law that ignorance of the law is no excuse; however, the conduct prohibited by the city ordinance here is passive. Mere presence in the city constitutes the violation and there is no requirement that the convicted person have any knowledge of the registration ordinance.

(2) It is true that the police power is broad, but due process places some limits on its exercise. Notice is a key part of due process and the principle of notice is appropriate where a person, wholly unaware of any wrongdoing, is brought before a court in a criminal case.

(3) The ordinance's only purpose is for the administrative convenience of the police. But when D became aware of the existence of the law, it was already too late; she was given no chance to comply and thereby avoid punishment.

(4) Therefore, to comply with due process, it must be shown that D had actual knowledge of the duty to register, or that there was a probability of such knowledge. Otherwise, D cannot be punished for conduct which would have been innocent if done by other members of the community.

d) **Dissent.** Numerous laws enacted under the police power of the state require no knowledge of the existence of the law on the part of the defendant. The majority bases its decision on an untenable distinction between affirmative and passive acts.

e) **Comment.** The rule that ignorance or mistake of law is no defense is less strictly applied where the accused's crime is one of omission. The Model Penal Code expresses this principle more generally, providing that ignorance or mistake of law is a defense when "the statute or other enactment defining the offense is not known to the actor and has not been published or otherwise reasonably made available prior to the conduct alleged." [Model Penal Code §2.04(3)(a)]

C. PROPORTIONALITY

1. **Cruel and Unusual Punishment.** The Eighth Amendment prohibits cruel and unusual punishment. This prohibition applies to inherently cruel punishments such as torture and execution by painful and lingering methods. It also prohibits punishments that, while conceptually permissible, are cruel and unusual in a given case because the punishment is so disproportionate to the crime. The courts must defer to legislative judgments as to what punishments are appropriate, but only up to a point; if the punishment is outrageously disproportionate in a given case, the courts may forbid enforcement of the punishment.

Harmelin v. Michigan

2. **No Proportionality Guarantee--Harmelin v. Michigan,** 501 U.S. 957 (1991).

a. **Facts.** Harmelin (D) was convicted of possessing 672 grams of cocaine and sentenced to life imprisonment without possibility of parole. D appeals his conviction, claiming that his sentence is cruel and unusual, because it is significantly disproportionate to the crime.

b. **Issue.** Does the Eighth Amendment prohibition against cruel and unusual punishment include a proportionality guarantee?

c. **Held.** No. Judgment affirmed.

1) In *Solem v. Helm,* 463 U.S. 277 (1983), a life sentence with no parole for committing a nonviolent felony under a recidivist statute, when the defendant's prior crimes were also nonviolent, was set aside as disproportionate in a 5-4 decision. We now conclude *Solem* was wrong.

2) "Cruel and unusual" refers to the mode of punishment, not to proportionality.

3) The proportionality factors in *Solem* invite imposition of subjective values concerning such things as: (i) the gravity of the offense; (ii) sentences imposed for similarly grave offenses in the same jurisdiction; and (iii) sentences imposed for the same crime in other jurisdictions.

d. **Concurrence** (Kennedy, O'Connor, Souter, JJ.). There are several principles governing proportionality: (i) courts should defer to the legislatures that have fixed prison terms for specific crimes; (ii) the Eighth Amendment does not require the adoption of one penological theory; (iii) marked divergence in sentences is the inevitable result of the federal structure; and (iv) proportionality review by federal courts should be informed by objective factors.

e. **Dissent** (White, Blackmun, Stevens, JJ.). Since the Eighth Amendment forbids "excessive" fines which suggest a consideration of proportionality, it must also permit the same consideration with respect to sentences. In applying the *Solem* reasoning and factors to the instant case, the punishment here violates the Eighth Amendment.

f. **Comment.** The Court notes that there are no absolutes and that one can always imagine extreme examples, "but for the same reason these examples are easy to decide, they are certain never to occur." But what of those punishments that fall below the outrageously egregious? Can they not be cruel and unusual?

D. LEGALITY

1. **Introduction.** Statutes should give fair warning of what conduct is prohibited. Some statutes which fail to define clearly the prohibitions have been held to be void for vagueness. Certainty is a desired feature of any system of law, but it is not always possible to precisely define illegal conduct.

2. **Fair Warning—The Problem of Open-Ended Criminality.**

a. **Common law.** At common law, absent a statute, the only conduct that was criminal was that which was deemed malum in se (inherently evil). The common law took a theological approach, which looked at the intrinsic quality of conduct.

b. **Criminal codes.** One of the reasons for the formulation of criminal codes is to safeguard conduct that is without fault from arbitrary condemnation as criminal and to give fair warning of the nature of the conduct that does constitute a criminal offense.

1) **Minority view--Shaw v. Director of Public Prosecutions,** House of Lords A.C. 220 (1962).

    a) **Facts.** Shaw (D), who published a booklet advertising the names and pictures of prostitutes, was convicted of conspiracy to corrupt the public morals. D argued that because his act was not a statutory offense, he could not be convicted. D appeals.

    b) **Issue.** May a person be punished for conduct that is not statutorily prohibited?

    c) **Held.** Yes. Judgment affirmed.

        (1) The courts have an inherent power to preserve the safety, order, and moral welfare of the state. Where no statute has intervened, the common law is broad enough to guard against novel attacks on the public welfare.

    d) **Dissent.** Criminal liability should be based on legislation, not by the passing opinion of a jury or judge as to what conduct is punishable.

2) **Majority view--Keeler v. Superior Court,** 470 P.2d 617 (Cal. 1970).

    a) **Facts.** Five months after receiving a divorce decree, Keeler (D) saw his former wife; she was pregnant by another man. D kicked her in the stomach, and the baby was born dead. D was charged with murder. The action is a proceeding for a writ of prohibition.

    b) **Issue.** May a person be guilty of murder for killing an unborn fetus when the law has not determined whether an unborn fetus is a "human being"?

    c) **Held.** No. Writ should issue.

        (1) The settled meaning of the term "human being" is a person born alive. Thus, D's act is not covered by current statute.

        (2) There are no common law crimes in California.

        (3) Due process prevents retroactive application of a penal statute even if the court had the power to rule that a fetus is a "human being."

    d) **Dissent.** Medicine now makes it possible for most viable fetuses to be born alive. This fact should be taken into account in interpreting the statute.

3) **Ex post facto laws.** Judicial determination, without statutory authority, that certain conduct is criminal makes that which was previously noncriminal into a criminal act. This is the definition of an ex post facto law. The United States Constitution prohibits both state and federal governments from passing such laws.

4) **Illegality as a matter of degree--Nash v. United States,** 229 U.S. 373 (1912).

    a) **Facts.** Nash (D) was indicted for violations of the Sherman Act (*i.e.,* conspiracy in restraint of trade and conspiracy to monopolize trade). D demurred to the counts of the indictment on the grounds that the statute was unconstitutionally vague, that no overt act was alleged, and that the contemplated acts would not be an offense if they had been done. The trial court overruled the demurrer, and D appeals.

    b) **Issue.** May a criminal statute apply sanctions for conduct the illegality of which is a matter of degree subject to dispute?

    c) **Held.** Yes. Judgment affirmed.

        (1) The Sherman Act outlaws combinations which are intended to, or inherently would, prejudice the public interests by unduly restricting competition or unduly obstructing the course of trade. Such a determination necessarily involves an element of degree subject to different estimates. However, in many instances, criminality is a matter of degree such as in homicide. A person may be punished for unforeseen consequences of his actions, when common social duty would have suggested more circumspect conduct than that exhibited by the defendant in any particular case. Such a result is not forbidden by the Constitution.

3. **Vagueness and Uncertainty of Prohibitions.**

  a. **Introduction.** The law should be certain enough so that persons who want to determine the legality of their conduct can do so without acting and then being held responsible for something they believed permissible.

    1) **Obscenity.** The standard of certainty can be an elusive one. For example, at one time the standard for "obscenity" as determined by the Supreme Court under the First Amendment provided as follows: "Obscene material is that which deals with the subject matter of sex in a manner appealing to prurient interests and is without redeeming social value (as tested by contemporary community standards)."

    2) **Novel construction.** Generally, the Supreme Court construes state laws as they have been interpreted by the state's highest court. Where a statute seems clear on its face, but the state supreme court applies a novel construction, thus making conduct criminal that otherwise was apparently outside the statute, the construction given cannot be applied retroactively. For example, in *Bouie v. City of Columbia,* 378 U.S. 347 (1964), the Court reversed a conviction under a state criminal trespass statute that referred to persons "coming onto another's land," but which the state supreme court construed as applicable to persons remaining on another's land after having been asked to leave.

4. **Crimes of Status—Preventive Criminality.**

a. **Introduction.** A crime of status is not a substantive crime but is predicated on a status, condition, or mode of life (*e.g.,* vagrancy).

Papachristou v. City of Jacksonville

b. **Vagrancy statute--Papachristou v. City of Jacksonville,** 405 U.S. 156 (1972).

1) **Facts.** Papachristou (D) and her codefendants were arrested while driving from a restaurant to a nightclub under a statute for "prowling by auto." The Jacksonville vagrancy statute forbade such activity as wandering without any purpose, being a habitual loafer, etc. D appeals the conviction.

2) **Issue.** Does a broad, generalized vagrancy statute violate due process?

3) **Held.** Yes. Conviction reversed.

a) The statute fails to give adequate notice of unlawful conduct. Its wording could apply to a wide variety of innocent activity.

b) The statute encourages arbitrary arrests in that it allows the police unfettered discretion. It allows police to treat as criminals those who do not present any threat to society.

IV. RAPE

A. MENS REA

1. **Introduction.** Rape is a difficult crime for the judicial system to address. Because it is one of the most violent and despicable crimes, fairness to victims and society in general requires effective enforcement. However, it is difficult to distinguish between truthful and false complainants. The necessary mens rea is not easily articulated, nor are the rules easily applied to specific cases. [*See, e.g.,*, Regina v. Morgan, *infra*, and Commonwealth v. Sherry, *infra*]

2. **Reasonableness of Mistake--Regina v. Morgan**, A.C. 182 (House of Lords 1976).

   Regina v. Morgan

   a. **Facts.** Morgan (D) invited three other men (Ds) to come to his house to have sexual intercourse with D's wife. They did so, and D's wife testified that she did not consent. Ds testified that she did consent after some struggle. Ds were convicted despite their defense that even if D's wife objected, Ds honestly believed that she did not object. The trial court had given an instruction that Ds would not be guilty of rape if they actually believed that D's wife had consented and that such belief was reasonable. Ds appeal.

   b. **Issue.** Should the reasonableness of a defendant's actual belief with respect to an element of the crime be determinative of his guilt?

   c. **Held.** No. Judgment affirmed for lack of any "miscarriage of justice."

      1) The perpetrator of rape must, to be guilty of the offense, have intended to have intercourse with the woman without her consent. Honest belief that the woman consented clearly negates such intent. Evidence of the reasonableness of the belief is useful only for determining whether the defendant actually held the belief, but a defendant may actually believe an unreasonable thing. A man may not be convicted of rape if he actually believed the woman was consenting to the intercourse and would not have attempted it but for his belief, whatever his grounds for so believing.

      2) Here, however, no reasonable jury could fail to convict Ds, even without being instructed about the reasonableness of D's belief.

   d. **Comment.** After this case, the English statute was amended to read that a man commits rape if he has unlawful sexual intercourse with a woman who does not consent and either knows she does not consent or is reckless as to whether she consents.

3. **Subjective Belief that Victim Consented--Commonwealth v. Sherry**, 437 N.E.2d 224 (Ma. 1982).

   Commonwealth v. Sherry

a. **Facts.** A registered nurse who worked with Sherry (D), a doctor at the same hospital, was at a party with D. While there, the nurse met Hussain and Lefkowitz (Ds). At various times during the party, each of Ds made sexual advances toward the nurse. Ds then grabbed the nurse and took her outside, saying they were going to Rockport. The nurse protested but did not physically resist, because she believed they were kidding and would leave her alone. Ds took her to Lefkowitz's home. They toured the house, and in a bedroom, Ds began to remove their clothes. The nurse protested, but each D in turn had intercourse with her. They then made the nurse bathe. Eventually, they returned her to her car. At their trial, Ds testified that the nurse voluntarily accompanied them and consented to the acts of intercourse. Ds moved to dismiss for lack of force or threat of bodily injury, but the trial judge denied the motions. The jury convicted each D of rape. Ds appeal.

b. **Issue.** Does the accused's subjective belief that the victim did not object to intercourse constitute a defense to the crime of rape?

c. **Held.** No. Judgment affirmed.

   1) The evidence in the case supports the jury's verdict. A rape victim need not use physical force to resist, as long as the resistance used demonstrates an honest and real lack of consent.

   2) Ds' request for an instruction that the jury had to find they had actual knowledge of the victim's lack of consent was properly rejected by the judge. This instruction essentially raised a defense of good faith mistake as to consent, although it was not based on a reasonable good faith mistake of fact and therefore could not be given.

   3) The crime of rape essentially requires the victim's lack of consent. A victim's statement of "no" can imply nothing but nonconsent. Even if the perpetrator does not believe the statement, he should be convicted. The subjective belief of the aggressor cannot constitute a defense.

B. ACTUS REUS

1. **Introduction.** The offense of rape generally consists of forcible sexual penetration. In the absence of force or threat of force, nonconsensual sexual penetration is generally a criminal offense only if the victim is underage, unconscious, or mentally incompetent.

State v. Rusk

2. **Reasonableness of Victim's Fears--State v. Rusk,** 424 A.2d 720 (Md. 1981).

   a. **Facts.** The prosecuting witness, Pat, met Rusk (D) at a bar. D knew Pat's girlfriend. Pat said she was leaving, and D asked for a ride home. Pat drove D to his house in a neighborhood Pat was unfamiliar with. D invited Pat to come into his house, but Pat declined. D reached over, turned off the car engine, and took the keys, repeating his invitation. Pat was afraid that D would rape her by the way D looked at her, but she went with D to his house. She made no attempt to leave when D momentarily left the room. She asked D if she could leave, but D told her he wanted her to stay. Pat begged to leave and told D he could get other girls, but D became insistent. Pat started to cry and D put his hands on her throat, lightly choking her. Pat asked D if he would let her go if she did what he wanted; D said yes, and Pat proceeded to perform the sex acts D wanted. Afterwards, D returned the car keys and Pat left. She immediately reported the incident to the police. D and two friends testified to the effect that Pat willingly accompanied D, and D stated that Pat got upset only after the sex acts. D was convicted of second degree rape, but the court of appeals reversed the conviction on the ground that Pat did not resist and did not possess fear great enough to overcome an attempt to resist. The State (P) appeals.

b. **Issue.** Is the reasonableness of a rape victim's fear a factual question for the jury?

c. **Held.** Yes. Judgment reversed.

1) Lack of consent is established through proof of resistance or by proof that the victim failed to resist because of fear. The victim must have actual and reasonable fear. The reasonableness of the victim's fear is a question of fact for the fact finder, based on the evidence.

2) The evidence in this case is sufficient to allow a reasonable jury to conclude that Pat's fear was reasonable and prevented her further resistance. The appellate court erred in substituting its own judgment for the jury's.

d. **Dissent.** All essential elements of a crime must be sustained by the evidence. There is no evidence that D did anything to create Pat's fears or made any intimidating threats. Pat may have actually feared D, but D did nothing reasonably calculated to give rise to such fear.

3. **Meaning of "Physical Force"--State in the Interest of M.T.S.,** 609 A.2d 1266 (N.J. 1992).

State in the
Interest
of M.T.S.

a. **Facts.** C.G., a fifteen-year-old girl, lived with her family and M.T.S., a 17-year-old boy. C.G. claimed to have awakened with D on top of her, having already penetrated her. C.G. slapped D and told him to get off her and leave, which D did. D claimed that the encounter had started consensually. At trial, the Court did not find that C.G. had been sleeping, but that she had not consented, and that second degree sexual assault had been proven. The verdict was overturned by the appellate division. The state petitioned for certiorari.

b. **Issue.** Does the statutory requirement of "physical force" mean the use of force to overcome lack of consent?

c. **Held.** No. Appellate division reversed.

1) To require that the element of force be extrinsic to the sexual act would not only reintroduce a resistance requirement into the sexual assault law, but would also immunize many acts of criminal sexual

force not required

contact short of penetration. Further, it would be fundamentally inconsistent with the legislative purpose underlying the relevant statute to eliminate any consideration of whether the victim resisted or expressed nonconsent.

(2) Any penetration done without the affirmative and voluntary consent of the victim to the specific act of penetration constitutes the offense of sexual assault.

d. **Comment.** The Court concedes that "cases such as this are inherently fact sensitive, and depend on the reasonable judgment and common sense of judges and juries." Does that make the standard so objective as to be unconstitutionally vague?

e. **Comment.** *Commonwealth v. Berkowitz,* 641 A.2d 1161 (Pa. 1994), discusses the element of force or compulsion, which is a part of the crime of rape. The court holds that the fact that a victim merely says "no" will not establish that force was used. Rather, such evidence will go to the issue of consent only. no = consent issue, not force

People
v. Evans
4. **Ambivalent Statements of Threat--People v. Evans,** 379 N.Y.S.2d 912 (1975).

a. **Facts.** Evans (D) met a petite 20-year-old college student at the airport. D told her he was a psychologist doing a magazine article and proceeded to ask her various questions. D took her to a bar for a "sociological experiment" where he observed her reaction to the people there. Then he took her to his apartment and, after a time, began to undress her. She resisted and D told her he was disappointed that she failed the test. He then told her, "Look where you are. You are in the apartment of a strange man . . . . I could kill you. I could rape you. I could hurt you physically." The girl became afraid as she realized her situation. Then D began telling her about his lost love who had died and how much the girl reminded D of the lost love. D thereby engaged her sympathy, and several sex acts followed throughout the night. There is no evidence that the girl resisted. D was charged with rape and brought to trial.

b. **Issue.** May a man be convicted of rape on the basis of allegedly threatening statements that may be consistent with either guilt or innocence?

c. **Held.** No. D is acquitted.

(1) There can be no rape that is achieved by fraud, trick, or stratagem. As long as there is actual consent to the act, fully understood by the victim, there is no rape.

2) Seduction has been made a statutory offense in some states. In New York, there are no existing penal sanctions against seduction.

3) The question is whether D's statements undermined the victim's will. The words could be interpreted as a threat, or as a mere statement of the position the girl was in and of the harm that could have come to her had she been with someone other than D. Because a crime is charged, the criminal intent of D must be shown beyond a reasonable

doubt. The ambiguity of D's statements falls short of proof beyond a reasonable doubt.

    d.   **Comment.** *Boro v. Superior Court,* 210 Cal. Rptr. 122 (1985), deals with a rape victim who was tricked into having intercourse, in the belief that it was part of a medical procedure. The court held that it would not find that deception vitiated consent, because the legislature had not specifically included such a principle in the rape statute.

5.   **Rejection of the Marital Exception--People v. Liberta,** 474 N.E.2d 567 (N.Y. 1984).

    a.   **Facts.** Liberta (D) was married to Denise. D began to beat Denise, to the point that she obtained a temporary court order of protection. D persuaded Denise and their son to accompany him to his motel. Once in his room, D forced Denise to have sexual intercourse with him. Denise later filed a complaint, and D was convicted of first degree rape. The appellate court affirmed, but D appeals, claiming that the marital exception applied because, under the rape statute, the term "female" did not include a female married to the actor.

    b.   **Issue.** Is a statutory marital exception to the crime of rape a valid defense?

    c.   **Held.** No. Judgment affirmed.

        1)   The statute D was convicted under had been amended prior to the offense to include in the definition of "not married" those situations in which a husband and wife are living separately under a court order. Therefore, in D's case he was "not married" to Denise for purposes of the statute.

        2)   D challenges the statute on the constitutional ground that it denies him equal protection as compared to others similarly situated. The distinction drawn by the statute—between married and unmarried males—originated in the common law concept that a married woman gives irrevocable implied consent to sexual intercourse, so that any intercourse between her and her husband could not be without consent. Another rationale was that the married woman was the property of her husband. Neither rationale has validity in the modern context. A marriage license is not a license for a husband to forcibly rape his wife.

        3)   The modern justification for the marital exception is that it protects against invasion of marital privacy. This rationale is no more persuasive than the notion that privacy would permit a husband to escape liability for beating his wife. Nor does the marital exception facilitate reconciliation, since a marriage subjected to forcible rape is hardly susceptible to reconciliation.

        4)   Another consideration involves the difficulty of proof, but the rules of evidence are designed to protect against false testimony. Finally, marital rape is no less serious than other types of rape, and should be

equally subject to prosecution. Because there is no justification for the marital exception, the statute denies equal protection.

5) The final issue raised by D is that the statute applies to males, but not females. As there is no justification for this distinction, the statute also denies equal protection on this ground.

strike exceptions that deny = protection under the statute.

6) The proper remedy for the aspects of the statute that deny equal protection is to strike the exceptions, so that the statute applies to any person who engages in forcible sexual intercourse. Accordingly, D's conviction must be affirmed.

C. PROBLEMS OF PROOF

1. **Introduction.** Because of the special difficulties involved in proving or disproving rape, the rules of evidence have been carefully considered in this area. Instructions about the complainant's credibility are carefully worded. Some corroboration of the complaint may be required. Special limitations on cross-examination also apply.

2. **Corroboration.** In *United States v. Wiley,* 492 F.2d 547 (D.C. Cir. 1974), the concurring opinion of Judge Bazelon examined the corroboration requirement for rape cases. Traditionally, rape was considered a charge easily made but, once made, difficult to defend against, even if the defendant was innocent. Most states have rejected the corroboration requirement for rape. The *Wiley* court adopted a rule whereby independent corroborative evidence is regarded as sufficient when it would permit a jury to conclude beyond a reasonable doubt that the victim's version of what happened was not fabricated. The following are some of the policies behind requiring corroboration.

   a. **False rape charges are more common than false charges of other crimes.** This notion arises from the contention that women may fantasize rape or may have motives to fabricate charges, such as revenge, explanation for pregnancy, etc. However, rape is actually one of the most underreported crimes because of the treatment a victim receives in society.

   b. **Rape is unusually difficult to defend against.** This policy stems from the usual absence of eyewitnesses and the supposed sympathy juries feel for the victim. However, the low rate of convictions where there is no corroborating evidence suggests that juries are actually skeptical of rape accusations.

   c. **Rape convictions result in severe sentences.** Corroboration is sometimes required because of the severity of punishment imposed, yet more lenient punishment would not reflect the serious nature of the offense.

   d. **Racial and sexual discrimination.** In the past, rape accusations may have been used to discriminate against blacks, who were disproportionately convicted of the offense. Corroboration was considered necessary to protect against this form of racism. It was also used to some extent to discriminate against women. Both forms of discrimination are disappearing in society.

3.   Cross-Examination of the Victim.

   a.   **Introduction.** Generally, character evidence is not admissible to prove conduct. Federal Rule of Evidence 608 allows such evidence for impeachment of a witness, but only under narrow restrictions. Formerly, a rape victim's character trait for unchastity could be used. Today, most jurisdictions have adopted "rape shield" laws that generally bar evidence of the victim's unchastity on the issue of consent. Most jurisdictions also do not allow proof of unchastity by specific instances of consensual intercourse with persons other than the defendant. Some jurisdictions have reached the same result by judicial decision.

   b.   **Use of character evidence--State *ex rel*. Pope v. Superior Court, 545 P.2d 946 (Ariz. 1976).**

   1)   **Facts.** Pope (P), a county attorney, brought a special action requesting the Arizona Supreme Court to reconsider existing law about the admissibility of evidence regarding the unchaste character of an alleged rape victim.

   2)   **Issue.** May evidence of a victim's unchaste character be used to impeach the victim's credibility?

   3)   **Held.** No.

      a)   Character evidence regarding unchastity may not be used to attack the credibility of the complaining witness in a forcible rape prosecution because there is no necessary connection between a witness's veracity and her sexual immorality.

      b)   Character evidence and evidence of prior bad acts have been admissible in the past when the defense of consent is raised, on the theory that a woman who has strayed from the path of virtue in the past is more likely to consent than a woman who has not strayed. However, such evidence injects collateral issues into the case and may divert the jury's attention from the defendant to the victim's past. Therefore, such evidence generally may not be used whenever a defense of consent is asserted.

      c)   In some situations, the probative value of evidence of prior unchaste acts may outweigh its inflammatory effect. These include evidence of prior consensual sexual intercourse with the defendant or testimony directly refuting physical evidence such as the victim's alleged loss of virginity, the origin of semen or disease, or pregnancy. *[handwritten: exception]*

      d)   Reputation evidence may sometimes be admitted if its value is great (*e.g.,* when the prosecution offers evidence of the victim's chastity, or in an attempted rape prosecution where the subjective intent of the defendant is an element).

4)   **Concurrence.** Reputation evidence has no place in other offenses and should not be used in rape prosecutions. Nor should a defendant be able to introduce evidence that a victim has made unsubstantiated charges of rape in the past.

c.   **Prior bad acts--State v. DeLawder,** 344 A.2d 446 (Md. 1975).

    1)   **Facts.** DeLawder (D) was charged with statutory rape of a girl less than 14 years old. D desired to discredit the prosecuting witness's testimony by revealing her possible biases, prejudices, or ulterior motives in making the allegations she did. D wanted to show that at the time of the alleged incident the girl thought she was pregnant by someone else and that she claimed D raped her because she was afraid to tell her mother that she had voluntarily had sexual intercourse with others. D would show that she had previously had sexual intercourse. The trial court sustained objections to this line of questioning and D was convicted. On appeal, the conviction was upheld. Then the United States Supreme Court decided *Davis v. Alaska,* 415 U.S. 308 (1974), which discussed the Confrontation Clause of the Sixth Amendment. The Court held that "the exposure of a witness's motivation in testifying is a proper and important function of the constitutionally protected right of cross-examination." The Court held that this principle outweighed the interests of protecting the confidentiality of juvenile adjudications of delinquency, the issue in the *Davis* case. In light of *Davis,* D seeks postconviction relief.

    2)   **Issue.** May a defendant use evidence of prior bad acts when such evidence may directly reveal the witness's biases, prejudices, or ulterior motives in testifying?

    3)   **Held.** Yes. Conviction overturned.

       a)   The rationale for not allowing evidence of prior bad acts was that consent was not an issue in a statutory rape prosecution, and any bad reputation for chastity was immaterial as an excuse.

       b)   The prosecution's case here relied entirely on the girl's veracity. D should have been able to show her biases or ulterior motives. His inability to cross-examine as to these questions was a denial of the right to confrontation. The desirability of allowing the girl to perform her public duty of testifying free from embarrassment or damage to her reputation must yield to D's right to seek out the truth in his defense.

    4)   **Comment.** In *Milenkovic v. State,* 272 N.W.2d 320 (Wis. 1978), the defendant sought to prove that the complainant accused him of rape falsely by showing that she had been promiscuous, had contracted venereal disease, thought she had infected her boyfriend, and wanted to explain the venereal disease by claiming the defendant passed it by raping her. The court held that the defendant could not introduce the evidence because the offer of proof was defective. The defendant did not offer to prove that the boyfriend did not know the girl had venereal disease before the alleged rape or that she did not know whether the boyfriend knew. The court criticized the *DeLawder* court for simply assuming that the mother was unaware of the pregnancy without requiring an offer of proof.

d. **Psychiatric examination--Government of the Virgin Islands v. Scuito,** 623 F.2d 869 (3d Cir. 1980).

   1) **Facts.** Scuito (D) was convicted of forcible rape. D and the victim told similar stories about the circumstances of the sex acts, the difference being whether D forced the woman. D sought a psychiatric examination of the woman because of her reputation for drug abuse and strange countenance and interests. The trial court refused to allow the exam. D appeals.

   2) **Issue.** Does a trial judge have discretion as to whether to order a psychiatric examination of an alleged rape victim?

   3) **Held.** Yes. Judgment affirmed.

      a) There are no evidence rules governing the use of a psychiatric examination, but many of the considerations regarding evidence of a rape victim's prior sexual conduct apply. [*See* Fed. R. Evid. 412] Both situations involve embarrassment to the victim, which may deter complaints and testimony by victims. The judge has discretion to allow the introduction of such evidence and to order such exams. The objective sought by D in this case could have been met by direct testimony of others in the community who observed the victim's behavior.

V. HOMICIDE

A. INTRODUCTION

Homicide is the killing of one human by another. Homicide is not necessarily a crime, but it is a material element for the crimes of murder and manslaughter.

1. **Types of Homicide.** There are three types of homicide.

   a. **Justifiable homicide.** A homicide is justifiable if it is commanded or authorized by law, such as when committed in execution of a sentence of death, in preventing an escape, or in pursuit of a dangerous fleeing felon.

   b. **Excusable homicide.** Excusable homicide may be either accidental or in self-defense.

      1) **Accidental.** For accidental homicide, the person must have committed the homicide while performing a lawful act with due care and without any intention of hurting the other.

      2) **Self-defense.** Self-defense involves killing another upon sudden affray, merely in one's own defense or in defense of one's spouse, child, or parent, and not from any vindictive feeling.

      3) **Comment.** Other homicides are excusable as a result of the status of the person committing the act (infants, feeble-minded persons, etc.), or because of an actual and reasonable mistake of fact.

   c. **Criminal homicide.** Criminal homicide is the killing of another human being but without justification or excuse. The two important classifications here are "murder" and "manslaughter."

2. **Elements of Criminal Homicide.**

   a. **Corpus delicti (the body of the crime).** The corpus delicti of a criminal homicide consists of two elements:

      (i) A person is deceased; and

      (ii) The death is a result of someone's criminality.

      1) **The victim.** There is controversy whether an unborn infant was "living" at the time of the act that purportedly resulted in its death.

         a) **Majority view.** The majority view presumes a child to be dead until proven otherwise. The proof of life required is that the child be expelled from the mother and using its own circulatory system.

         b) **Minority view.** The minority view holds that the killing of a fetus is homicide.

2) **Omission to act.** Where there exists a legal duty to act, an omission to so act will constitute criminal homicide if such omission results in the killing of another human being. For example, the court found a legal duty existed where two elderly women lived together and one became incapacitated; the other did nothing to help her, creating culpable negligence when the first woman died.

b. **Time limit.** At common law, the death had to occur within one year and a day after the defendant's unlawful act causing the injury or there could be no prosecution for murder. This is still the law in most jurisdictions.

c. **Criminal state of mind.** Determination of the mental element (mens rea) is usually more difficult to establish than the physical element (actus reus). The classification of the mens rea distinguishes murder from manslaughter and the various degrees thereof.

B. GRADING OF INTENDED KILLINGS—MURDER

Murder is the unlawful killing of a human being by another human being with malice aforethought. This malice may be actual or may be implied by law.

1. **Malice Aforethought.**

   a. **Introduction.** The term "malice aforethought" does not approximate its literal meaning. Rather than relying on this misleading phrase, it is more appropriate to consider the various types of mens rea for murder that the common law came to recognize and that exist today in most jurisdictions:

      1) **Intent to kill.** Conduct, accompanied by an intent to kill, that causes another's death constitutes murder, unless there are mitigating circumstances present, or the homicide is either justifiable or excusable.

      2) **Intent to inflict serious bodily harm.** Conduct coupled with an intent to do serious bodily injury but without an intent to kill, which causes another's death, constitutes murder.

      3) **Depraved heart.** Reckless conduct that a reasonable person would realize creates a high degree of risk of death or serious bodily injury to another, which actually causes the death of another, may constitute murder.

2. **First and Second Degree Murder.**

   a. **Introduction.** At common law, there were no degrees of murder. All homicide with "malice aforethought" was murder and punished by death. In order to reduce the punishment for less grievous homicides, most states classify murder. The typical classification is into first degree (homicide with "premeditation") and second degree (without "premeditation") murder.

b. First degree murder. First degree murder is all homicide with malice aforethought that is either (i) encompassed within the felony-murder rule of the jurisdiction (usually heinous felonies); or (ii) willful, deliberate, and premeditated.

1) **Willful.** The defendant must actually intend to kill.

2) **Deliberate.** The defendant must be possessed of a cool mind that is capable of reflection.

3) **Premeditated.** The defendant, having a cool mind, must in fact reflect before his act of killing. The defendant's state of mind is decisive during the length of time between the formation of the idea to kill and the actual killing.

4) **Proof of state of mind.** Premeditation, deliberation, and willful intent are subjective states of mind. The existence of these elements must be determined from the defendant's conduct in light of the surrounding circumstances.

5) **Presumption of premeditation for certain homicides.** Homicides perpetrated by poison or torture or after lying in wait for the victim, etc., are presumed by common law to have been premeditated.

a) **"Irresistible impulse" does not preclude premeditation--Commonwealth v. Carrol,** 194 A.2d 911 (Pa. 1963).

(1) **Facts.** Carrol (D) was convicted of first degree murder after he took a gun from near the bed and shot his wife twice in the back of the head while she was lying on the bed with her back to him. D's wife suffered from mental disorders and was allegedly sadistic and nagging. A psychiatrist testified that, in his opinion, D's act was an impulsive automatic reflex homicide as opposed to an intentional premeditated homicide. D appeals, claiming that his crime was at most second degree rather than first degree murder.

(2) **Issue.** May a person be guilty of first degree murder when acting out of an "irresistible impulse"?

(3) **Held.** Yes. Judgment affirmed.

(a) The intent to kill necessary to first degree murder may be found from D's own words or conduct or the surrounding circumstances together with all reasonable inferences therefrom, and may be inferred from the intentional use of a deadly weapon on a vital part of another's body.

(b) Whether the time period between forming the intent to kill and committing the killing was short or long is immaterial if the homicide was in fact intentional, willful, deliberate, and premeditated. The fact that D

Common-
wealth v.
Carrol

may not have established a plan to dispose of the body or escape is no defense if he acted deliberately.

    (c)   A psychiatrist's testimony that there was no premeditation need not be believed by the jury and was entitled to little weight since it was contradicted by D's own testimony that he "remembered the gun, took it down, and fired two shots" into the head of his sleeping wife.

    (d)   The relationship between D and his wife leading up to the murder may have created an irresistible impulse or an inability of D to control himself, but could not excuse his deliberate act.

    b)   **Elements of proof--People v. Anderson,** 447 P.2d 942 (Cal. 1968).

    (1)   **Facts.** Anderson (D) was convicted of first degree murder and sentenced to death. D killed the 10-year-old daughter of the woman with whom he had lived for about eight months. Over 60 knife wounds were inflicted upon the victim's body. No one witnessed the killing, but D had been drinking heavily. D appeals.

    (2)   **Issue.** Must there be clear evidence of premeditation to justify a first degree murder conviction?

    (3)   **Held.** Yes. Judgment modified. Evidence is sufficient only to find second degree murder. The following types of evidence are necessary to find first degree murder:

    (a)   Facts showing that the defendant was engaged in planning the murder prior to its occurrence.

    (b)   Facts about the defendant's prior relationship with or conduct with the victim that would justify a finding of motive to kill the victim, plus facts of type (a) or (c) that justify an inference that the homicide was premeditated.

    (c)   Facts about the nature of the homicide so that it may be inferred that it was intentional (*i.e.,* it was so particular and exacting that it must have been premeditated) and done for a reason as indicated in (b).

    (4)   **Comment.** The court here found insufficient evidence that D planned the murder, that D had any motive to kill the victim, or that the stabbings were deliberately placed blows; thus, premeditation could not be inferred.

c.   **Second degree murder.** In most states, murder not falling within the first degree murder category is second degree murder.

1)   **No premeditation.** Those murders committed with the intent to kill but lacking premeditation and deliberation are of the second degree.

a) **Intentional.** Both first and second degree murder include "intentional" homicide. Since it may actually be impossible for the mind to function in a way so that an intentional homicide occurs without at least some premeditation, the only difference between first and second degree murder exists in the degree of the premeditation (a difficult distinction to make).

b) **Voluntary manslaughter.** However, if the rationale of second degree murder is that it does not involve premeditation, then a conflict between it and intentional (voluntary) manslaughter inevitably arises. Voluntary manslaughter does not include malice (since it is a homicide which arises from a sudden passion and on adequate provocation); therefore, it seems that the difference between voluntary manslaughter and second degree murder is in the adequacy of the provocation that causes the killer's act—a more substantial provocation must be required to classify the homicide as voluntary manslaughter.

2) **Felony-murder.** Those felony-murders where the felony in question is not enumerated in the first degree murder statute are considered to be second degree murder.

3) **Wanton disregard for human life.** Killings that indicate the defendant's wanton and willful disregard for human life are also second degree murder (*e.g.*, playing "Russian roulette" with a loaded revolver).

a) This standard seems to approach the negligence standard, but in order for second degree murder to exist, the defendant's act must be sufficiently wanton to imply malice.
   (reckless)

b) Involuntary manslaughter may also arise from criminal negligence (although sufficient wantonness is not present to imply malice aforethought). Here again, the distinction between second degree murder and involuntary manslaughter is a difficult one to draw.

c) Criminal negligence, even of a wanton nature, cannot ever amount to first degree murder because negligence necessarily rules out the possibility of premeditation.

d) The element of provocation, which is discussed *infra* in connection with manslaughter, may reduce murder to manslaughter.

e) The character of the defendant (*e.g.*, personal turpitude) may also have an effect on whether the murder is held to be first or second degree murder.

3. **Provocation.**

   a. **Common law reasonable person test.** At common law, sufficient provocation is that which causes a reasonable person to lose his normal self-control. Although a reasonable person who has lost control over himself would not kill, his homicidal reaction to the provocation is at least understandable. The provocation defense is available only if the offender moves quickly (*i.e.,* succumbs to the provocation right away); too much delay can lose the defense.

b. **Provocation of adultery--State v. Thornton,** 730 S.W.2d 309 (Tenn. 1987).

1) **Facts.** Thornton (D) found his wife and her lover engaged in sexual relations in D's home. He fired a single shot at his wife's lover, striking him in the left hip. The victim died 16 days later from massive infection of the wound. At the time of the incident, D and his wife were separated, but D was attempting a reconciliation. The couple's three-year-old daughter was asleep in an upstairs bedroom at the time of the shooting. D's wife stated that she had informed D that she might want to "date" someone else, and that she considered that to mean having sexual relations. D had apparently gone to the family home to try to convince his wife that his attempts at reconciliation were sincere. He observed his wife and the victim in the kitchen with the child. D decided to go get his camera. D returned and spent over an hour observing the two. When he heard the sounds of intercourse he burst into the house and bedroom and attempted to take pictures. Stating that he believed the victim was about to attack him, D drew his pistol, and fired once. D gave directions to the ambulance dispatcher and remained until the police arrived. D testified that he lost control and exploded when he found the couple in bed. D was convicted of first degree murder. D appeals.

2) **Issue.** Will the provocation of finding one's wife *in flagrante delicto* serve as a defense to the charge of first degree murder?

3) **Held.** Yes. Reversed and remanded for sentencing for voluntary manslaughter.

   a) D actually found his wife in bed with a stranger, at the time he was trying to save his marriage. D had attempted no harm to the victim until that point. The passions of any reasonable person would have been inflamed and intensely aroused.

4) **Comment.** The court's disapproval of the wife's behavior is quite apparent in its opinion. The specific reference to the fact that D's wife had only met the victim a few nights before, but had engaged in intercourse with him each night since, would seem to indicate that the court believes that she was equally, if not more, at fault than D.

c. **Traditional common law limits on provocation--Girouard v. State,** 583 A.2d 718 (Md. 1991).

1) **Facts.** During an argument with his wife, Girouard (D) stabbed her 19 times after she graphically disparaged his sexual ability, said she did not love him, demanded a divorce, and told him she had filed charges to have him court-martialed. D then non-fatally slit his own wrists and called the police. Police found D wandering around, despondent, and tearful. D was convicted of second degree murder and sentenced to 22 years in prison, 10 of which were suspended. D appeals.

2) **Issue.** Should the mitigating factor of provocation be limited only to the traditional circumstances of: extreme assault and battery upon a defendant; mutual combat; illegal arrest; injury or serious abuse of a close relative; or sudden discovery of a defendant's spouse committing adultery?

3) **Held.** Yes. Judgment affirmed.

    a) This state holds, as do most jurisdictions, that words alone, even "fighting words," do not constitute provocation adequate to reduce the crime of murder to manslaughter.

4) **Comment.** Most cases of provocation involve inflammatory words being used by one person to another, who reacts with force. What if the disparaging remarks in this case were said to other people about D and in D's presence? Or, what if the remarks were made to D, but loudly enough for others to hear? Would the added factor of "humiliation" tip the scales?

d. **"Mere words."** In *State v. Shane,* 590 N.E.2d 272 (Ohio 1992), the defendant killed his wife after she admitted her infidelity. The court noted its disapproval of a rule that "mere words" cannot be sufficient provocation to reduce murder to manslaughter generally, but which makes a specific exception when one spouse informs the other of infidelity. The court held that words alone will not constitute reasonably sufficient provocation to incite the use of deadly force in most situations; the trial judge must decide this issue as a matter of law, in view of the specific facts of the individual case.

Maher v. People

e. **Provocation out of presence of defendant--Maher v. People,** 10 Mich. 212 (1862).

1) **Facts.** Maher (D) was convicted of assault with intent to kill. D tried to kill a man he had been told had had sexual intercourse with his wife. The trial court excluded evidence of provocation on the rule that the provocation had to be committed in the presence of the defendant. D appeals.

2) **Issue.** To be admissible, must provocation have been committed in D's presence?

3) **Held.** No. Judgment reversed.

    a) The evidence should have been admitted. The acts amounting to the provocation need not be committed in D's presence. Adequate provocation is that which would provoke a reasonable person, before a reasonable time has elapsed for the passion to cool, and is the result of temporary excitement.

    b) Here, D seeing his wife and another man go into the woods, and being told that his wife had had sexual relations with the man the day before, was sufficient evidence to go to the jury on the issue of provocation. New trial is granted.

4) **Comment.** The common law did not permit a jury to find provocation in any and all situations in which the jury could find the circumstances reasonably provocative. The more lenient approach in *Maher* is recognized in most states today.

f. Model Penal Code--People v. Casassa, 404 N.E.2d 1310 (N.Y. 1980).

1) **Facts.** Casassa (D) became infatuated with Lo Consolo, who rejected D's advances. D eavesdropped on Lo Consolo's apartment. Finally, D took several bottles of liquor to Lo Consolo's apartment, but she rejected his offer. D then stabbed her to death. D eventually confessed and was charged with second degree murder. D claimed as a defense that he acted under the influence of extreme emotional disturbance based on his obsession with Lo Consolo. A state witness testified that D's mental state was the result of stress he created within himself. The trial court found D guilty on the ground that the test of extreme emotional disturbance was objective, not subjective, and that D's emotional state was so peculiar to him that it could not be considered reasonable. D appeals.

2) **Issue.** Does the defense of extreme emotional disturbance require a completely subjective evaluation of reasonableness?

3) **Held.** No. Judgment affirmed.

a) Under the criminal statute, D has the burden of proof as to the affirmative defense of extreme emotional disturbance. The defense is broader than the traditional "heat of passion" defense that it replaced, because extreme emotional disturbance need not be spontaneous; it can be one that affects the accused's mind for a substantial period of time before becoming manifest. It requires a mental infirmity short of the level of insanity but sufficient to render the accused less culpable for his actions.

b) There are two elements to the defense: (i) an act done under the influence of extreme emotional disturbance; and (ii) a reasonable explanation for the disturbance as viewed by a person in the defendant's situation under the circumstances as the defendant believed them to be.

c) D claims that the extreme emotional disturbance defense is based on a subjective standard of reasonableness. The first element of the defense is clearly subjective, but the second requires an objectively reasonable explanation. The jury evaluates the defense by viewing the accused's internal situation and his perception of the external circumstances, and then determining whether from that viewpoint the explanation for the emotional disturbance was reasonable. By this means, an accused has a fair opportunity for mitigation, while the fact finder is not required to find mitigation whenever emotional disturbance exists.

d) The trial court applied the correct standard when it considered D's mental disability but found that D's excuse was so peculiar to him that it did not merit mitigation. D acted out of malevolence, not pursuant to an understandable human response that deserves mercy.

g. Objectivity and defendant's age and sex--Director of Public Prosecutions v. Camplin, 2 All E.R. 168 (House of Lords, 1978).

1) **Facts.** Camplin (D), a 15-year-old boy, was with the deceased, a middle-aged man, in the deceased's apartment. The deceased buggered D in spite of D's resistance and then laughed at D. D lost his self-control and hit the deceased with a heavy cooking pan, splitting his skull. At trial, D asked for an instruction that his conduct be measured by the reaction expected of a reasonable boy. The judge refused and gave a reasonable man instruction. D was convicted of murder. On appeal, the court substituted a conviction for manslaughter on the ground that the jury should have considered D's age. The Director of Public Prosecutions (P) appeals.

2) **Issue.** In deciding questions of provocation, should the fact finder consider the reaction expected of a reasonable person of the defendant's same age and sex?

3) **Held.** Yes. Judgment affirmed.

   a) Homicide is the only crime in which provocation may affect the nature of the offense committed. In other crimes, provocation is relevant only in determining the appropriate penalty.

   b) Prior cases held that the defendant's own temperament or physical defect should not be a factor in applying the reasonable person test. A modern statute has changed the law in pertinent ways, however. It still requires that the provocation actually cause the defendant to lose his self-control and that a reasonable person would react as did the defendant, but it also removes all limitations as to what may be a provocation and it clearly leaves it to the jury to apply the reasonable person test.

   c) The rationale for the reasonable person test is to avoid allowing pugnacious persons to easily excuse loss of self-control. The old rule required that words alone were insufficient unless accompanied by violence. Under the new rule, words alone may be sufficient provocation. This necessarily means that the defendant's characteristics should be considered in analyzing the gravity of the provocation.

   d) A jury should hold a defendant to a standard of self-control possessed by a reasonable person, but should consider the defendant's characteristics in determining whether the provocation would make a reasonable person lose self-control. The reasonable person is one of the defendant's same sex and age.

C. GRADING OF UNINTENDED KILLINGS

1. **Manslaughter.** Manslaughter is a catch-all category that includes homicides that are not bad enough to be murder but that are too bad to be of no criminal consequence whatever.

a. **Voluntary manslaughter.** Voluntary manslaughter is an intentional homicide committed under extenuating circumstances that mitigate but do not justify or excuse the killing. The principal extenuating circumstance is that the defendant acted in a state of passion engendered by adequate provocation.

   1) **Heat of passion.** The elements of heat of passion are:

      a) There must have been a reasonable provocation.

      b) The defendant must have been in fact provoked.

      c) A reasonable person so provoked would not have cooled off in the interval of time between the provocation and the delivery of the fatal blow.

      d) The defendant must not in fact have cooled off during that interval.

b. **Involuntary manslaughter.** Involuntary manslaughter is an unintentional homicide committed without excuse, justification, or malice. Involuntary manslaughter may result from the commission of a lawful act in a negligent manner, or from the commission of an unlawful act that is not a felony (the misdemeanor-manslaughter rule).

   1) **Criminal and tort negligence compared.** Most states require a higher degree of negligence for criminal liability than that required for ordinary (tort) negligence. The negligence required is either one or both of the following two elements:

      a) The defendant's conduct must involve a high degree of risk of death or serious bodily injury, in addition to the unreasonable risk required for ordinary negligence.

      b) Whatever the degree of risk required, the defendant must be aware that his conduct creates this risk.

      c) Note that if both are required, then "recklessness" is a more appropriate term than negligence.

   2) **Hazardous business conditions--Commonwealth v. Welansky, 55 N.E.2d 902 (Mass. 1944).**

      a) **Facts.** Welansky (D) was hospitalized for an illness. At the same time, in a nightclub D owned, a 16-year-old employee used a lighted match in trying to see to replace a burned-out light bulb. In so doing, he lit some flammable decorations. The fire spread throughout the club and several customers died. D was convicted of manslaughter because he permitted the flammable decorations, defective wiring, overcrowding, and absence of suitable means of escape, all of which proximately led to the deaths. D appeals.

      b) **Issue.** May a person be convicted of manslaughter merely for permitting hazardous conditions to exist on his business premises?

      c) **Held.** Yes. Judgment affirmed.

Common-
wealth v.
Welansky

(1) Involuntary manslaughter consists of death resulting through wanton or reckless conduct. If there is a duty of care for the safety of business visitors invited to premises which D controls, wanton or reckless conduct may consist in intentional failure to take such care in disregard of the probable harmful consequences to them.

(2) Knowing facts that would cause a reasonable person to know the danger is equivalent to knowing the danger, even if the person is so heedless as to not actually know the danger. Even if D actually thought he was careful, the facts showed the risk was so great that his inaction was wanton and reckless.

(3) D was more than just negligent or even grossly negligent. Fire in a public place is always a danger, and D's disregard of the safety of his patrons in the event of a fire from any cause was wanton and reckless.

3) Homicide through the use of automobiles.

    a) Simple negligence. In *State v. Barnett,* 63 S.E.2d 57 (S.C. 1951), Barnett was convicted of involuntary manslaughter because of a homicide resulting from his negligent operation of a car. He appealed, claiming that the court erred in charging that ordinary negligence is sufficient for conviction. The court held that ordinary negligence in the handling of a dangerous instrumentality is equivalent to culpable negligence. Generally, involuntary manslaughter requires that the accused's negligence be "gross." However, because of the inherent danger of an automobile, simple negligence is sufficient for an involuntary manslaughter conviction.

    b) Special statutes. Some states, such as California, provide for a special category of manslaughter—manslaughter in the operation of a motor vehicle:

        (1) It is a felony to unintentionally kill a person while operating an automobile in a criminally negligent manner.

        (2) It is a misdemeanor to kill a person while operating an automobile in a negligent manner.

State v. Williams

    c. Objective and subjective standards--State v. Williams, 484 P.2d 1167 (Wash. 1971).

        1) Facts. The Williams (Ds), husband and wife, were both Indians who did not graduate from high school. The wife had two children from a prior marriage, the younger of whom was 17 months old. This child developed a toothache from an abscessed tooth. Within a two-week period, an infection of the mouth and cheeks developed and became gangrenous. Because he could not eat, the child's resistance was lowered and he contracted pneumonia, from which he died. During this time, Ds knew the child was ill and they gave him aspirin. They did not take him to a doctor for fear that the authorities would keep him because of his condition. The autopsy surgeon testified that, even if the child had seen a doctor in the last week, the child's life could not have been saved. Ds were charged with manslaughter for negligently failing to provide necessary medical attention. Ds were convicted and now appeal.

2) **Issue.** May simple negligence suffice to render a person criminally liable?

3) **Held.** Yes. Judgment affirmed.

   a) The common law rule required more than ordinary or simple negligence for a determination of involuntary manslaughter; gross negligence was essential. A Washington state statute has modified the law by imposing criminal liability where death is the proximate result of only simple or ordinary negligence.

   b) Ds were required to exercise ordinary caution. They knew that the child was sick while there was still time to take him to a doctor and save his life. They had taken him to a doctor previously. They could see that his condition was deteriorating. Ds breached their duty of caution, and the child died as a proximate result of the breach; thus, they are guilty.

d. **Distinguishing murder and manslaughter.**

1) **Intent to do a dangerous act--Commonwealth v. Malone, 47 A.2d 445 (Pa. 1946).**

   Common-wealth v. Malone

   a) **Facts.** Malone (D), age 17, was convicted of second degree murder for killing his friend, age 13, during a game of "Russian poker." D and the victim were on friendly terms; both had consented to play, neither intending harm to the other. D appeals, contending that he is only guilty of manslaughter.

   b) **Issue.** Is malevolence toward the victim an essential element of malice?

   c) **Held.** No. Judgment affirmed.

       (1) When an individual commits an act of gross recklessness for which he must reasonably anticipate that death to another is likely to result, he exhibits that wickedness of disposition, hardness of heart, and a mind regardless of social duty that proves that he possessed malice.

   d) **Comment.** D did not intentionally kill the victim. He did act in a "maliciously reckless" manner, however.

2) **Malice based on reckless and wanton conduct--United States v. Fleming, 739 F.2d 945 (4th Cir. 1984).**

   United States v. Fleming

   a) **Facts.** Fleming (D) had a blood alcohol level of .315 and was driving in the wrong direction on a one-way road at between 70 and

80 miles per hour. The speed limit was 30 miles per hour. D lost control of his vehicle and collided with a car driven by Mrs. Haley. The impact killed Mrs. Haley. D was convicted of second degree murder. D appeals, claiming that the evidence did not show malice aforethought, so he could be convicted at most of manslaughter.

b) **Issue.** May a person be convicted of murder for a death caused by reckless driving while intoxicated?

c) **Held.** Yes. Judgment affirmed.

(1) Malice aforethought is the element that makes a homicide a murder instead of manslaughter. Such malice does not require an intent to kill or injure, nor does it require ill will against the victim or other persons. Evidence of reckless and wanton conduct that is a gross deviation from a reasonable standard of care, sufficient to support an inference that the accused was aware of a serious risk of death or serious bodily harm, may demonstrate malice.

(2) In this case, the prosecution only had to prove that D intended to drive the way he did without regard for the life and safety of others. The evidence presented supports the verdict.

(3) D claims that if he could be convicted of murder without proof that he intended to cause death or injury, then all drunk driving homicides would be murder. However, the difference between malice for murder and gross negligence which only supports manslaughter is a difference of degree. D's conduct is markedly different in degree from most vehicular homicides. While the typical drunk driver puts others in danger simply by attempting to drive, in this case, D was drunk but also drove in a reckless manner that was especially dangerous because he was drunk.

2. **Commission of Crime.**

a. **Unlawful act doctrine.** "Unlawful act involuntary manslaughter" covers an unintentional homicide in the commission of a dangerous, unlawful (malum in se) act. If the unlawful act is malum prohibitum, the defendant generally is held not guilty of manslaughter unless the death is the foreseeable consequence of his conduct in committing the act. Thus, if A ran into B, a pedestrian, while driving in excess of the speed limit (although not recklessly), he would not be guilty of involuntary manslaughter since the act is only "malum prohibitum," not "malum in se."

State v. Hupf

1) **Application--State v. Hupf,** 101 A.2d 355 (Del. 1953).

a) **Facts.** Hupf (D) was convicted of involuntary manslaughter after a passenger in his car was killed when D was involved in an automobile accident. The State (P) proved that the death was the proximate result of D's vehicle code violations, but failed to prove that D drove recklessly. The trial court certified the issue to the state supreme court.

b) **Issue.** May a person be convicted of involuntary manslaughter without proof of conduct evidencing reckless disregard for the lives or safety of others, as long as a death resulted proximately from the commission of an unlawful act?

c) **Held.** Yes.

    (1)   It is unnecessary for the State to prove conscious or reckless disregard for the lives or safety of others. Mere violation of a statute, coupled with the violation's being the proximate cause of death, is sufficient to constitute involuntary manslaughter. The circumstances of the particular case are relevant in mitigation of punishment.

d) **Comment.** This case follows the common law definition in that both "malum in se" and "malum prohibitum" acts may constitute the "unlawful" act. Most courts do not go as far as *Hupf* did. Courts take three different views of malum prohibitum crimes as being manslaughter:

    (1)   D is not guilty unless the death that occurs is the foreseeable or natural consequence of D's unlawful conduct.

    (2)   Did the unlawful excess cause the death, or would it have happened even if D had been acting lawfully?

    (3)   D is not guilty of manslaughter unless the unlawful conduct (malum prohibitum) amounts to criminal negligence.

b. **Felony-murder rule.** At common law, any homicide committed while perpetrating or attempting to perpetrate a felony was murder. Most jurisdictions have limited this rule.

1) **The basic rules.**

    a) **Types of felonies.** Some jurisdictions have amended the felony-murder rule to hold that it will be applied only to certain types of felonies (*e.g.,* rape, robbery).

    b) **"In perpetration of" felony.** The homicide must occur "in the perpetration of" the felony. Most courts interpret this to mean that it is sufficient if the homicide takes place at any time within the "res gestae" of the other felony, and this includes all acts in the immediate preparation, actual commission, and immediate escape. A few courts require that the homicide occur at the actual moment of technical perfection of the felony (if the felony is burglary, it must occur during the breaking and entering).

    c) **Dangerous felony--Regina v. Serné,** 16 Cox Crim. Cas. 311 (1887).   Regina v. Serné

(1) Facts. Serné (D) insured his property and the life of one of his boys. While the family was sleeping, D allegedly set fire to the house. Everyone but D's two boys escaped. D was charged with murder, and the judge gave instructions to the jury.

(2) Issue. Does the felony-murder doctrine apply regardless of the dangerous nature of the felony involved?

(3) Held. No.

    (a) Malice aforethought includes knowledge that the act will probably cause the death of a person as well as acts done with an intent to commit a felony. However, the common law rule is too broad unless it is limited to dangerous felonies. The felony-murder rule should only apply when the act is known to be dangerous to life and likely in itself to cause death, and is done for the purpose of committing a felony and does cause death.

d) Comment. In *People v. Stamp*, 82 Cal. Rptr. 598 (1960), the victim died from a heart attack partly brought on by fright when he was robbed at gunpoint by the defendant. The defendant's conviction of first degree murder was affirmed on the grounds that a felon is strictly liable for all killings committed by him in the course of the felony and takes his victim as he finds him.

People v.
Phillips

2) Inherently dangerous felonies--People v. Phillips, 414 P.2d 353 (Cal. 1966).

a) Facts. Phillips (D) was convicted of second degree murder by application of the felony-murder rule based on his commission of grand theft. D, a chiropractor, induced the victim's parents not to allow an operation, representing falsely that he could treat her. D charged them a substantial sum, but the child died. D appeals his conviction.

b) Issue. Must the felony D is charged with be an "inherently dangerous" one in order to apply the felony-murder rule?

c) Held. Yes. Judgment reversed.

    (1) Grand theft is not inherently dangerous to life, and only such dangerous felonies will support a felony-murder conviction. No prior case has applied the doctrine when the death resulted from felonious perpetration of a fraud.

    (2) It makes no difference that the acts of D may themselves have been inherently dangerous. The court must look in the abstract to the felony with which D is charged. Otherwise there would be no limitation on the doctrine, which has been severely criticized.

    (3) There is no proof that D acted with conscious disregard for life in this case. The felony-murder rule allowed a conviction without proof of express or implied malice.

d) Comment. In *People v. Satchell*, 489 P.2d 1361 (Cal. 1972), the court found that the felony possession of a concealable weapon by an ex-felon was not a "felony inherently dangerous to human life." Looking to the genus of crimes known as felonies, the court determined that it could not conclude that the "possession of a concealable firearm by one who has been convicted of *any crime within that genus* is an act inherently dangerous to human life which, as such, justifies the extreme consequence (*i.e.,* imputed malice) which the felony-murder doctrine demands."

3) **Merger doctrine--People v. Smith,** 678 P.2d 886 (Cal. 1984).

a) **Facts.** Smith (D) became angry with her two-year-old daughter Amy when Amy refused to sit on the couch instead of the floor while eating a snack. D began spanking Amy, then she and her boyfriend began hitting her repeatedly with their hands and a paddle. They also bit Amy. Finally, D knocked Amy backwards, causing her to hit her head on the closet door. Amy went into respiratory arrest and died shortly thereafter. D was tried for murder. Among other things, the jury was instructed on second degree felony murder, using the felony of child abuse. D was convicted of second degree murder and felony child abuse and appeals, claiming that the crime of child abuse was an integral part of and included in fact within the homicide and thus merged into the homicide.

b) **Issue.** May felony child abuse that produced the death be used as the underlying felony to support a conviction of second degree murder on a felony-murder theory?

c) **Held.** No. Judgment reversed.

(1) Felony murder is a disfavored doctrine; it is usually unnecessary and it erodes the relation between criminal liability and moral culpability. The doctrine should be given the narrowest possible application consistent with its purpose of deterring those who engage in felonies from killing negligently or accidentally.

(2) The felony-murder doctrine does not apply to felonies that are an integral part of and included in fact within the homicide. Most homicides are committed as a result of a felonious assault; to apply the rule in such cases would preclude the jury from considering the issue of malice aforethought. Such an application would have no deterrent effect.

(3) Such felonies as assault with a deadly weapon, burglary with intent to assault, and discharging a firearm at an inhabited dwelling have been held to merge into the resulting homicide. On the other hand, felonies such as furnishing narcotics, driving under the influence of narcotics, poisoning food, drink or medicine, armed robbery, kidnapping, and child abuse by malnutrition and dehydration have been used to support application of the doctrine.

(4) Despite these general principles, the doctrine may apply if the underlying offense was committed with an independent felonious purpose. In this case, there was no independent purpose for D's beating of her daughter; the purpose was the very assault that resulted in death.

Criminal Law - 65

4)   Killing by the victims.

a)   No liability for death of a co-felon--State v. Canola, 374 A.2d 20 (N.J. 1977).

(1)   Facts. Canola (D) and three others were robbing a store when shooting started. The store owner shot and killed one of the robbers and was, in turn, killed by another of the robbers. D was indicted on two counts of murder and was convicted of both counts. On appeal, the conviction for the murder of the store owner was upheld but the homicide of the co-felon prompted a petition of certification to the New Jersey Supreme Court.

(2)   Issue. May a felon be guilty of murder for the killing of a co-felon by a victim of the felony?

(3)   Held. No. The count relating to the death of the co-felon is dismissed.

(a)   The applicable statute states simply that "if the death of anyone ensues from the committing" of a felony, then the felon may be guilty of murder. The common law felony-murder rule was never applied to hold a felon guilty of the death of his co-felon at the hands of the intended victim. Nor have any of the states so held, although some, at times, have imposed criminal liability on the felons for the killing of nonfelons by police or victims.

(b)   The statute uses broad language that could include the death of a co-felon. The language could also mean to include accidental deaths or any death within the res gestae of the felony. Because of multiple possible interpretations, public policy must guide the application of the statute.

(c)   The general doctrine of felony murder is based on an agency theory, because one may not be criminally liable for acts not actually or constructively his own. Thus, the statute should not be construed to expand the rule beyond the common law notion.

(4)   Concurrence. The statute was clearly intended to impose liability for any killing that ensues during the felony, even though not committed by any of the felons. The only exception would be the killing of a co-felon by other than another co-felon, which is justifiable homicide.

b)   Vicarious liability theory--Taylor v. Superior Court, 477 P.2d 131 (Cal. 1970).

(1)   Facts. Taylor (D), a getaway driver in a robbery of a liquor store, was charged with the murder of his accomplice, who was conducting the robbery and was killed by one of the proprietors. D sought to have the murder count of the information dismissed.

(2) **Issue.** If the conduct of a co-perpetrator is sufficiently provocative of lethal resistance to support a finding of implied malice, may he be charged with murder when the victim of the crime kills his fellow perpetrator?

(3) **Held.** Yes. Writ of prohibition is denied.

Agency theory followed here

(a) The charge of murder is not based on the felony-murder rule, but upon vicarious liability for the intentional acts of an accomplice.

(b) The mens rea requirement is implied by the felon's "conscious disregard for life." If the felon provokes lethal resistance by the victim, the requirement is met.

(c) It is reasonable to find that the felons sufficiently provoked the proprietor to hold the felons responsible for initiating the gun battle.

(4) **Dissent.** Criminal defendants should be responsible only for their own acts.

D. CAPITAL PUNISHMENT

1. **Introduction.** Under common law, crimes were classified as treason, felony, and misdemeanor. Crimes classified as felonies under common law were punishable by the death penalty. Although the penalties have changed, the offenses have generally retained that status under modern statutes. The type of penalty used today to distinguish a felony from a misdemeanor is usually the type of prison to which the offender may be sent, or the length of sentence which can be imposed. Two other classifications continue in modern times: capital/noncapital crimes, and infamous/noninfamous crimes.

2. **Capital Punishment Constitutional--Gregg v. Georgia,** 428 U.S. 153 (1976).

Gregg v. Georgia

a. **Facts.** Gregg (D) was found guilty of murder and sentenced to death under Georgia law. In an earlier case, *Furman v. Georgia*, 408 U.S. 238 (1972), the Supreme Court had held the Georgia capital punishment statute unconstitutional because it allowed imposition of the death penalty in a capricious and arbitrary manner. D challenges the state statute as amended.

b. **Issue.** Is capital punishment per se "cruel and unusual punishment" and therefore unconstitutional under the Eighth and Fourteenth Amendments?

c. **Held.** No. Judgment affirmed.

1) Although unappealing to many, capital punishment is essential to an ordered society that requires reliance on the legal process instead of self-help. On a number of occasions, we have both assumed and asserted the constitutionality of capital punishment. In fact, 35 states enacted capital punishment statutes since the *Furman* decision, indicating continued public acceptance of capital punishment.

2) Because statistical attempts to evaluate the deterrent effect of the death penalty have been inconclusive, the resolution of this complex factual issue properly rests with state legislatures.

3) Under Georgia's sentencing procedure, the jury's discretion is always circumscribed by legislative guidelines. The death penalty is available for only six categories of crime: murder, kidnapping for ransom or where the victim is harmed, armed robbery, rape, treason, and aircraft hijacking. After a verdict of guilty, a separate sentencing hearing is conducted, and the jury must find that one of ten specified aggravating circumstances exists before imposing the death penalty. This satisfies the concerns of *Furman* as to those defendants who were being condemned to death capriciously and arbitrarily.

d. **Dissent** (Brennan, J.). Our civilization and the law have progressed to the point that the punishment of death, for whatever crime and under all circumstances, is "cruel and unusual."

e. **Dissent** (Marshall, J.). The death penalty is unnecessary to promote the goal of deterrence or to further any legitimate notion of retribution, and is thus "cruel and unusual punishment."

McClesky
v. Kemp

3. **Statistical Challenges to the Fairness of the Death Penalty--McClesky v. Kemp,** 481 U.S. 279 (1987).

a. **Facts.** McClesky (P) was convicted of murder for killing a white policeman during the course of a robbery. P was black. P was sentenced to death based on the aggravating circumstances that the murder was committed during the course of an armed robbery and the victim was a police officer who was performing his duties. The state courts upheld the conviction and sentence. P then petitioned for a writ of habeas corpus in federal court, claiming that the capital sentencing process was racially discriminatory. To support his claim, P produced a statistical study that showed that a black person convicted of killing a white victim was significantly more likely to be sentenced to death than a white person convicted of killing either a white person or a black person. The district court dismissed the petition and the court of appeals affirmed. P appeals.

b. **Issue.** May an accused rely on statistical evidence of racial disparity in sentencing to prove that the sentencing procedure is unconstitutional?

c. **Held.** No. Judgment affirmed.

1) A defendant claiming deprivation of equal protection must prove purposeful discrimination that had a discriminatory effect on him. P failed to prove that the decision makers acted with discriminatory purpose in this case. Instead, P relied on the statistical study. While

statistics may be useful in some types of cases, they are inapplicable to capital sentencing decisions.

2) Sentencing procedures require consideration of innumerable factors that depend on the facts of each particular case. An appropriate inference that would apply to a specific decision may not be drawn from general statistics. The sentencing procedure, as well as the entire criminal justice system, relies on discretion as a basic principle, and the exercise of such discretion should not be overturned by resort to general statistical analysis.

3) Even if the procedure in individual cases results in statistical disparities, this does not show that the state had a discriminatory purpose in using the system. There is no evidence that the state legislature adopted the capital punishment statute to further a racially discriminatory purpose.

4) P also claims the sentencing system violates the Eighth Amendment. This attack on the discretionary nature ignores the substantial benefits to the defendant that accrue from the discretion in the system, such as the jury's ability to exercise leniency. The system is designed to minimize racial bias, while preserving the fundamental value of a jury and the benefits of discretion.

5) Another problem with P's approach is that there is no limiting principle. Any statistical disparity based on an arbitrary variable, including physical attractiveness or facial characteristics as well as race, would support an attack. P's claims are matters for the legislature, not the courts.

d. **Dissent** (Brennan, Marshall, Blackmun, Stevens, JJ.). The fact in this case is that P's chance of a death sentence was more likely because he was black. The Court has in the past been concerned with the risk of an arbitrary sentence, even if the accused cannot prove racial bias in any particular sentencing decision. The statistical study shows that race is more likely than not to influence the sentence. If a conviction is not permissible if the chance of error is less likely than not, then a death sentence should not be imposed if the chance of irrational imposition is more likely than not. While discretion is important, it is a means, not an end.

e. **Dissent** (Blackmun, Marshall, Brennan, Stevens, JJ.). The Court is applying a lesser standard of scrutiny in this capital punishment case than it ordinarily applies to equal protection challenges. The statistical study shows that race better explains differential treatment than any other grounds.

f. **Dissent** (Stevens, Blackmun, JJ.). The racial disparity shown by P is contrary to the Court's prior requirement that capital punishment not be imposed unless it is done fairly and with reasonable consistency. The state could limit capital punishment to those serious offenses in which it can be shown that the sentence is not influenced by race.

VI. THE SIGNIFICANCE OF THE RESULTING HARM

A. CAUSATION—ACCOUNTABILITY FOR THE RESULTS OF CONDUCT

1. **Introduction.** Criminal culpability generally requires not only conduct but also a specified result of that conduct.

    a. Some crimes do not require a specific result; for example, conspiracy.

    b. The causation question is conveniently divided into two topics: actual causation and proximate causation.

2. **Actual Cause.**

    a. **"But for" rule.** The defendant's act must have actually caused the unlawful result before he can be held criminally liable. The defendant is the cause if "but for" his antecedent conduct the result would not have occurred.

    b. **Foreseeability--People v. Acosta,** 284 Cal. Rptr. 117 (1991).

People v.
Acosta

   1) **Facts.** Acosta (D), driving a stolen motor vehicle, led the police on a 48-mile chase, driving recklessly much of time. Two police helicopters, assisting in the chase, collided with each other, killing three occupants. Expert testimony at trial indicated the crash was due to pilot error and was not affected by ground activity. D was convicted of three counts of second degree murder. D appeals.

   2) **Issues.** a) Was there sufficient evidence that D's conduct was the proximate cause of the deaths? b) Was there sufficient evidence of malice?

   3) **Held.** a) Yes. b) No. Judgment reversed.

      a) The crash was not a "highly extraordinary result" which would absolve D. Rather, it was foreseeable that in the heat of the chase, a pursuer might act negligently or recklessly. But for D's conduct, the crash would not have happened.

      b) There was no malice, however, because no showing was made that D consciously disregarded the risk to the helicopter pilots.

   4) **Dissent.** D certainly represented a threat to other vehicles on the road, but to extend that responsibility to persons in the air, whose role was to merely observe D's movements, defies common sense.

People
v. Arzon

    c. **Exclusive and sole cause not required--People v. Arzon,** 401 N.Y.S.2d 156 (1978).

1) Facts. Arzon (D) set fire to a couch in an abandoned multistory building. Fire fighters responded to the resulting fire but were unable to control it. When they decided to leave the building, they were engulfed in smoke from a separate fire on a lower floor. The added smoke made evacuation more dangerous, and one fire fighter received fatal injuries. D was charged with second degree murder for his reckless conduct and with second degree felony murder. D seeks to have these charges dismissed for lack of a causal connection.

2) Issue. Must a defendant's actions be the sole cause of another's death in order to support a murder conviction?

3) Held. No. Motions denied.

    a) When a person acts with "depraved indifference to human life," it is not necessary that the ultimate harm be intended by the actor. As long as the ultimate harm should have been foreseen as being related to the action taken, criminal liability may exist. The conduct must be an actual cause of the death; however, it need not be the sole and exclusive factor.

    b) Here, D's conduct indicated a depraved indifference to human life. The response of the fire fighters was easily foreseeable, as was their exposure to a life-threatening danger. The spread of the fire further increased the danger and placed the fire fighters in a position of particular vulnerability to the separate and independent fire on a lower floor. Therefore, D's conduct was a sufficiently direct cause of the death to make D liable. The ultimate harm was a result foreseeably related to D's acts.

d. Sufficiently direct cause. In *People v. Warner-Lambert Co.*, 414 N.E.2d 660 (N.Y. 1980), Warner-Lambert and its officers were indicted for manslaughter after an explosion at one of its chewing gum factories. The company used potentially explosive substances in the manufacturing process and had been warned by its insurer of the explosion hazard. There was no hard proof of what triggered the explosion. The court found the evidence before the grand jury was not legally sufficient to establish the foreseeability of the immediate, triggering cause of the explosion and dismissed the indictment. The court stated, "We subscribe to the requirement that the defendants' actions must be a *sufficiently direct cause* of the ensuing death before there can be any imposition of criminal liability . . . ."

e. Substantial factor test. The test here is: "Was D's conduct a substantial factor in bringing about the forbidden result?" If the result would not have occurred "but for" D's conduct, this conduct is a substantial factor in bringing about the result, but D's conduct will sometimes be a substantial factor even though not a "but for" cause.

f. Example. A is falling from a window; midway down B shoots him dead. Is B to be held? Did he cause A's death? B certainly sped it up. The decision to hold B is not as easy as in tort cases where the courts would simply give damages for the worth of A's life at the time he was shot. In the criminal law, it is an all-or-nothing proposition. B is either guilty or not guilty. [*See* People v. Ah Fat, 48 Cal. 61 (1874)—he is guilty]

g.   **Neglect or maltreatment of injury.** D remains responsible for the death of another if he wounds or injures another and such injury results in death. It is irrelevant that the death is only an indirect result of a chain of natural causes or the result of unskilled or improper medical treatment. All persons are criminally liable for the consequences of their acts even though other causes produced the fatal result.

   1)   **Application.** In *Hall v. State*, 159 N.E. 420 (Ind. 1927), D struck several blows to the head of the deceased, fracturing his skull. However, the cause of death was determined to be blood poisoning resulting from the skull fracture. Further evidence was presented indicating that the wounds to the head received improper medical treatment. Consequently, D appealed his conviction of first degree murder. The court sustained the conviction, holding that D would not be relieved of responsibility even though improper medical treatment aggravated the wound and contributed to the death.

h.   **Subsequent injury inflicted by another.** When one willfully and with malice aforethought wounds another with a deadly weapon, and immediately thereafter a third person willfully and maliciously inflicts another wound and thereby accelerates or hastens the victim's death, both offenders can be found guilty of murder under the majority view.

People v.
Campbell

   1)   **Subsequent human actions--People v. Campbell,** 335 N.W.2d 271 (Mich. 1983).

      a)   **Facts.** Campbell (D) and Basnaw were drinking heavily. D, angry at Basnaw for having had sex with D's wife, encouraged Basnaw to kill himself, giving Basnaw his own gun and five bullets. After D left, Basnaw shot himself. D was charged with murder. D moved to quash the information and dismiss. The motion to quash was denied. D appeals.

      b)   **Issue.** Does providing a weapon to one who subsequently uses it to commit suicide constitute murder?

      c)   **Held.** No. Reversed and remanded with instructions to quash.

         (1)   The prosecution and trial court relied on *People v. Roberts,* 178 N.W. 690 (Mich. 1920), in which a husband left a poisoned brew within reach of his terminally ill wife who knowingly ingested it. Roberts was convicted of murder in the first degree.

         (2)   We hold that *Roberts* no longer represents the law of Michigan.

         (3)   "Homicide" involves the killing of another. "Suicide" by definition cannot include homicide. Inciting someone to commit suicide cannot qualify as a homicide because D did not kill another.

         (4)   D hoped Basnaw would commit suicide, but hope does not provide the degree of intent required for murder.

i. **Intervening act--Stephenson v. State,** 179 N.E. 633 (Ind. 1932).

  1) **Facts.** Stephenson (D) abducted the deceased woman and took her to a train, on which he assaulted her with the intent to rape. D and his accomplice then took her to a hotel room. D permitted her to leave with his accomplice to buy a hat. The deceased also bought poison, which she took back at the hotel. After she became ill, D took her home. She died about a month later as a result of the combination of shock, loss of food and rest, infection from the wounds D inflicted, the effects of the poison, and the failure to obtain prompt medical attention. None of these factors alone would have caused death. D was convicted of second degree murder. D appeals.

  2) **Issue.** May a person be convicted of murder for inflicting an injury that contributes substantially to a death, although other causes also contributed to the death?

  3) **Held.** Yes. Judgment affirmed.

    a) All of D's actions were so closely connected that they constitute one transaction. D's actions, taken as a whole, make him criminally responsible for the homicide.

    b) The fact that the deceased took poison is directly related to D's conduct. The deceased was under D's control at all times. The poisoning was part of the attempted rape because of the effect the assault had on the deceased.

  4) **Comment.** A victim's voluntary self-infliction of harm may break the causation unless the victim is rendered irresponsible by the defendant's acts. The *Stephenson* case has been criticized, though, because the motive for taking the poison appeared to be to escape the shame and disgrace of what had happened, rather than to escape further assault.

  5) **Comment.** In *People v. Lewis,* 57 P. 470 (Cal. 1889), Lewis (D) shot the deceased in the abdomen, inflicting a wound that would produce death within an hour. While in D's house, the deceased got hold of a knife and cut his own throat, inflicting a wound that would produce death within minutes. D appealed his conviction, alleging that it was this intervening cause that shortened D's life. The court sustained the conviction, holding that when the deceased cut his throat, he was already actually dying from the mortal wound to his abdomen. Thus, the gunshot wound contributed to the deceased's death.

3. **Proximate Cause.** Even though A's conduct may actually cause B's death, this conduct is not necessarily the "legal" or proximate cause of B's death.

  a. **Direct causation.** Where direct causation exists, courts will hold that there is proximate cause also. In other words, if a reasonable person standing in the position of the defendant at the time of the act could have foreseen the result which in fact occurred (absent intervening forces), the defendant will be held responsible.

Common-
wealth
v. Root

1) **Comparison to tort law--Commonwealth v. Root,** 170 A.2d 310 (Pa. 1961).

a) **Facts.** Root (D) and the deceased were in a drag race on a highway, going about 90 miles per hour, when the road narrowed to two lanes at a bridge. The deceased tried to pass D and hit an oncoming car. Appeal is from D's conviction for involuntary manslaughter.

b) **Issue.** Do tort concepts of proximate cause apply equally in criminal cases?

c) **Held.** No. Conviction reversed.

(1) The deceased was aware of the risk and caused his own death by his own independent, reckless act. D's conduct was not a sufficiently direct cause of the death.

(2) The tort concept of proximate cause is inapplicable in criminal cases, where a more direct causal connection is required. Otherwise the expansion of tort liability principles could extend criminal liability to those whose conduct is not generally considered to present the likelihood of a resultant death.

d) **Dissent.** D's unlawful conduct was a direct cause of the death. The decedent's action was a natural reaction to the situation.

e) **Comment.** This case tends to distort the meaning of legal cause. The true reason for the court's holding is probably the feeling that D should not be held liable for the death of the deceased, who was an equally willing and foolhardy participant in the drag race which caused his death. The court pointed out that if the tort principles applied in criminal cases, the conduct of the deceased would have to be considered to determine whether it superseded D's conduct. The deceased's attempt to pass would be a superseding cause. However, in *Jacobs v. State*, 184 So. 2d 711 (Fla. 1966), where an innocent victim was killed, as well as one of the race participants, the court held all three drag racers criminally liable for the death of the innocent party. The court stated that the deaths were proximately caused by the negligent operation of a motor vehicle while drag racing.

State v.
McFadden

2) **Proximate cause/vicarious liability--State v. McFadden,** 320 N.W.2d 608 (Iowa 1982).

a) **Facts.** McFadden (D) and Sulgrove engaged in a drag race on a city street. Sulgrove lost control of his vehicle, swerved into oncoming traffic, struck a third vehicle, and killed six-year-old Ellis. Sulgrove was also killed. D's vehicle did not impact with either of the other cars. D was charged with two counts of involuntary manslaughter. After a bench trial, D was convicted and sentenced. D appeals.

b) **Issue.** Is there sufficient causation to uphold a conviction of involuntary manslaughter of a defendant who participates in a drag race with another person who strikes another vehicle and kills someone, when the defendant did not impact with any other cars?

c) **Held.** Yes. Convictions affirmed.

(1) The trial court found D guilty under three separate theories: (i) aiding and abetting; (ii) vicarious responsibility; and (iii) proximate cause.

(2) While vicarious liability would support D's conviction as to Ellis, it would not support the conviction as to Sulgrove. D could not be guilty of vicarious liability as to Sulgrove's death because there is a statutory requirement of proof that the perpetrator caused the death of another.

(3) Sulgrove's voluntary participation does not, in itself, bar D's conviction.

(4) The civil standard of proximate cause, *i.e.*, that there be a sufficient causal relationship between the defendant's conduct and a proscribed harm to hold him criminally responsible, may be properly applied to criminal matters, since there are no specific policy differences that would justify a different standard.

3) **Causation established--Commonwealth v. Atencio,** 189 N.E.2d 223 (Mass. 1963).

Commonwealth v. Atencio

a) **Facts.** Atencio (D), his friend (D), and the deceased played a game of Russian roulette. Each D placed the gun to his own head and pulled the trigger once before the deceased took his turn. The gun fired when the deceased pulled the trigger. Ds were convicted of manslaughter. Atencio appeals.

b) **Issue.** When a person shoots himself to death as part of a game of Russian roulette, are the other players criminally liable for the death?

c) **Held.** Yes. Judgment affirmed.

(1) Ds' concerted action and cooperation in the game constituted wanton or reckless conduct which brought about the death. The deceased's act was not an intervening act so as to exculpate Ds; it was part of a joint enterprise.

(2) Ds may not have had a duty to prevent the deceased from playing, but they had a duty not to participate and thereby encourage him.

(3) This case differs from the drag racing cases in which the death results from lack of skill or judgment. Here, the outcome is a certainty and mere luck determines who will die.

d) **Comment.** Compare this case to *Commonwealth v. Malone, supra*, in which D was found guilty of murder.

b. Intervening causes.

1) Introduction. D's criminal responsibility terminates if, subsequent to his act, a new and independent force that was neither contemplated nor reasonably foreseeable supersedes and itself becomes the proximate cause of the injury.

2) Examples.

a) If A receives a nonmortal wound at the hands of B, is negligently treated by Doctor C, and dies, B will be held for homicide. Such negligent treatment is a reasonably foreseeable risk; *contra* where the negligence amounts to gross negligence.

b) If D assaults someone, leaving him helplessly lying on the highway, and a car then runs the victim over, killing him, D must be held for the death (the intervening force was certainly foreseeable).

c. Summary on proximate cause.
Note that if a court finds that there is proximate cause, this is simply a determination by the court that, weighing all the facts of the case, it thinks that responsibility is sufficient to find the defendant guilty as charged. Other hypotheticals:

1) D shot the victim, inflicting a mortal wound that would produce death in an hour. Then the victim took a knife and cut his own throat, which also would cause death in five minutes. The court held that concurrent causes existed and found the defendant guilty.

2) A mortally wounds B; C comes along and kills B. C is held. If A materially increased the risk to B by putting him in a position to be killed, A may also be held. Similarly, both may be held if A and C are working in concert.

3) A gave B a poison pill. She attempted to swallow it and choked on the pill, dying of suffocation. Here there is "but for" causation, but the result is certainly bizarre. But since B would have died from the pill anyway, A is liable.

B. ATTEMPT

1. **Introduction.** Both at common law and under most modern statutes, it is a crime to attempt the commission of any felony or misdemeanor. Merely taking steps toward the completion of a crime, if done with the requisite intent, may be a crime itself. Attempt consists of (i) a specific intent to commit a crime and (ii) an act in furtherance of that intent which goes far enough toward completion of the crime.

2. **Mens Rea.** The mens rea of attempt has two components: (i) the intent to commit the acts or cause the result constituting the crime; and (ii) the intent necessary for the completed crime. Therefore, if the crime allegedly attempted requires specific intent, such as burglary, the defendant must have had the specific intent to commit burglary.

a. **Application to attempted murder--People v. Kraft,** 478 N.E.2d 1154 (Ill. App. Ct. 1985).

1) **Facts.** Kraft (D) prevented the Grossis from passing him as they were both driving down the highway. D then pulled over to the side of the road. As Grossi pulled up to his truck, D fired a shot over the Grossis' car. D then fired another two or three shots, one of which struck the Grossis' car. Grossi found a police officer, who drove to D's truck. D then initiated a gunfight. D surrendered after being wounded. D was charged with attempted murder. At his trial, D explained that he had become afraid of Grossi and only intended to scare him away. Once he shot, he went into shock and "wanted to die," so he shot at the police. D's psychiatrist testified that D had a schizotypal personality disorder with depression and was under the influence of alcohol and marijuana at the time of the incident. He also testified that D was sane and had full knowledge of what he was doing. D's defense was essentially that he never intended to kill anyone and could not be convicted of attempted murder because he lacked the necessary intent. The jury was instructed that attempted murder occurs if one knows that the act creates a strong probability of death to an individual. D was convicted. D appeals, claiming the jury instructions were incorrect.

2) **Issue.** May a person be convicted of attempted murder in the absence of evidence of an intent to kill the victim?

3) **Held.** No. Judgment reversed.

a) The crime of murder includes an act performed with the knowledge that such act creates a strong probability of death or great bodily harm to the victim or another. Attempt is defined to be any act that constitutes a substantial step toward the commission of an offense, committed with intent to commit the specific offense. As a result of these definitions, there is a discrepancy between the culpable mental states for the two crimes; *i.e.,* attempt requires an intent to commit the offense, but murder includes intents other than an intent to kill.

b) The jury instruction given in this case is similar to the holding in *People v. Morano*, 387 N.E.2d 816 (Ill. App. 1979), to the effect that knowledge of a probability of death resulting from the act is sufficient to support a conviction for attempt. In *People v. Jones*, 405 N.E.2d 343 (Ill. 1979), however, the state supreme court noted that specific intent to kill is required to support a conviction for attempted murder. Therefore, knowledge that the consequences of an act might include death does not satisfy the specific intent requirement. This is the better approach.

3. Actus Reus.

a. Introduction. The actus reus of attempt is an act that progresses sufficiently toward the commission of the offense. Whether a defendant has done enough in furtherance of his intent to have committed attempt is not subject to any precise rule. Various approaches have been used.

b. Traditional approach.

1) Perpetration vs. preparation. Some courts hold that the defendant's acts must have gone beyond mere "preparation" into the zone of "perpetration." However, because there is much confusion as to when preparation ends and perpetration begins, this formula is not always useful.

Common-
wealth v.
Peaslee

2) Dangerous proximity to success--Commonwealth v. Peaslee, 59 N.E. 55 (Mass. 1901).

a) Facts. Peaslee (D) was arrested for arranging combustibles in a house, soliciting someone to start the fire (who refused), and driving toward the building with intent to light the materials. However, when D was within a quarter of a mile of his destination, he changed his mind and drove away. D was convicted of attempted arson. D appeals.

b) Issue. Is it necessary that an accused carry through with the last act of his criminal purpose to be held liable for attempt?

c) Held. No. Judgment reversed on other grounds.

(1) The arranging of combustibles on its face indicated the intent to commit arson.

(2) All the circumstances and facts must be weighed before a decision can be reached as to perpetration, however. Some preparations may constitute attempts if the preparation comes near to accomplishing the act and the intent to complete makes the crime probable.

d) Comment. This decision, written by Justice Holmes, is the source of the "dangerous proximity to success test" for attempt.

c. Alternative approaches. The difficulty in applying the traditional approach in a consistent and fair manner has led some courts to apply alternative analyses.

1) The last step. In *King v. Barker*, N.Z.L.R. 865 (1924), the court cited the rule stated in *R. v. Eagleton*, 169 E.R. 826 (1855):

"the accused must have taken the last step which he was able to take along the road of his criminal intent."

2) **Physical proximity test.** Some have suggested that the defendant's conduct must be physically proximate to the intended crime, the focus being on what remains to be done as opposed to what was already done. In applying this test, courts may take into account such factors as the seriousness of the crime, the time and place at which it is to occur, and the uncertainty of the result.

3) **Control over all indispensable elements.** An alternative test requires that the defendant go far enough to have obtained control over all factors that are indispensable to the commission of the crime. Thus, nothing must be left undone that would prevent the defendant from committing the crime.

4) **"Probable desistance" test.** Another approach is to find an attempt only when the act is such that in the ordinary course of events it would lead to completion of the crime in the absence of intervening outside factors. Thus, the emphasis here is upon the likelihood that the defendant would cease his efforts to commit the crime, given the conduct he has already committed.

5) **"Equivocality" or "res ipsa loquitur" test.** Still another variation suggests that an act amounts to attempt only if—when considered alone—it firmly shows the actor's intent to commit the crime. Hence, the accused's behavior is considered without reference to other evidence that may demonstrate criminal intent (such as a confession); the act relied upon to constitute attempt must "speak for itself" in establishing intent.

6) **Act falling short of an attempt punishable by statute--State v. Young,** 271 A.2d 569 (N.J. 1970).

    a) **Facts.** A group of students staged a protest sit-in over the dismissal of a student for refusing to stand for a flag salute. Young (D), a lay minister, entered the school grounds and participated in the sit-in. D was arrested and convicted under a state law prohibiting the entering on school grounds with the intent to disrupt the peace and order of the school. D appeals.

    b) **Issue.** May the state punish a person who commits an otherwise innocent act because of the person's unlawful purpose in so acting?

    c) **Held.** Yes. Judgment affirmed.

        (1) The state may punish innocent acts, if they are done with unlawful intent. The act itself need not be criminal. Many statutes prohibit otherwise innocent acts if they are done with the forbidden purpose or intent. Examples are possession of burglar tools or weapons with improper intent.

        (2) At common law, a crime required both an act and wrongful intent, but the act could by itself, if not accompanied by the wrongful intent, be innocuous. The common law crime of "attempt" required an act short of actual commission of a crime,

as long as the necessary evil purpose was connected with the act.

(3) In attempt cases, a distinction is made between an attempt and mere preparation, which would not be a crime. Yet conduct short of an attempt may be punishable at common law, such as solicitation or conspiracy to commit a crime. While not in itself an attempt, a solicitation or conspiracy presents a likelihood of evil consequences sufficient to merit criminal sanctions.

(4) In modern times, legislatures may protect society by criminalizing an act because of the evil purposes associated with it, regardless of whether the act would constitute a common law attempt to commit the crime which the legislature desires to prevent. Therefore, even if D did nothing more than enter the school with the forbidden intent, he was guilty. It does not matter that his conduct fell short of an actual disruption, or even an attempted disruption.

McQuirter v. State

7) **Lingering as attempt--McQuirter v. State,** 63 So. 2d 388 (Ala. 1953).

a) **Facts.** McQuirter (D), a black man, was sitting in the cab of his truck one evening. Mrs. Allen, who was white, and her children walked by, and D got out of his truck. D walked behind Mrs. Allen down the street. Mrs. Allen stopped at a friend's house for 10 minutes while D passed by. When she left, D came toward her. Mrs. Allen then went to another friend's house, and D turned and walked back down the street, then leaned on a stop sign for about 30 minutes. After D finally went back toward his truck, Mrs. Allen went home. D was charged with assault with intent to rape. At the trial, three police officers testified that D claimed that he intended to get a white woman that night and that he intended to take Mrs. Allen into a nearby cotton patch. D denied having made these statements and gave an innocent explanation for his actions. He was found guilty of an attempt to commit an assault with intent to rape. D appeals.

b) **Issue.** May a person be convicted of an attempt to commit an assault with intent to rape if he merely follows the victim and lingers near her home, as long as he later expresses his intent to "get" her?

c) **Held.** Yes. Judgment affirmed.

(1) An attempt to commit an assault with intent to commit rape is merely an attempt to commit rape that has not proceeded far enough to constitute an assault. To justify a conviction of attempt to assault with intent to commit rape, the jury must find beyond a reasonable doubt that D intended to have sexual intercourse with the woman against her will.

(2) If the jury was satisfied beyond a reasonable doubt that D intended to have sexual intercourse with Mrs. Allen against her will, by force or by putting her in fear, then the conviction was not improper. Intent is a jury question, and the evidence here was sufficient to sustain the verdict.

d) **Comment.** Attaching criminal liability merely for manifesting an intent in one's actions comes very close to violating the fundamental criminal law requirement of an actus reus.

d. Model Penal Code approach.

1) **Basic approach.** Departing from the approaches considered above, the Model Penal Code would require an act constituting a "substantial step" in the course of conduct intended to result in the crime. In addition, the conduct must be "strongly corroborative" of the defendant's criminal purpose, although it need not establish purpose by itself.

2) **Application--United States v. Jackson,** 560 F.2d 112 (2d Cir. 1977), *cert. denied*, 434 U.S. 941 (1977).

United States
v. Jackson

a) **Facts.** Jackson (D) and Allen were contacted by Hodges to help her carry out a bank robbery. The group planned to enter the bank with the manager on Monday morning and take the weekend deposits. They armed themselves and drove to the bank, but did not rob it because they had arrived late. They decided they needed another man and went and got Scott. They returned to the bank. Allen entered to check for cameras and D made a false license plate. Because customers were in the bank, the group decided to wait until the next Monday. In the meantime, Hodges was arrested for a separate crime and began cooperating with the government, warning them of the imminent robbery. Allen told Hodges he would not rob the bank, but on Monday morning the three men, heavily armed and otherwise prepared, went to the bank, alternately parking and driving around for about an hour. During this time, D removed the front license plate (the false plate had been placed over the rear plate). When making a pass by the bank, the men detected the government agents and sped off. They were arrested and convicted of attempted robbery. Ds appeal.

b) **Issue.** May a defendant be convicted of attempt when he did not commit the last proximate act necessary to effect a particular result that is an element of the offense?

c) **Held.** Yes. Judgment affirmed.

(1) Commission of the "last proximate act" is sufficient, but not necessary, to constitute an attempt.

(2) To be convicted, D must have (i) been acting with the kind of culpability otherwise required for conviction of a crime, and (ii) taken a "substantial step" toward the commission of the crime.

(3) The substantial step must "strongly corroborate" the firmness of the defendant's criminal intent. The substantial step, in addition to an affirmative act, can be an omission or possession. The substantial step requirement eliminates remote preparation from criminal liability.

(4) This approach assures firmness of criminal design while allowing apprehension of dangerous persons without risking the ultimate harmful result.

(5) The evidence here supports the findings made at trial that D's acts were substantial. The steps taken were not "insubstantial" as a matter of law.

e. **Solicitation.**

1) **Common law.** At common law, it is a misdemeanor to counsel, incite, or induce another to commit or to join in the commission of any offense, whether that offense is a felony or a misdemeanor.

a) **Mens rea.** The common law crime of solicitation apparently requires a showing that the defendant acted volitionally and with the intent or purpose of causing the person solicited to commit the crime.

b) **Actus reus.** The only act required for the commission of the crime is the counseling, inciting, or inducing of another to commit the offense. The crime of solicitation is complete upon the performance of this act.

2) **Modern statutes.** While statutes traditionally have not dealt comprehensively with solicitation, the tendency has been to limit the crime to the incitement, counseling, etc., of serious offenses, such as murder, rape, kidnapping, robbery, and so forth. A lesser penalty is generally imposed for solicitation than for the commission of the crime itself, an attempt to commit it, or even a conspiracy to commit it.

3) **Comparison with attempt.** Unlike solicitation, attempt requires that the defendant have progressed far enough in his criminal scheme to have gone beyond mere preparation. Generally, a person who does the bare minimum that suffices for solicitation will not be liable for attempt. At the same time, however, if the defendant continues to assist the person solicited, he may well incur liability as a party to an attempt to commit the crime.

State v. Davis

4) **Application--State v. Davis,** 6 S.W.2d 609 (Mo. 1928).

a) **Facts.** Davis (D) was convicted of attempted murder for paying an undercover police officer to kill the husband of his lover. D had given the officer various maps and photographs of the house and its occupants. D appeals.

b) **Issue.** Does solicitation of a planned murder amount to a perpetration of an overt act in a criminal attempt?

c) **Held.** No. Judgment reversed.

(1) Solicitation is a separate crime; therefore, more needs to be shown than mere solicitation in order to establish an overt act.

(2) Intent was clearly established but an overt act going to the very essence of the murder attempt is required.

    d) **Comment.** In *United States v. Church*, 29 Mil.J.Rptr. 679 (Ct. Milit. Rev. 1989), Church "contracted out" the murder of his wife; the hired killer was an undercover agent, and the "murder" was staged. The court expressed its disagreement with *Davis,* and found Church's actions constituted a substantial step toward commission of the crime and established the requisite overt act amounting to more than mere preparation. Church, the court stated, did all he could do to effect the crime.

4. Impossibility.

    a. **Negation of intent.** If the actor knows that it is impossible for him to commit the crime because of some physical impossibility, then no attempt can exist because the required intent element will not be present. There must be at least an apparent ability to commit the crime (a reasonable person standing in the defendant's position must think the crime could be committed).

    b. **Factual and legal impossibility.** The tough cases are the ones where the defendant thinks that it is possible for him to commit the crime, but for some reason unknown to him, it is factually impossible. For example, A picks B's pocket, which happens to be empty. There has been an attempt. In contrast, mistake of law is a defense when the defendant mistakenly believes that his conduct is prohibited by law.

    c. **Mistake regarding attendant circumstances--People v. Jaffe,** 78 N.E. 169 (N.Y. 1906). People v. Jaffe

        1) **Facts.** Jaffe (D) made an offer to buy goods which he thought were stolen; but before he had purchased them, they had been returned to their rightful owner. The goods were no longer stolen property but D was under the impression that they were. D was convicted of attempting to receive stolen property. D appeals.

        2) **Issue.** May a person be convicted of an attempt to receive stolen goods if the goods were not in fact stolen goods?

        3) **Held.** No. Judgment reversed.

           a) D is not guilty of an attempted crime. If D had completed the crime, he would not have received stolen property. He could not know it was stolen, an essential element of the defense, because it was not in fact stolen. Belief that property is stolen does not satisfy the statutory requirement of knowledge.

        4) **Comment.** Modern statutes would reach a contrary result by defining attempt so as to include the kind of mistake that D made.

    d. **Elimination of impossibility defense--People v. Dlugash,** 363 N.E.2d 1155 (N.Y. 1977). People v. Dlugash

1) **Facts.** Dlugash (D) was out drinking with Bush and Geller, the victim, with whom Bush was staying. Geller demanded that Bush pay part of the rent, and Bush threatened Geller with a shooting unless Geller "shut up." They went to Geller's apartment and Geller again demanded money. Bush shot Geller three times in the chest, one shot piercing Geller's heart. Two to five minutes later, D went to Geller's body and fired five shots into Geller's head. D was tried for murder. No expert witnesses could determine at what point Geller died, although the estimates ranged from "very rapidly" to about 10 minutes after Bush first shot him. The jury was instructed on intentional murder and attempted murder. D was convicted of murder. On appeal, the murder conviction was reversed for failure of proof beyond a reasonable doubt that Geller was still alive when D shot him. The court declined to find an attempted murder because D thought Geller was dead when he shot him. The People (P) appeal.

2) **Issue.** May a person be guilty of an attempt if completion of the crime was impossible?

3) **Held.** Yes. Judgment modified.

   a) The general rule has been that legal impossibility is a good defense to a charge of attempt but that factual impossibility is no defense. This rule has been changed by the Model Penal Code, substantially adopted in New York. The new rule eliminates the defense of impossibility in virtually all situations. It emphasizes the actor's mental frame of reference because it is that intent that actually presents the danger to society.

   b) If a person intends to commit a crime and takes action that tends to effect a commission of the crime, he is guilty. Impossibility is irrelevant if the crime could have been committed if the circumstances had been as the actor thought them to be. Here, the jury must have found that D intended to kill the victim. There is evidence to support that finding, although there was insufficient evidence that Geller was still alive. Therefore, D is guilty of attempted murder.

United States
v. Berrigan

e. **Federal law--United States v. Berrigan,** 482 F.2d 171 (3d Cir. 1973).

1) **Facts.** Berrigan (D), a priest, and McAlister (D), a nun, were convicted of sending letters out from prison by courier without permission of the warden. Prison officials, unbeknownst to D, intercepted the first letter and knew of subsequent letters. D was convicted of trying to take something out of a federal prison not permitted by regulation. D appeals.

2) **Issue.** Under federal law, may one commit a criminal attempt when it is legally impossible to commit a crime?

3) **Held.** No. Judgment reversed.

   a) Because the warden knew and consented to the carrying out of letters, even though that consent was not communicated to Ds, there was a legal impossibility of Ds' actions being criminal.

4) **Comment.** While most states and the Model Penal Code would hold otherwise based on common law theory, federal law is purely statutory. Gaps in federal statutes cannot be filled by a common law theory. Thus, in *United States v. Oviedo*, 525 F.2d 881 (5th Cir. 1976), the court reversed D's conviction of attempt to distribute heroin because of insufficient proof of intent. D had agreed to sell heroin to an undercover agent at an agreed place and time. D appeared with what he claimed to be heroin and gave it to the agent. D was subsequently arrested and prosecuted for distribution of what still appeared to be heroin. However, later testimony revealed that the powder that was transferred was a nonnarcotic, uncontrolled substance. The court held that D cannot be convicted of attempting to sell heroin when he in fact only transferred a nonnarcotic substance. The court further held that in order to obtain a conviction, it is necessary that D perform objective acts that are criminal in nature. It is insufficient to show that D believed the substance to be narcotic if it was not narcotic.

VII. GROUP CRIMINALITY

A. ACCOUNTABILITY FOR THE ACTS OF OTHERS—PARTIES TO A CRIME

1. **Introduction.** Suppose X is going to kill A and Y goes along with X to watch the spectacle. Is Y guilty of the crime for standing around and watching? This section is concerned with ascertaining the extent of a person's liability for a crime that he did not commit personally but to which he has some relationship.

   a. **The dividing line.** In the hypothetical above, Y would not be guilty of any crime. He did not aid X in any way. If aid or encouragement is the dividing line, consider the following cases:

      1) Y is prepared to jump in and render assistance to X if he has trouble killing A. Does Y's presence aid X? Does it hinder A?

      2) What if Y has told X that he will help him, but A does not know this?

      3) What if during the fight Y yells, "Get him"?

      4) What if Y yells encouragement to X, but X is deaf and cannot hear a word he says?

      5) What if there is a crowd of 50 people and they are all yelling encouragement to X?

      6) What if Y is standing in the crowd, knowing this will encourage a fight, but he has no intent or purpose to so encourage it (he just wants to see what happens)?

   b. **Common law categories.**

      1) **Principal in the first degree.** This is one who actually commits the crime, or who gets an innocent third party to do it for him. For example, A may give poison to B (who does not know it is poison) to give to C. A is guilty of murder; B is not a party to the crime because she is an innocent agent.

      2) **Principal in the second degree.**

         a) **Definition.** A principal in the second degree is one who is present when the crime is committed and who aids in its commission (for example, the driver of the getaway car).

         b) **Constructive presence.** Presence need not be actual (that is, at the immediate scene of the crime); it may be constructive. A person is constructively present where she acts pursuant to a common design with the one who commits the criminal act and aids that person (as by keeping lookout), or is situated so as to be able to help him in committing the crime. One who conspires with another, but who is not on the scene during the crime's commission, is treated as constructively present.

    c)   **Aiding and abetting.** To be guilty as a second degree principal, the defendant must make some "substantial contribution" to the commission of the crime by aiding or encouraging its commission.

3)   Accessory before the fact.

    a)   **Definition.** An accessory before the fact is one who is absent at the time the crime is actually committed but who procured, incited, counseled, advised, encouraged, or commanded that the crime be committed.

    b)   **Knowledge.** Mere knowledge that a crime is going to be committed is not sufficient. There has to be some actual encouragement that it be committed.

    c)   **Proceeds.** A person can be such an accessory even though he does not share in the proceeds from the commission of the crime.

4)   Accessory after the fact.

    a)   An accessory after the fact is a person who, knowing that a felony has been committed, aided, assisted, comforted, or received the felon.

    b)   Mere failure to notify the police about a felony that one knew has been committed does not make a person such an accessory. There has to be some actual intent or motive to assist the felon.

5)   The derivative principle. According to the derivative principle that existed at common law, a principal of the second degree or an accessory could not be convicted unless the principal in the first degree had already been convicted, since until this time there was said to be no crime in which these persons could have aided.

6)   Where distinctions are made. The distinction between first and second degree principals is recognized for all crimes. But only in felonies are distinctions made between principals and accessories (all persons involved in misdemeanors are treated as principals).

7)   Punishment. At common law, little distinction was made in the punishment given to the various parties to a crime. This has been changed by modern statutes, which typically differentiate, giving lesser punishment to accessories, for example, than to principals.

c.   Modern rules. The common law has been changed to some degree by statute. The parties to a crime are classified as either principals or accessories.

1)   Principals. All persons who participate in the commission of any crime, whether they directly commit the act, or aid, abet, advise, or encourage its commission, and whether they are present at the scene of the crime or not, are principals.

a)   Thus, there are no accessories before the fact, and no distinction is made between principals of the first degree and principals of the second degree.

b)   One may "commit a crime" (by aiding and abetting) that he is technically incapable of committing. So, for example, a husband can aid another man to rape his wife and be guilty of rape.

2)   **Accessories.** Every person who, after a felony has been committed, conceals or aids a principal in such felony with the intent that said principal escape arrest and punishment, having knowledge that said principal has committed or been charged with such felony, is an accessory.

2.   **Mens Rea.** Criminal liability for the acts of others is predicated on the individual's criminal intent. When the defendant did not actually perform the crime, but only assisted in some way, determination of the necessary mens rea is often difficult.

Hicks v.
United States

a.   **Intent to assist--Hicks v. United States,** 150 U.S. 442 (1893).

1)   **Facts.** Hicks (D), a Cherokee Indian, and Colvard, a white who was friendly with the Indians and had a Cherokee wife, rode their horses together down a road and were met by Rowe, another Cherokee, who was armed. The three conversed but the witnesses could not hear or understand what was said. Twice Rowe pointed his rifle at Colvard and D laughed. Then D removed his coat and told Colvard to take off his hat and die like a man. Rowe then shot Colvard dead and D and Rowe rode off together. D testified that Rowe was in a dangerous mood and that he did not know whether Rowe would kill Colvard or D himself. D also said he rode off with Rowe at his demand and soon left him. The trial judge instructed the jury that if the intentional use of words had the effect of encouraging Rowe to shoot Colvard, D would be presumed to have intended the effect. D was convicted of murder. D appeals.

2)   **Issue.** May a person be found guilty of murder when the words he intentionally uttered had the effect of encouraging the murder, but he did not intend that effect?

3)   **Held.** No. Judgment reversed and remanded for a new trial.

a)   The judge should have instructed the jury that the words of encouragement must have been used by D with the intention of encouraging and abetting Rowe. The effect of the words is irrelevant to D's criminal liability. If he did not intend to encourage Rowe, he may not be found guilty. The facts are not conclusive as to D's intent, so a new trial with proper instructions is necessary.

State v.
Gladstone

b.   **Intent to associate with perpetrator--State v. Gladstone,** 474 P.2d 274 (Wash. 1980).

1) **Facts.** The police hired Thompson as an informant and told him to buy marijuana from Gladstone (D). Thompson visited D but D did not sell him any marijuana. Instead, D told Thompson that Kent might sell him some. D showed Thompson how to get to Kent's place. Thompson bought marijuana from Kent and D was charged with aiding and abetting the sale. There was no evidence of communication between D and Kent. D was convicted of the crime charged. D appeals.

2) **Issue.** May one be guilty of aiding and abetting when he does nothing in association or connection with the principal to accomplish the crime?

3) **Held.** No. Judgment reversed.

   a) A Washington state statute makes a principal of one who aids and abets another in the commission of a crime. The aider and abettor need not be present at the commission of the crime, but to be guilty he must do something in association or connection with the principal.

   b) Here there was no such nexus between D and Kent. D's only involvement was communication that Kent might commit a criminal offense. This is not aiding and abetting.

4) **Dissent.** The jury could properly conclude that D intended that his information would encourage Kent's participation in the crime.

5) **Comment.** A couple of states have created a crime of criminal facilitation, which imposes criminal liability for providing a person the means or opportunity to commit a crime.

c. **Acts of others--People v. Luparello,** 231 Cal. Rptr. 832 (1987).

People v. Luparello

1) **Facts.** Luparello (D) tried to locate his former lover through Martin, a friend of the former lover's current husband. D told his friends that he wanted the information at any cost. After Martin failed to provide the information sought, D's friends, without D present, lured Martin outdoors and killed him. D was charged and convicted of murder. D appeals.

2) **Issue.** Is a defendant liable for the unplanned and unintended act of co-conspirators?

3) **Held.** Yes. Judgment affirmed.

   a) Accomplice liability derives from the aider and abettor's intent to commit or encourage the commission of a crime. Liability is extended to reach the actual crime committed as opposed to the crime "intended" based on the policy that aiders and abettors should be responsible for the criminal harms they have naturally, probably, and foreseeably put in motion. D is guilty of any foreseeable offense committed by anyone he aids and abets.

4) **Concurrence.** I concur because of the controlling case law, but find said law to be unsound. It is illogical to assess D's degree of culpability by the mental state of the perpetrator and/or the circumstances of the crime. If the jury found that the shooter lay in wait, demonstrating malice, D would

be guilty of murder in the first degree. But if the shooter was drunk and unable to form malice, D would then only be guilty of voluntary manslaughter. Such fortuity of result is irrational.

State v. McVay

d. **Mens rea related to final act--State v. McVay,** 132 A. 436 (R.I. 1926).

1) **Facts.** Three people were killed by escaping steam when a boiler aboard a steamer exploded. McVay (D), the captain, and his engineer were indicted for manslaughter as principals. Kelley was indicted as an accessory before the fact. Kelley challenged the indictment on the ground that no one could be an accessory before the fact to manslaughter that arose out of criminal negligence. The issue was certified to the state supreme court.

2) **Issue.** May a defendant be indicted as being an accessory before the fact to manslaughter that arose through criminal negligence?

3) **Held.** Yes.

a) The indictment charged that Kelley "feloniously and maliciously" did "aid, assist, abet, counsel, hire, command and procure" Ds to commit the manslaughter. Ds in turn were charged with manslaughter "without malice." Kelley claims that a sudden and unpremeditated crime cannot be maliciously incited ahead of time. This may be true when the actual crime involved a sudden and unpremeditated act, but not all manslaughter occurs in that manner.

b) Manslaughter also includes unlawful acts that result in unintentional homicide, and gross negligence in doing lawful acts. These may be premeditated acts that a person such as Kelley could aid or abet.

c) In this case, Kelley was indicted for procuring the commission of the crime before it happened. Ds need not have consciously intended to kill, but their negligence in creating excess steam may have been sufficiently gross to permit imposition of criminal liability. Ds chose this course of action, allegedly with Kelley's participation, and the jury could find Kelley an accessory if he acted with knowledge of the possible danger to human life when he advised Ds to take the chance of the negligent acts.

People v. Abbott

e. **Intent to participate--People v. Abbott,** 445 N.Y.S.2d 344 (1981).

1) **Facts.** Abbott (D) challenged Moon to a drag race on a public highway. Moon was traveling about 85 miles per hour and D was going about 93 miles per hour when D struck a car driven by Hammond. Hammond and her two passengers were killed. D and Moon were both convicted of criminally negligent homicide. Moon appeals, claiming that he could not be liable for criminally negligent homicide unless his conduct resulted in the death.

2) **Issue.** Is a participant in a drag race criminally liable for a death caused by the collision of the other participant's vehicle with the deceased's vehicle?

3) **Held.** Yes. Judgment affirmed.

a) A person may be criminally liable for criminal conduct engaged in by another person if he (i) acts with the necessary mental culpability and (ii) intentionally aids the other person to engage in the conduct.

b) In this case, Moon's participation in the drag race demonstrated a gross deviation from the reasonable person standard of care sufficient to sustain a criminally negligent homicide conviction. By participating, Moon intentionally aided D in the unreasonably dangerous activity, and actually made D's actions possible. There would have been no race without Moon's participation. The jury could reasonably find that Moon acted with the culpable mental state of criminal negligence and assisted or encouraged D to act in a manner dangerous to life.

3. Actus Reus.

a. **Introduction.** In deciding whether particular conduct is such as would justify criminal liability, the materiality of aid or encouragement is a major factor. The "but for" test used to determine causation need not be satisfied for a determination of accessorial liability, as long as the necessary mens rea is present. The threshold of materiality of the act is not always clear, however.

b. **Application--Wilcox v. Jeffery,** 1 All E.R. 464 (1951).

Wilcox v. Jeffery

1) **Facts.** Aliens were forbidden to take employment, paid or unpaid, while in the United Kingdom. Hawkins, a United States saxophone player, was invited to the United Kingdom. Wilcox (D), who owned a jazz music magazine, greeted Hawkins upon his arrival, attended a jazz concert given by Hawkins, and wrote and published an article praising the illegal concert. D was convicted of aiding and abetting Hawkins in violating the alien order. D appeals.

2) **Issue.** May a person be guilty of aiding and abetting a criminal act simply by being a paid spectator at the event and by publishing an article about it?

3) **Held.** Yes. Judgment affirmed.

a) If D's presence had been accidental, he would probably not be guilty. But D took part in the illegal act by encouraging it. D knew the act was illegal, yet affirmatively encouraged its commission.

4) **Comment.** Similarly, in *State ex rel. Attorney General v. Tally, Judge,* 15 So. 722 (Ala. 1894), the court found the judge was an accomplice in the killing of the deceased in that he deprived the deceased of a chance of life. There, the deceased's relatives had sent him a telegram warning him that he was being sought after for the seduction of the judge's sister-in-law. The judge, however, advised the telegraph operator not to deliver the warning telegram. Ultimately, the assailants caught up with the deceased and killed him. The court concluded that one can be held criminally responsible if one

renders it easier for the principal actor to accomplish the intended act, even though it would have been attained without such help.

4. Comparison of the Parties' Liability.

a. **Introduction.** In some cases, the parties will not share the same motive for their actions. For example, the aider and abettor may be intending to assist the commission of a crime when the other does not so intend, as when the aider and abettor forces the other to act through threats. Alternatively, the principal may not be subject to conviction (*e.g.,* diplomatic immunity). The general rule, however, is that an aider and abettor may not be convicted unless a crime was actually committed.

State v.
Hayes

b. **Principal without intent--State v. Hayes,** 16 S.W. 514 (Mo. 1891).

1) **Facts.** Hayes (D) and Hill agreed to burglarize a store. Hill actually pretended to agree in order to obtain the arrest of D. The two men arrived at the store, then D boosted Hill into the store, and Hill handed a side of bacon out to D. They were then arrested. The trial court charged that if D, with felonious intent, assisted and aided Hill to enter the building, D would be guilty of burglary, even though Hill (who actually entered the building) had no criminal intent. D appealed his conviction.

2) **Issue.** Should a party who does not actually enter a building, but only assists someone into the building who has no criminal intent, be found guilty of burglary?

3) **Held.** No. Conviction reversed.

a) Trial court erred in charge to the jury. D did not commit every overt act necessary to make up the crime. To make D responsible for the acts of Hill, they must have had a common motive or design. The motives here were dissimilar, since Hill had no intention to burglarize. The act of Hill can thus not be imputed to D.

4) **Comment.** Other courts have taken a position contrary to *Hayes*.

B. CORPORATE CRIMES

1. **Introduction.** Business crimes include traditional crimes committed in the course of doing legitimate business as well as violations of criminal regulatory statutes. The latter types of business crime, including antitrust violations, environmental protection violations, etc., present policy problems because they deviate in substantial ways from traditional criminal activity and therefore require a different kind of justification. In addition, when the crime is committed by a corporation, the liability of individual agents versus that of the entity is a major issue.

2. **Use of Criminal Law.**

    a. **Policy considerations.** When the criminal law is used to regulate the economic conduct of business (antitrust, price controls) or to promote public welfare objectives (environmental protection, consumer safety), the result is to undermine the restraints imposed on the use of criminal law generally.

        1) **Specificity.** A basic limitation on criminal statutes is that they must clearly describe the proscribed conduct. Many statutes have been declared void for vagueness. Yet the antitrust laws especially are notorious for not specifically defining what conduct is illegal.

        2) **Personal guilt.** Criminal justice requires that the person to be punished be personally guilty of the illegal act. Yet criminal sanctions on corporations fall on stockholders rather than on those who commit the crimes.

        3) **Deserved punishment.** Intent is a fundamental principle of criminal law because the stigma of criminal sanction should be reserved for those who intended the harm for which they are punished. Yet corporate punishment is far removed from those who intend the harm.

    b. **Deterrence.** Some commentators feel that criminal sanctions may make business too timid, stifling innovation; criminal sanctions provide excessive deterrence. Others feel that criminal sanctions would have an ideal deterrent effect. However, criminal penalties have not been effective in the area of business regulation.

        1) One explanation is that business regulatory violations are not commonly regarded as morally reprehensible. The spirit of the free enterprise system denies moral culpability, thereby rendering criminal sanctions unjust.

        2) Generally, the cases are complex. It is difficult to prove unlawful intent, and it is difficult to carry the burden of proof necessary to gain a criminal conviction.

        3) Often the law is unclear as to what constitutes unlawful conduct.

        4) Law enforcement is in the hands of members of a social class who are likely to sympathize with those in business.

3. **Corporate Criminal Liability.**

    a. **Introduction.** Once particular business conduct has been declared illegal, the question remains as to how sanctions will be imposed, and on whom.

        1) **Acts for which the corporation is bound.**

            a) When is a corporation punished as a substitute for punishment of individuals?

b)   What acts of what corporate employees justify criminal penalties imposed on the corporation?

2)   **Vicarious liability.** When may higher corporate officials be held liable for the acts of lesser ones? This question raises the possibility that corporate officials may be held liable even when they would not be held under normal legal doctrines as an accomplice.

b.   **Corporate liability.**

New York
Central &
Hudson River
Railroad Co.
v. United
States

1)   **Corporate liability for employee activity--New York Central & Hudson River Railroad Co. v. United States,** 212 U.S. 481 (1909).

a)   **Facts.** An employee of the New York Central & Hudson River Railroad Co. (D) made arrangements with a shipper whereby D would pay the shipper rebates in return for its use of D's lines. D and the employee were each convicted of violating a federal law. D appeals, contending that the law was unconstitutional.

b)   **Issue.** May Congress make a corporation criminally liable for the acts of its employees?

c)   **Held.** Yes. Judgment affirmed.

(1)   D claims that the law allowing punishment of corporations actually punishes innocent stockholders without giving them an opportunity to be heard. The early common law rule did exclude corporations from criminal liability.

(2)   The modern rule reflects the realization that what a corporation does, it can intend to do. If a corporation can lay down tracks and run railroad cars on them, it can also intend to do so. A corporation acts by its officers and agents, and must be held accountable for their acts.

(3)   The payment of rebates inures to the benefit of D, and if only the individuals may be held liable, the law against rebates cannot be effectively enforced.

United States
v. Hilton
Hotels Corp.

2)   **Corporate liability for employee acts in violation of corporate policy--United States v. Hilton Hotels Corp.,** 467 F.2d 1000 (9th Cir. 1972).

a)   **Facts.** Hilton Hotels Corp. (D) was one of several hotels, restaurants, and hotel and restaurant supply companies that organized an association to attract conventions to their city. Members were to contribute specified amounts, and D and other hotels allegedly agreed to buy supplies only from suppliers who contributed. The agreement, if proved, constitutes a per se violation of the Sherman Act. D's purchasing agent admitted that he had been instructed not to participate in a boycott against noncontributing suppliers but that he had threatened one such supplier with a boycott because he personally disliked the supplier's agent. This threat was the evidence upon which D was convicted. D appeals, claiming that it should not be held responsible when its agent had violated express instructions not to participate in the illegal activity.

b) **Issue.** May a corporation be held criminally liable for acts of its agents, done within the scope of their employment, even though the corporation's policy and specific instructions prohibited such acts?

c) **Held.** Yes. Judgment affirmed.

   (1) Congress has power to impose criminal liability on corporations through general principles of agency, so that the illegal acts of employees acting within the scope of their employment are imputed to the corporation. This is so even when the agent is disobeying express instructions.

   (2) Congress may reasonably conclude that corporate exposure to criminal conviction provides an incentive to prevent illegal actions by employees. In many cases it is impossible to pinpoint particular corporate agents who acted illegally, although the participation of the corporation is evident. Even when particular agents can be identified, their conviction and punishment is ineffective as a deterrent to the corporation.

   (3) D could not avoid liability by giving general instructions without taking appropriate steps to enforce the instructions.

3) **Corporate liability for acts committed without authorization--Commonwealth v. Beneficial Finance Co.,** 275 N.E.2d 33 (Mass. 1971).

a) **Facts.** Beneficial (D) was convicted of bribery and conspiracy to engage in bribery; it appeals. Two employees of D, one a vice-president, together with other companies and several of their employees, bribed members of state regulatory boards to get favorable action in setting maximum interest rates on loans. D argues that it cannot be held liable for the acts of its employees since they were not authorized by the board of directors or someone high enough in the corporate hierarchy to indicate that the acts were acts of "corporate policy."

b) **Issue.** Is the corporation liable when its agent, who has the authority to act for and on behalf of the corporation in handling its business, commits a crime while engaged in corporation business?

c) **Held.** Yes. Conviction sustained.

   (1) The standard that must be met is that the corporation placed a person in a position where he had the power, responsibility, and authority to act for and on behalf of the corporation in handling the particular business or operation of the corporation in which he was engaged at the time the criminal act was committed, and that he had the power to decide what he would or would not do while acting for the corporation. It must also be shown that he was acting for and on behalf of the corporation in the accomplishment of that particular business or operation, and that he committed a criminal act while so acting.

(2) In reaching a determination on this standard, the jury may consider (i) the extent of the agent's control and authority, (ii) the extent of use of corporate funds in the crime, and (iii) a repeated pattern, if any, of criminal conduct that might show corporate toleration or ratification of the agent's acts.

(3) In effect, this is a respondeat superior doctrine.

State v. Ford Motor Co.

4) **Criminal and products liability--State v. Ford Motor Co.**, No. 5324 (Ind. 1979).

a) **Facts.** Ford (D) allegedly negligently designed Pinto gas tanks and failed to notify Pinto purchasers of the defect. Deaths were caused when the decedent's car erupted into flames upon being struck in the rear by another car. Ford (D) was indicted under the state reckless homicide statute.

b) **Issue.** Is the reckless homicide statute applicable to corporations?

c) **Held.** Yes.

(1) Under the Indiana statute, a corporation can be prosecuted and convicted for any offense when the offense was committed by its agents within the scope of their authority.

d) **Comment.** Although D was indicted in the case, the jury found the company not guilty.

c. **Corporate agent liability.** In the corporate context, courts have applied general principles of accomplice liability. However, when applied to corporate bureaucracy, liability may be difficult to impose on the highest officers without adopting a form of vicarious liability.

Gordon v. United States

1) **Basic rule--Gordon v. United States**, 203 F.2d 248 (10th Cir. 1953), *rev'd*, 347 U.S. 909 (1954).

a) **Facts.** Gordon (D) was a partner in an appliance selling business. Certain salespeople violated the Defense Production Act by making sales without collecting the required down payment. D and the other partners were charged individually with the violation on the theory that the knowledge of their agents could be imputed to them personally. Ds were convicted and appeal.

b) **Issue.** When an employee knowingly commits a criminal act in the course of his employment, may that knowledge be imputed to individual partners (employers) who did not actually know of that act?

c) **Held.** Yes. Judgment affirmed.

(1) The statute requires willfulness as an essential element of the crime. However, D, by being an employer, had constructive knowledge of the acts of his employees. Therefore, D was properly convicted.

d)   **Dissent.** D lacked the necessary intent. An employer is not criminally liable for acts of his employees unless he directs the acts or has guilty knowledge thereof. The majority has erroneously applied principles of corporate liability to individual partners. A corporation may be deemed to have constructive knowledge of what its employees know. However, that rule exists because a corporation can only act through its agents, not because it is an employer.

e)   **Comment.** The Supreme Court later reversed, essentially for the reasons given by the dissent here. [347 U.S. 909 (1954)] However, the Court has held that a partnership itself, as an entity, may be held criminally liable for the acts of its employees. [United States v. A & P Trucking Co., 358 U.S. 121 (1958)]

2)   **Position of authority justifying liability--United States v. Park,** 421 U.S. 658 (1975).

a)   **Facts.** Park (D) was the chief executive officer of a national supermarket chain. One of the company's regional warehouses was infested with rodents and food stored therein was contaminated in violation of the Federal Food, Drug and Cosmetic Act. The company pled guilty to charges of violations but D, who was also charged, pled not guilty. The evidence at trial showed that D had the responsibility of running the corporation and that he delegated the various phases of its operation to subordinates. D admitted that by virtue of his position he was responsible for the entire operation of the company, including the provision of sanitary food storage conditions. The jury was instructed that the issue was whether D, "by virtue of his position in the company, had a position of authority and responsibility in the situation out of which these charges arose." D was convicted, but the court of appeals reversed. The United States (P) petitioned for certiorari.

b)   **Issue.** May a corporate officer be convicted of a criminal offense without proof of any wrongful action, as long as he was in a position of authority to prevent or to correct the violation which formed the basis for the complaint?

c)   **Held.** Yes. Judgment reversed.

   (1)   D was convicted under a statute that does not require an awareness of some wrongdoing, but simply that the person stand in responsible relation to a public danger. The statute can extend to all who have a responsible share in the furtherance of the transaction that the statute outlaws. The question of responsibility depends on the evidence of each case and on the judgment of the jury.

   (2)   This type of statute imposes both a duty to seek out and remedy violations and a duty to take measures to insure that violations do not occur.

   (3)   A defendant may raise the defense of powerlessness to prevent or correct the violation.

d) **Dissent.** The instructions given were inadequate because they did not require a finding beyond a reasonable doubt that D engaged in wrongful conduct amounting at least to common law negligence.

3) **Strict liability--United States v. MacDonald & Watson Waste Oil Co.,** 933 F.2d 35 (1st Cir. 1991).

a) **Facts.** MacDonald & Watson Waste Oil Co. ("MacDonald") was hired to remove solid waste. A company employee supervised removing the contaminated soil to an improper location. D'Allesandro (D), president of MacDonald, was convicted under the "responsible corporate officer" doctrine of knowingly transporting and causing the transportation of hazardous waste to an improper facility. MacDonald was also convicted. The case against D was proven by showing he had knowledge as a "responsible corporate officer" which is shown by proving that a person: (i) is a corporate officer; (ii) had direct responsibility for the alleged illegal activity; and (iii) knew or believed the alleged illegal activity occurred. D appeals.

b) **Issue.** May a district court properly adapt the "responsible corporate officer" doctrine traditionally applied to strict liability offenses, thus allowing the jury to find a defendant guilty without finding that he had actual knowledge, which is required by statute?

c) **Held.** No. Conviction reversed.

(1) The seminal cases of *United States v. Dotterweich*, 320 U.S. 277 (1943), and *United States v. Park,* 421 U.S. 658 (1975), eliminated the scienter requirement and established the "responsible corporate officer" doctrine. However, when Congress has specifically included a knowledge requirement, there is no precedent for ignoring it, especially where the offense charged is a serious felony as in the instant case.

(2) The trial court properly instructed the jury that knowledge could be inferred. However, under its instructions, the jury's belief that D lacked actual knowledge of, and had not willfully blinded himself to, the criminal transportation alleged would be insufficient for acquittal if the jury found that the responsible corporate officer knew or erroneously believed that the same type of illegal activity had occurred on another occasion.

(3) Belief of a prior illegal action does not necessarily show knowledge of a subsequent illegal action. In a crime having knowledge as an express element, a mere showing of official responsibility is not an adequate substitute for direct or circumstantial proof of knowledge.

4. **Sentencing.** Once a person has been convicted of a business crime, an appropriate sentence must be administered. A typical complaint is that business offenders "get off easy" when compared with other types of criminals. Others suggest that large fines replace imprisonment because fines provide more benefits to the public while serving equally well the purposes of punishment. There is no consensus on these points, however.

C. CONSPIRACY

1. **Definition.** Conspiracy is an agreement between two or more persons to do an unlawful act or to do a lawful act in an unlawful manner. At common law, conspiracy was a misdemeanor, and if the substantive crime was actually committed, then the misdemeanor merged into the actual crime committed. Today, however, conspiracy is punishable as a separate and distinct crime. Therefore, the defendant may be prosecuted for both the conspiracy and the complete crime and the sentences added together on conviction.

2. **Particular Aspects of Conspiracy.**

   a. **Relationship to the law of evidence.**

      1) **Introduction.** It is difficult to understand the law of conspiracy unless one understands the law of evidence.

         a) **Hearsay rule.** The hearsay rule requires that one testify only about those things that he has actually observed; that is, one cannot put into evidence the out-of-court statement of another to prove the truth of that statement.

         b) **Exceptions to hearsay rule.** There are exceptions to the hearsay rule. One of these is the "admissions exception" —anything that the defendant himself has said out of court can be introduced in court to prove the truth of the fact asserted in the out-of-court statement. Also, admissions by the agent of a party will often be received against the party. For example, if a truck driver hits A, then admits to A that he was going too fast, A may testify in court about the statement and such testimony will be used against the owner of the truck and the employer of the driver (*i.e.,* the principal).

      2) **Admissions of one admissible against all--Krulewitch v. United States, 336 U.S. 440 (1949).**

         Krulewitch v. United States

         a) **Facts.** Krulewitch (D) and a woman defendant allegedly conspired to persuade another woman to travel interstate (from New York to Florida) for the purpose of prostitution, and then did transport her for that purpose. Such activity is illegal under the Mann Act. After D was arrested, the complaining witness (the prostitute) told the prosecution of an alleged conversation she had with the woman defendant. The conversation occurred after the witness had returned to New York and involved a suggestion not to implicate D. D was tried alone, and this conversation was admitted over objection. D was convicted. The court of appeals affirmed. D appeals.

b)   **Issue.** May a conspirator's statements against a co-conspirator be admitted into evidence if the statements were not made in furtherance of the crime charged?

c)   **Held.** No. Judgment reversed.

(1)   The complaining witness's testimony about the alleged conversation was hearsay, and thus not admissible unless covered by an exception to the hearsay rule.

(2)   An exception to the hearsay rule does apply to out-of-court statements made by one conspirator, but only if made in furtherance of the objectives of an ongoing conspiracy. The government asserts that the statement was made in furtherance of a subsidiary phase of the conspiracy; *i.e.,* to avoid detection. But the conversation took place well after the criminal act was completed. It was too far removed from the conspiracy alleged to have been made in furtherance of that conspiracy. The exception to the hearsay rule should not be extended to such statements or the hearsay rule would effectively cease to exist in conspiracy cases.

d)   **Concurrence** (Jackson, J.). When prosecutors resort to charging conspiracy instead of the underlying substantive offense, they threaten the fairness of the justice system. Conspiracy to commit a misdemeanor may be a felony, so the stakes are higher. Conspiracy itself is difficult to define. In proving a conspiracy, the prosecution may use the specific acts of the co-conspirators, regardless of the involvement of the defendant in those particular acts. The defendant may be tried wherever any conspirator did any of the acts, giving the prosecution wide latitude. These dangers to defendants require that limits placed on conspiracy charges be carefully followed, and an expansion of the hearsay exception in conspiracy cases is clearly unwarranted.

3)   **Hypotheticals.**

a)   Suppose A recruits B to do a bank job saying, "Come on, do it with us. We've got C, a great safecracker." The police want B to testify against C. Such testimony is admissible, since it was said by one of the members of the conspiracy during the course of and in furtherance of the conspiracy. Conspiracy is like the partnership idea—each member of the conspiracy is said to have authorized all of the other members to do all of the acts that they do.

b)   Suppose A came into the bar and said, "Boy, are we lucky. We've got C to be the safecracker." This statement is not admissible (except against A), since it was not made in furtherance of the conspiracy.

4)   **Imputing the acts of one conspirator to the others.**

a)   **Introduction.** The general rule is that each conspirator is held accountable for any and all crimes which result from the furtherance of the conspiracy.

It is no defense to say that the crime committed was not part of the original plan (even if it was expressly agreed that the act should not be done) if it can be said that the commission of such an act or crime was reasonably foreseeable. The courts are generally liberal in finding that acts were the natural and probable consequence of the conspiracy.

b) **Application--Pinkerton v. United States,** 328 U.S. 640 (1946).

Pinkerton v. United States

(1) **Facts.** The Pinkertons (Ds), Daniel and Walter, were prosecuted for conspiracy to commit violations of the Internal Revenue Code and for substantive violations. Only Walter committed the actual violations, but both brothers were convicted of conspiracy and certain of the substantive violations. Daniel appeals.

(2) **Issue.** May a conspirator be convicted of committing the offense intended by the conspiracy although he had no direct participation in the actual commission?

(3) **Held.** Yes. Judgment affirmed.

(a) Once Daniel conspired with Walter, he became equally responsible with Walter for acts done in furtherance of the conspiracy. The conspiracy was continuous. There is no evidence that Daniel withdrew from the conspiracy before Walter acted. The criminal intent necessary was established by the formation of the conspiracy. Thus, Daniel was properly convicted of the substantive offenses.

(4) **Dissent** (Rutledge, J.). All the government proved was that Daniel had, in the past, conspired with Walter to commit violations similar to those committed in this case. There is no evidence that Daniel conspired to commit the particular acts that Walter committed here. Daniel was even in prison when Walter committed some of the acts.

(5) **Comment.** In *People v. McGee*, 399 N.E.2d 1177 (N.Y. 1979), the court expressly refused to follow the *Pinkerton* rule in state prosecutions, requiring participation in the substantive offense to support a conviction for the substantive offense.

c) **Relation back doctrine.** If a new person joins a conspiracy and has an awareness as to its general purpose and the past acts that have been committed in its furtherance, the doctrine of "relation back" applies and such a person becomes responsible for all of the acts of the conspirators up to that time.

b. **Actus reus—the agreement itself--Interstate Circuit, Inc. v. United States,** 306 U.S. 208 (1939).

Interstate Circuit, Inc. v. United States

1) **Facts.** Interstate Circuit, Inc. and Texas Consolidated Theaters (Ds), film distributors that dominated the market for film exhibition in various cities, entered into contracts with each of eight film distributors which, in total, controlled 75% of all first run films. The individual contracts were

permissible, but the Government showed that the eight distributors had an agreement with one another. The showing was made by introducing a letter from Interstate to each of the eight distributors, that showed each of the eight as addressees, and that made certain pricing demands as a condition of Interstate doing further business with the distributor. Subsequently, each distributor agreed and on that basis the trial court found that the distributors had conspired with one another. The district court restrained Ds from continuing in a combination and conspiracy condemned by the court as a violation of section 1 of the Sherman Antitrust Act. Ds appeal.

2) **Issue.** Where evidence shows that members of a group independently entered into an agreement with one party, and each of the members were aware that the other members of the group were considering the same agreement, will such evidence support a finding that the group members entered into an agreement among themselves?

3) **Held.** Yes. Affirmed.

a) Since the letter named as addressees the eight distributors, each distributor knew that the proposal was being considered by the others.

b) Each distributor knew that group cooperation would lead to increased profits, while nonparticipation would lead to losses.

c) Knowing that concerted action was being invited, each distributor participated in the plan.

d) Each distributor became aware that the others had joined and, with that knowledge, they renewed the arrangement and carried it into effect for two successive years.

e) An unlawful conspiracy does not require simultaneous action or agreement among the conspirators.

3. **Concert-of-Action Requirement.**

United States
v. Alvarez

a. **Necessity of an agreement--United States v. Alvarez,** 625 F.2d 1196 (5th Cir. 1981).

1) **Facts.** An undercover Drug Enforcement Agency ("DEA") agent made arrangements with co-conspirators to import marijuana into the United States from Colombia by airplane. Although Alvarez (D) was not involved in making the plans, he drove two of the co-conspirators to the airport in a truck. When asked by the undercover agent if he would be at the unloading cite, D responded by shaking his head, signifying "yes." D unloaded certain appliances from the truck at the airport. When the co-conspirators outlined their plan to the DEA agent, they were arrested, as was D. D was convicted of conspiracy and appealed on the ground of insufficient evidence. The court of appeals reversed, finding that although D may have intended to commit the unlawful act of unloading the marijuana, the fact that this act would assist the conspiracy did not prove that D knew of the

conspiracy or intended to join it. The court of appeals granted a rehearing.

2) **Issue.** Must a defendant actually join in an agreement to violate the law in order to be guilty of conspiracy?

3) **Held.** No. Conviction affirmed.

   a) We find the evidence sufficient to convict. D's joining the illegal compact can be inferred on two fronts: (i) there is direct evidence D intended to be at the off-loading site; a jury could reasonably conclude that this manifested a prior agreement to assist in the unloading; and (ii) D's nodding of his head may be viewed as assurance to assuage jittery accomplices.

4) **Dissent.** We do not view D's assurances as an indication of guilty knowledge. D may have been a humble workman performing a lawful act unrelated to the conspiracy.

5) **Comment.** Similarly, in *Weniger v. United States*, 47 F.2d 692 (9th Cir. 1931), the appellate court found that the evidence was insufficient to show that the particular conspiracy in question was organized by city officials and joined in by the appellants. The court held that in order to show that a conspiracy existed, the law requires proof of the common and unlawful design and the knowing participation of the persons charged as conspirators before a conviction is justified. Thus, the evidence falls short of showing that the appellants were part of the conspiracy. On the other hand, in *Williams v. United States*, 218 F.2d 276 (4th Cir. 1954), the court found ample evidence to show that the appellants were engaged in a well-organized conspiracy to violate the federal internal revenue laws relating to liquor. The evidence was quite comprehensive and provided by numerous witnesses, thus indicating a consistent pattern of agreement between the appellants.

4. **Mens Rea Requirement.**

a. **Introduction.** Conspiracy is generally held to be a specific intent crime; that is, the defendant must have the specific intent to commit the act that is a crime.

b. **Is knowledge enough?** To be guilty of a conspiracy, one must have more than mere knowledge. There has to be an improper purpose or desire; *i.e.,* the defendant must in some sense promote the venture herself, make it her own, or have a stake in its outcome.

   1) **Application--People v. Lauria,** 59 Cal. Rptr. 628 (1967).

   People v.
   Lauria

   a) **Facts.** Lauria (D) ran a telephone answering service. Among his customers were nine or 10 prostitutes. D knew they were prostitutes, but he did not charge them extra, nor did they provide him with a major part of his business. D was charged with conspiracy to commit prostitution, but the indictment was dismissed. The People (P) appeal.

      b)   **Issue.** May a person be guilty of conspiracy for knowingly providing services that are used to commit misdemeanors when he has no stake in the venture?

      c)   **Held.** No. Judgment affirmed.

           (1)   Knowledge of another's criminal activity is not necessarily a conspiracy to further the activity. A supplier of goods and services has a variable duty to screen his customers. In *United States v. Falcone*, 311 U.S. 205 (1940), distributors of sugar, yeast, and cans were not guilty of conspiracy to produce illegal liquor. However, in *Direct Sales Co. v. United States*, 319 U.S. 703 (1943), a drug wholesaler was convicted of conspiracy with the buyer, who was supplying addicts.

           (2)   Knowledge of criminal activity must be combined with one of the following to justify a conspiracy conviction:

                (a)   A "stake in the venture," such as an inflated price for the service, so the seller has an interest in having the activity go on;

                (b)   No legitimate use for the goods or services (*e.g.,* a prostitution directory);

                (c)   An unusual volume of business not proportionate to any legitimate demand.

United States
v. Feola

  c. **Unknown status of victim--United States v. Feola,** 420 U.S. 672 (1975).

      1)   **Facts.** Feola (D) and three others arranged a false heroin sale. Unknown to D, the buyers were federal narcotics agents. The plan was to rob the buyers if they did not accept the bags of powder represented to be heroin (later shown to be sugar). One agent became suspicious and was able to stop an assault on another agent. Ds were arrested and later convicted of conspiring to assault and of assaulting federal officers. Ds appealed, and the court of appeals reversed the conspiracy convictions. The United States (P) appeals.

      2)   **Issue.** Must a conspirator have knowledge of the status of the intended victim in order to be guilty of conspiracy to assault a federal officer in the performance of his official duties?

      3)   **Held.** No. Convictions for assault on and for conspiracy to assault a federal officer affirmed; judgment of the court of appeals with respect to the conspiracy conviction reversed.

           a)   In order to incur liability for assaulting a federal officer in violation of 18 U.S.C. section 111, an actor must entertain merely the criminal intent to do the acts therein specified—all the statute requires is an intent to assault, not an intent to assault a federal officer. The fact that the victim is a federal officer creates the liability irrespective of knowledge of the victim's official capacity by the actor.

b) Similarly, knowledge of the official identity of the victim is irrelevant to the essential nature of an agreement to commit an assault, the entrance into which agreement is made criminal by the law of conspiracy.

c) There are two independent values served by the law of conspiracy:

(1) Society should be protected from the dangers of concerted criminal activity.

(2) The agreement to engage in a criminal venture is an event of sufficient threat to social order to permit the imposition of criminal sanctions for the agreement alone, plus an overt act in pursuit of it, regardless of whether the crime agreed upon is actually committed.

d) In the instant case, imposition of a requirement of knowledge of the official identity of the victim (which serves only to establish federal jurisdiction) would render it more difficult to serve the policy behind the law of conspiracy without serving any other apparent social policy.

4) **Dissent** (Stewart, Douglas, JJ.). An assailant must know or have reason to know that the person assaulted is an officer to be so convicted.

d. **Types of conspiracies.**

1) **The "hub of the wheel" conspiracy--Kotteakos v. United States,** 328 U.S. 750 (1946).

Kotteakos v.
United States

a) **Facts.** There were originally 32 defendants. Brown (D) was the key figure; he acted as a broker for the others in getting loans under the National Housing Act (charging them all a commission). D knew that when these loans were gotten they were taken for illegal purposes under the Act. None of the parties dealing through D knew of the others. Seven of the defendants were convicted. The appellate court held that there were actually several conspiracies rather than one, but that there was no prejudicial error. Ds appeal.

b) **Issue.** Where one person deals with others having no connection with each other, are all defendants guilty of one conspiracy?

c) **Held.** No. Judgment reversed.

(1) There are several conspiracies, not just one big one. By allowing the case to proceed on the theory of one conspiracy, the court improperly allowed the specific acts of unrelated conspirators to be considered against all the others.

d) **Comment.** The "hub of the wheel" conspiracy might be diagrammed as follows:

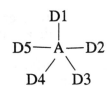

```
        D1
         |
  D5 — A — D2
       /   \
     D4     D3
```

If the hub of the wheel acts alone, then there are five different conspiracies (there is no connection between the individual radii). But if the hub is a **known** source for all of the radii or the scheme depends on all radii to function, then there is one big conspiracy.

Similarly, in *Blumenthal v. United States*, 332 U.S. 539 (1947), the Court found that only one large conspiracy in fact existed. The Court held that the two separate agreements (one between the distributor and an unidentified man and the other between the distributor and two local businessmen) were merely steps in the formation of a larger and more general conspiracy. The schemes were the same and the salesmen knew, or should have known, that they were sharing in a larger project. The Court stated that it is not necessary that one know everyone involved or exactly what part each person is playing in carrying out the common design of the conspiracy. Here, all knew of and joined in the scheme of disposing of whiskey at prices over the ceiling.

For example, in *Anderson v. Superior Court*, 177 P.2d 315 (Cal. 1947), Stern was performing abortions. He had several people referring women to him, the defendant being one of them. The court found one large conspiracy. The rationale: The doctor is a full-time abortionist; the defendant who brings him one woman a week knows that there have to be other suppliers also. If the doctor were an osteopath, knowledge of the others would less easily be imputed to the defendant.

e) **Summary.** If one large conspiracy is found, one conspirator can be held liable for possibly hundreds of crimes. Also, all co-conspirators can be tried together, which makes the defense of any one defendant more difficult.

United States v. Bruno

2) **The "fork-chain" conspiracy--United States v. Bruno,** 105 F.2d 921 (2d Cir. 1939), *rev'd on other grounds,* 308 U.S. 287 (1939).

a) **Facts.** There are 88 defendants (two on trial here) being prosecuted for conspiracy to import, sell, and possess narcotics. The defendants argue that there are several separate conspiracies, not one large one. Appeal is from conviction of conspiracy to import, sell, and possess narcotics.

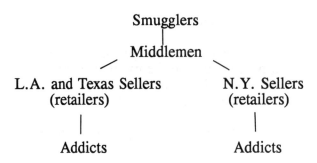

```
              Smugglers
                  |
             Middlemen
            /           \
L.A. and Texas Sellers    N.Y. Sellers
      (retailers)          (retailers)
           |                   |
        Addicts             Addicts
```

b) **Issue.** Can a single conspiracy exist even though none of the conspirators either cooperated or communicated with each other?

c) **Held.** Yes. Judgment affirmed.

   (1) The trial court allowed the jury to find that there was one great conspiracy. The evidence showed no communication between the smugglers and the retailers, or between retailers, etc., but each part of the organization knew of the others and the success of the individual parts was dependent on the success of the whole.

d) **Comment.** This is a "fork-chain" conspiracy:

5. **Parties to a Conspiracy.**

   a. **Introduction.** There must be two or more persons to a conspiracy.

   b. **Two-party crimes.**

      1) **General rule.** Certain crimes require an agreement *and* the active participation of at least two persons. For example, bribery requires action by the giver and the receiver of the bribe. In these situations, there can be no separate offense of conspiracy, since the agreement between the two persons is a necessary part of the substantive crime.

      2) **Three or more persons.** Note, however, that if three persons become involved in such a crime, there can be a conspiracy.

      3) **Application--Gebardi v. United States,** 287 U.S. 112 (1932).

         Gebardi v.
         United States

         a) **Facts.** Gebardi (D) and the woman he transported across state lines to have sexual relations with were charged with a conspiracy to violate the Mann Act. Gebardi made all of the arrangements; the woman voluntarily consented to go. Ds were convicted of conspiracy to violate the Mann Act. Ds appeal.

         b) **Issue.** May a woman be convicted of conspiracy to violate the Mann Act when she has not actually violated it?

         c) **Held.** No. Judgment reversed.

            (1) Congress intended the Mann Act to exempt the woman of the substantive crime. Therefore, the woman may not be convicted of conspiracy to violate the Act. Since she is

not guilty, the man cannot be either, since it takes two persons for a conspiracy (there must be an "agreement").

    d)   **Comment—Model Penal Code.** The Code would convict the man in *Gebardi*; that is, if one agrees with another to commit a crime, one is guilty of a conspiracy even if the other person is not. Most courts, however, follow the *Gebardi* rule.

Garcia v.
State

c.   **Feigned acquiescence by one party--Garcia v. State,** 394 N.E.2d 106 (Ind. 1979).

    1)   **Facts.** Garcia (D) complained to Young that her husband beat her and her children, and she asked Young to find someone to kill her husband. Young contacted the police, who set up a meeting between D, Young, and a plainclothes detective. D made a down payment to the detective and provided information to help him kill her husband. D was then arrested and later convicted of conspiracy to commit murder. D appeals, claiming there was no conspiracy because the detective only feigned acquiescence in the plan.

    2)   **Issue.** May one commit a conspiracy with a police officer who merely feigns acquiescence to the conspiracy?

    3)   **Held.** Yes. Judgment affirmed.

        a)   The traditional view of conspiracy is termed "bilateral" and requires that two or more persons conspire to commit a crime, each with the intent to do so. If all but one co-conspirator merely feign acquiescence, there is no conspiratorial agreement and no conviction for conspiracy is possible.

        b)   The Model Penal Code adopts a "unilateral" approach by which a culpable party's guilt is unaffected by whether other co-conspirators are also guilty. The rationale is that the unequivocal evidence of a firm purpose to commit a crime, which is the basis of conspiratorial liability, is the same regardless of the true intentions of co-conspirators.

        c)   Indiana makes illegal an agreement with another to commit a felony. This term does not require a meeting of the minds but rather reflects the unilateral approach.

d.   **RICO statute.**

    1)   **Introduction.** Title 18, U.S.C. sections 1961-1964, provides for criminal penalties and civil remedies involving Racketeer Influenced and Corrupt Organizations—hence the name RICO. The statute provides a broad definition of "racketeering activity" and prohibits any person who has profited from racketeering to use or invest such profits to acquire an interest in an interstate enterprise. Any interest acquired in violation of the statute is subject to forfeiture to the United States. The maximum punishment provided is a fine of $25,000 and 20 years' imprisonment. Any person injured by violations of this law can sue for damages.

2) The enterprise concept of conspiracy--United States v. Elliott, 571 F.2d 880 (5th Cir. 1978).

a) **Facts.** Elliott (D) and five other defendants were indicted under a single indictment for conspiracy to violate RICO. RICO makes it unlawful to engage in any racketeering activity which affects interstate commerce. The criminal enterprise in which Ds were alleged co-conspirators engaged in murder, numerous thefts, arson, illicit drug transactions, and obstruction of justice. Not all the Ds had contact with all the other Ds, but all had participated in some way in the criminal activities of the enterprise. At trial, the prosecutor introduced evidence of multiple conspiracies. All six Ds were convicted and now appeal.

b) **Issue.** In a trial for conspiracy to violate RICO, does proof of multiple conspiracies under an indictment alleging a single conspiracy constitute a material variance requiring reversal?

c) **Held.** No. All the convictions are affirmed but Elliott's. The evidence against Elliott was insufficient to prove that he had agreed to participate in the enterprise through a pattern of racketeering.

(1) A single conspiracy could not be demonstrated by applying pre-RICO conspiracy concepts to this case, but through RICO Congress intended to authorize the single prosecution of a multifaceted, diversified conspiracy through the enterprise concept.

(2) RICO creates a substantive offense that ties together diverse parties and crimes. Each conspirator need not participate in or have knowledge of all the crimes of the enterprise, only two or more. It is irrelevant to one conspirator what another conspirator has agreed to do because, under RICO, a defendant is charged with agreeing to participate in the enterprise through his own crimes, not with agreeing to commit each of the enterprises.

(3) Our society disdains mass prosecutions, but we recognize that conspiracy must be punished because it is more dangerous than individual action. When many conspire, they invite mass trial by their conduct.

d) **Comment.** Before this case, the United States Supreme Court had held that proof of multiple conspiracies under an indictment alleging a single conspiracy constituted a material variance requiring reversal. [*See* Kotteakos v. United States, *supra*] At issue was the right not to be tried en masse for the conglomeration of distinct and separate offenses committed by others. This case takes the opposite position where conspiracy to violate RICO is involved. Note the importance the Fifth Circuit places on Congress's intent to take strong action against criminal enterprises.

VIII. JUSTIFICATION AND EXCUSE (EXCULPATION)

The commission of what would otherwise be a crime may be justified or excused by the circumstances under which the act was committed.

A. DEFENSE OF PERSONS

1. **Self-Defense.** Generally, a person is privileged to use such force as reasonably appears necessary to defend herself against an apparent threat of unlawful and immediate violence from another. In all cases where the defendant claims that she acted in self-defense, the following elements must be established.

    a. **Reasonable belief in necessity.** The defendant must have believed that the force used was necessary for her own protection and this belief must have been reasonable (*i.e.,* a belief that a reasonable person in the same or similar circumstances would have formed). But, at the same time, an honest and reasonable belief is enough—the defense is still available even though it turns out that the belief was wrong and there was, in fact, no actual need to use force in self-defense.

    b. **Threatened harm imminent.** The defendant must have reasonably believed that the threatened harm was imminent; *i.e.,* that it would be inflicted immediately if she did not act in self-defense. Thus, it is necessary to consider whether the threatening person was actually present and, if so, whether the person appeared willing and able to injure the defendant.

    c. **Threatened harm unlawful.** The threatened harm must have been unlawful. This raises the issues of whether force can be used to resist an unlawful arrest and whether one who is the initial aggressor in an affray can claim the defense at all, an issue discussed below.

    d. **Reasonable force.** The force which the defendant used must have been reasonable. In other words, it must have been no greater than appeared necessary under the circumstances to prevent the victim from inflicting the harm.

2. **Special Limits on the Use of Deadly Force.** "Deadly force" is force used with the intent to cause death or serious bodily injury or which is known by its user to create a substantial risk of death or serious bodily injury. Although there is no absolute prohibition against the use of deadly force in self-defense, there are some special limits on when it may be used.

    a. **Perceived threat of death or serious bodily injury**. All courts agree that deadly force may be used in self-defense only if the defendant reasonably believed that the other person was about to inflict death or great bodily injury upon her and that deadly force was necessary to prevent the harm.

perfect SD — imperfect SD

3. **Objective Standard for Self-Defense--People v. Goetz,** 497 N.E.2d 41 (N.Y. 1986).

People
v. Goetz

110 - Criminal Law

a. **Facts.** Goetz (D) entered a subway car and sat on a bench. He was approached by two black youths, one of whom stated to D, "Give me five dollars." These two youths were accompanied by two others who were also in the subway car. D pulled out a handgun and shot four shots, hitting three of the youths. He then fired another shot at the youth he had missed, severing his spinal cord. D then told the conductor who responded that the youths had tried to rob him. D fled the scene, but turned himself in about a week later. D told the police that he was carrying a gun because he had been mugged and injured three years earlier and had successfully protected himself on two prior occasions by displaying the gun to would-be assailants. D also described his deliberate intent to hurt the youths and to shoot each of them, and stated that he would have shot more times if he had had more bullets. D was charged with attempted murder, assault, and weapons possession. The prosecutor instructed the grand jury that the defense of self-defense applies only when the defendant's beliefs and reactions are those of a reasonable person, an objective standard. D was indicted, but the appellate court reversed. The People (P) appeal.

b. **Issue.** Must a claim of self-defense be evaluated based on what a reasonable person in the defendant's position would have believed?

c. **Held.** Yes. Judgment reversed.

   1)   The use of force may be justified in certain circumstances, such as the defense of a person, but only to the extent the person "reasonably believes" the use of force to be necessary to defend himself from what "he reasonably believes" to be the use or imminent use of unlawful force by the aggressor. The use of deadly physical force is permitted only when the person "reasonably believes" that the aggressor is using or about to use deadly physical force, or is committing or attempting to commit a robbery or other such violent crime.

   2)   In explaining the meaning of the term "reasonably believes," the prosecutor stated that the jurors should consider whether D's conduct was "that of a reasonable man in D's situation." The lower court in reversing held that the statute requires consideration of whether D's reactions and beliefs were "reasonable to him," which is a subjective standard. This is incorrect.

   3)   The common law required an objective standard of reasonableness when applying self-defense, and the legislature followed this approach when they modified the Model Penal Code section on self-defense. Whereas the Model Penal Code permits self-defense where the defendant believes that the use of deadly force is necessary, the New York statute requires that the defendant "reasonably" believe.

   4)   An interpretation that permits a subjective standard would fundamentally change the law; it would allow a defendant to escape responsibility simply for believing the actions taken were reasonable and necessary to prevent a perceived harm. Citizens may not be free to set their own individual standards for the justifiable use of force.

   5)   Even under the objective standard, however, the individual defendant's personal knowledge and experience must be considered when assessing the reasonableness of the defendant's belief.

4. Battered-Woman's Syndrome--State v. Kelly, 478 A.2d 364 (N.J. 1984).

a. **Facts.** The day after Kelly (D) got married, her husband got drunk and knocked her down. Thereafter, for seven years, he beat her frequently while drunk, threatening to kill her and cut off parts of her body if she left him. One day, they went shopping and did not have enough money to buy the week's food. D's husband told D he would give her more money the next day, but when D asked for the money he became angry and began beating her in public. D escaped, but then her husband ran toward her again with his hands raised. D took some scissors from her purse to scare him, but she stabbed him instead, killing him. At D's murder trial, she claimed self-defense and sought to call as a witness an expert on battered-woman's syndrome. The court refused to permit the expert's testimony and D was convicted of reckless manslaughter. D appeals.

b. **Issue.** Is expert testimony regarding the battered-woman's syndrome admissible to prove a claim of self-defense?

c. **Held.** Yes. Judgment reversed.

1) The battered-woman's syndrome is increasingly accepted as an identifiable set of common characteristics shared by women who are abused physically and psychologically over time by a dominant male figure. The male figure coerces the woman to do what he wants regardless of her rights. The syndrome takes effect once the woman remains in a situation after she has been abused at least twice.

2) The battering cycle that develops in physically abusive relationships consists of: (i) the tension-building stage, when the woman placates relatively minor abuse; (ii) the acute battering stage, in which the violence escalates; and (iii) the contrition stage, in which the male seeks forgiveness and promises to change. The cycle repeats itself over time, with the final stage giving the woman hope that the relationship will improve.

3) The effect of the battering cycle is to give the victim low self-esteem, a feeling of guilt for a failed marriage, and acceptance of responsibility for the batterer's actions, as well as resistance to leaving the relationship for fear of the batterer's response. These effects create a special state of mind that experts are able to explain.

4) D's claim of self-defense was based primarily on her own testimony about her belief that her husband was about to kill her. The expert testimony she sought to present was relevant to her belief, and would have bolstered D's credibility by showing that her experience was common to other women in similar situations; *i.e.,* that she would remain in the marriage despite her fears and the abuse she suffered. The testimony was also relevant to the reasonableness of D's belief regarding the danger she faced. These aspects of battered-woman's syndrome are not within the normal knowledge and experience of a jury.

5) The offered testimony satisfies the three basic requirements for admissibility of expert testimony: (i) that the subject matter is beyond

the average juror's knowledge; (ii) that the area of expertise is sufficiently developed that the testimony is reliable; and (iii) that the witness is qualified by expertise to testify.

5. **No Perfect Self-Defense--State v. Norman,** 378 S.E.2d 8 (N.C. 1989).

a. **Facts.** Norman (D) had been badly abused by her husband during most of their 25-year marriage. He frequently punched and kicked her, threw things at her, and burned her with cigarettes and hot coffee. He forced her into prostitution, humiliated her in public, and forced her to eat pet food from a bowl on the floor. For years he threatened to maim and kill her. This behavior continued until D shot her husband three times in the back of the head, while he slept. The day before the killing, D was beaten to the point that police were summoned. However, the police would do nothing unless D filed a complaint, which she was afraid to do. D was convicted of voluntary manslaughter and sentenced to six years in prison. D appealed to the court of appeals which found in favor of D, holding that the trial court should have instructed the jury that it could acquit D by reason of perfect self-defense. The Government appeals.

b. **Issue.** Should the trial court have instructed the jury as to the right of perfect self-defense?

c. **Held.** No. Reversed.

    1) In a perfect self-defense, at the time of a killing, a defendant believes it necessary to kill to save herself from imminent death or harm. That belief must be reasonable based on the circumstances as they appear, and as would create the same belief in an ordinary person.

    2) In an imperfect self-defense, a defendant is the initial aggressor, but does not have intent to kill or seriously injure, and the victim escalates aggression to such a point that the defendant reasonably believes she is in imminent danger of death or great bodily harm.

    3) The evidence here shows no danger of imminent death or bodily harm. The deceased was sleeping at the time D shot him three times in the back of his head.

d. **Dissent.** The evidence presented showed a 20-year history of beatings and dehumanizing treatment suffered by D, who believed escape was impossible. She reasonably believed that the law could neither help nor protect her. D could reasonably believe that the next potentially fatal attack was imminent, especially in view of how the husband's behavior worsened during the three days prior to the shooting.

6. **Exception to Self-Defense--State v. Abbott,** 174 A.2d 881 (N.J. 1961).

a. **Facts.** Abbott (D) shared a common driveway with the Scaranos. When the Scaranos paved their portion of the driveway, D made a doorstop to keep his garage door from swinging onto the Scarano's property. Nicholas Scarano objected and a fight ensued. Nicholas's parents came to his aid with a hatchet and a carving knife. All of the parties were wounded by the hatchet. D claimed that they were injured during a struggle for the hatchet. D was separately indicted for atrocious assault and battery. At trial, the jury acquitted D of the charges relating to the parents, but found D guilty as to Nicholas. D appeals.

b. **Issue.** Is a person who is being attacked required to retreat only if he intends to use deadly force?

c. **Held.** Yes. Conviction reversed.

  1) Deadly force is not justifiable when an opportunity to retreat is available. Deadly force is force used with the purpose of causing, or that the actor knows will create, a substantial risk of death or serious bodily harm.

  2) It is not the nature of the force defended against that raises the issue of retreat, but the nature of the force that D employed in his defense.

  3) If a person does not resort to deadly force, one who is assailed may hold his ground and defend himself against the attack.

  4) The jury should be instructed that D could have held his ground when Nicholas came at him with his fists and when the parents came at him with the instruments. The issue of retreat could arise only if D resorted to deadly force.

7. **Duty to Retreat.** Contrary to the common law position, most American jurisdictions no longer require the defendant to retreat before using deadly force. However, a substantial minority of states still adhere to the common law rule, requiring retreat before resort to the use of deadly force in self-defense. Of course, there is no duty to retreat where retreat cannot be done safely, or where the attack takes place in the defendant's own home

8. **Aggressor's Right to Defense.** Generally, a person cannot use force to defend herself if she was the initial aggressor in the situation. By beginning the altercation, she forfeits her right to assert self-defense later. However, there are two situations in which a person, although an initial aggressor, may regain her right to act in self-defense:

a. **Nondeadly aggressor met with deadly force.** If the victim responds to the aggressor's use of nondeadly force with deadly force, the aggressor can use whatever force appears reasonably necessary (including deadly force) to repel the attack. The rationale is that because nondeadly force cannot be met with deadly force, the victim by responding with deadly force has threatened unlawful harm.

b. **Aggressor withdraws.** An aggressor may regain her right to act in self-defense by withdrawing from the affray. Ordinarily, the defendant must actually notify her adversary of the desire to desist, but some jurisdictions hold that even unsuccessful efforts to do so, if reasonable, will suffice.

United States v. Peterson

c. **Aggressor's duty to withdraw--United States v. Peterson,** 483 F.2d 1222 (D.C. Cir. 1973).

1) **Facts.** Keitt and two others drove to the rear of Peterson's (D's) house and began taking the windshield wipers from D's wrecked car. D came out and protested and a verbal fight ensued. D went back in his house, got a gun, and came back out, warning the others not to move. He also threatened to kill Keitt if he came into D's yard. Keitt left the car, challenged D, and then got a lug wrench, which he raised. Keitt advanced toward D, who warned that he would kill Keitt if he took "another step." Keitt did not stop and D shot him in the face, immediately killing him. D was convicted of manslaughter and now appeals.

2) **Issue.** May an aggressor claim self-defense if he does not first withdraw from the conflict?

3) **Held.** No. Judgment affirmed.

   a) The general rule is that a claim of self-defense may not arise from a self-generated necessity to kill. Such a killing is not defensive because the necessity could have been averted. A claim of self-defense may arise, however, if the aggressor communicates to his adversary an intent to withdraw and then in good faith attempts to do so.

   b) Here, Keitt may have been the original aggressor, but he was about to leave, or withdraw, when D challenged him with a gun. D never made an attempt to withdraw and, having become the aggressor, may not claim self-defense.

4) **Comment.** The Model Penal Code allows self-defense against any escalation of the confrontation. If the original defender uses excessive force to respond, the original aggressor may defend against the excessive force, unless his original aggression was intended to provoke a necessity to kill in self-defense.

B. PROTECTION OF PROPERTY AND LAW ENFORCEMENT

1. **Protection of Property.** The right to use force in the protection of property is much more limited than the right to use force in the protection of persons.

   a. **Deadly force not allowed.** A person cannot use deadly force simply to defend her property against unlawful interference, even if there is no other way to prevent the threatened harm. This rule is based on the premise that the interest in security of property does not justify jeopardizing the lives of others.

   b. **Nondeadly force.** Nondeadly force may be used to protect both real and personal property in one's possession if it reasonably appears necessary to prevent or terminate an unlawful intrusion onto or interference with that property.

1) **Request to desist.** But force is not reasonable unless a *prior request* has been made for the other to desist from interfering with the property.

2) **Property in possession of another.** Moreover, the traditional rules apparently require that the property defended be in the *possession* of the person using the force. Thus, there is *probably* no right to use force in defense of property in the possession of another.

3) **Compare—use of force to regain or reenter property.** Traditionally, one illegally dispossessed of property cannot use force to regain it or, in the case of real property, to reenter it. An exception is made, however, where action is taken immediately after the loss of the property or in "hot pursuit" of the dispossessor.

People v. Ceballos

c. **Use of mechanical device--People v. Ceballos,** 526 P.2d 241 (Cal. 1974).

1) **Facts.** Ceballos (D) lived alone in a garage and in an apartment above the garage. D had some tools stolen from his house and a few months later noticed pry marks on one of the garage doors. One of the locks had also been bent. D set up a trap gun. Two boys who decided to break in and see if there was anything to steal opened the door. The gun fired and hit one of the boys in the face. D was convicted of assault with a deadly weapon. D appeals, claiming the trap gun was justified.

2) **Issue.** May a person use a trap gun to protect property in his house while he is away?

3) **Held.** No. Judgment affirmed.

a) The general rule imposes criminal and civil liability for setting up a deadly mechanical device which actually kills or injures another. An exception has arisen when the intrusion is such that the person, if present, could inflict the harm with his own hands. That exception should not apply to criminal cases, however, because under it liability depends on fortuitous events, and because the use of trap guns presents an unacceptable danger to children, fire fighters, etc.

b) Even if the exception applied, D would be liable. Although homicide is justifiable as a defense against a forcible and atrocious crime, the burglary by the boys here did not threaten death or serious injury to anyone since they were the only persons present. Neither can the use of deadly force be justified solely for the protection of property.

2. **Law Enforcement.** The dangers of law enforcement present many difficult questions as to the scope of justified violence. Problems arise when citizens assist law enforcement officers, when officers effectuate arrests, and when suspects resist arrest.

a.   **Assistance to police.** Citizens may properly assist law enforcement agencies in good faith. However, the use of force as part of such assistance could endanger others. The defense of aiding law enforcement agencies does not exonerate a citizen from all liability for his conduct. The defense essentially nullifies criminal intent. The fact finder must scrutinize the defendant's conduct to determine whether it shows a lack of criminal intent. A private citizen called upon by a police officer to assist in making an arrest, however, has the same privilege as the officer because the citizen is required by law to comply with the police officer's order.

b.   **Effectuating arrest.** Both private citizens and police officers may use force in making an arrest, but different standards apply to the two groups.

   1)   **Police officers.** A police officer is entitled to act on reasonable appearances in using force in making an arrest. A police officer may use whatever nondeadly force reasonably appears necessary to make an arrest for a felony or misdemeanor. The right to use deadly force has traditionally been limited to situations in which the officer reasonably believes the suspect committed a felony. The modern approach is more restricted; deadly force is permitted only if the suspect has committed a dangerous felony or presents a significant risk of harm to others.

   2)   **Traditional rule--Durham v. State,** 159 N.E. 145 (Ind. 1927).

        Durham v. State

   a)   **Facts.** Durham (D), a game warden, arrested Long for illegal fishing. Long fled to his boat to attempt an escape. D pursued Long; Long hit him with an oar. D shot Long in the arm and was prosecuted for assault and battery. D appeals his conviction.

   b)   **Issue.** May an arresting officer use injuring force to capture a fleeing misdemeanant?

   c)   **Held.** Yes. Judgment reversed.

   (1)   For misdemeanors, the officer may use all the force necessary to make the arrest, except that he may not use deadly force or inflict serious bodily harm on one merely fleeing arrest. However, if the person resists the officer such that the officer's life is in danger or serious bodily harm is threatened, the officer may take the person's life if necessary. Because the victim resisted arrest, D was justified in using the force he did.

   3)   **Modern approach—use of deadly force to stop fleeing burglar not permitted--Tennessee v. Garner,** 471 U.S. 1 (1985).

        Tennessee v. Garner

   a)   **Facts.** The Tennessee fleeing felon statute authorized police officers to use deadly force to capture unarmed suspects fleeing from nonviolent felonies. One night an unarmed 15-year-old boy broke into an unoccupied house to steal money and property. Two police officers responded and yelled at the boy to stop as he fled. As the boy tried to get over a fence, the police shot and killed him. Garner (P) sued the Memphis Police Department for wrongful death. The State of Tennessee (D) intervened to defend the statute. The district court upheld the state law, but the court of appeals reversed. D appeals.

b) **Issue.** May a state authorize police officers to use deadly force to capture an unarmed suspect fleeing from a nonviolent felony?

c) **Held.** No. Judgment affirmed.

(1) Under state law, the reasonableness and necessity of using deadly force to capture a fleeing felon is a jury question. However, once it is determined that the officer could not have caught the felon without shooting, shooting is reasonable under the statute. The nature of the felony or the actual dangerousness of the felon is irrelevant.

(2) The Fourth Amendment protects against unreasonable seizures. Killing a fleeing suspect is certainly a "seizure" of the person. Under common law, killing a felon who resisted arrest was permitted, but at that time, all felonies were capital crimes. Any felon at large would be executed if caught and tried, so such outlaws were considered automatically dangerous. The use of deadly force was not permitted when the fleeing suspect's crime did not require execution.

(3) Tennessee's law is inconsistent with the rationale of the common law. There are now hundreds of state and federal felonies not recognized at common law, including white collar crimes and possession of contraband. To permit the use of deadly force against a suspect without regard to the risk of danger presented to the community presents an unnecessarily severe and excessive police response that violates the Fourth Amendment.

(4) The officers as individuals cannot be held liable because they reasonably relied on the state statute. D, however, is liable for constitutional damages even though it relied on the state statute.

d) **Dissent.** The reasonableness of the officer's seizure of P depends on the public interest involved and the intrusion on P's legitimate interests. The public interest in using deadly force to apprehend a fleeing burglar relates to the seriousness of the crime. Burglary is a serious and dangerous felony, and the public has a compelling interest in preventing and detecting the burglaries. Apprehension of the suspect is critical. On the other hand, while P has an obvious interest in his life, he does not have a right to flee unimpeded from the scene of a burglary. Use of deadly force as a last resort to apprehend a fleeing burglar at night is not unreasonable.

United States
v. Hillsman

4) **Arrest by private citizen--United States v. Hillsman,** 522 F.2d 454 (7th Cir. 1975).

a) **Facts.** Hillsman (D) and several others were attending a downtown funeral. Two plainclothes DEA agents were in the crowd to observe narcotics dealers. A fight erupted when one of the agents refused the request of a group of mourners to stop taking pictures. The other agent (Rhodes) drew his gun and prepared to shoot the principal instigator. He was bumped and accidentally shot and killed an innocent bystander. After announcing he was a federal agent, Rhodes told his partner, "Let's get out of here," and they both fled in their respective cars. D and others chased Rhodes's car and fired shots at it, but did not injure Rhodes. D was convicted of assaulting a federal officer. He appeals, claiming he was justified in trying to stop what he believed was a fleeing felon.

    b)   **Issue.** May a private citizen arrest a suspected felon when he believes a felony has been committed, although in fact no felony has been committed?

    c)   **Held.** No. Judgment affirmed.

        (1)   A person may be liable for assaulting a federal officer even when he did not know the victim was a federal officer. [*See* United States v. Feola, *supra*]

        (2)   D might be justified because of the agent's actions if, assuming the agent had been a civilian, he would have been justified. Indiana law allows a private citizen to arrest one who commits a felony in his presence, or one he reasonably believes has committed a felony, as long as the felony was actually committed. Here, however, D requested only an instruction as to voluntary manslaughter. The jury did not find that Rhodes committed this felony, so D was properly convicted.

    d)   **Concurrence.** Except for the *Feola* case, I would reverse because D's conduct was socially desirable.

C.   RESIDUAL JUSTIFICATION

1.   **General Principle of Justification.**

    a.   **Problem.** The problem is illustrated by *Regina v. Dudley and Stephens, supra*, where a ship went down and the crew on a lifeboat ate the cabin boy in order to survive. One of the most difficult problems to solve is to determine when people really do act out of necessity. If those who take others' lives out of necessity are to be exculpated, then the test for their excuse should be formulated around the conditions that existed at the time they acted and not on conditions that happened long after the act was completed.

    b.   **General rule.** Criminal acts, done out of necessity, may be excused if the accused can show that they were done to avoid otherwise unavoidable consequences to himself or others he is bound to protect, the results of which would have been irreparable; that no more was done than was absolutely necessary; and that the evil inflicted was not out of proportion to the evil that was threatened. Some courts hold that acts of "economic" necessity are not justified. Almost all courts hold that acts that result in taking another's life are never justified.

    1)   For example, most courts would not excuse the defendants in the *Dudley and Stephens* case. However, had such a group taken food that did not belong to them from the ship, this would have been excused.

c. **Model Penal Code.** The Code formulates rules different from that of the majority of jurisdictions:

  1) Conduct the actor believes to be necessary to avoid an evil to himself or another is justifiable, provided:

    a) The evil sought to be avoided by such conduct is greater than that sought to be prevented by the law defining the crime; and

    b) The law does not provide for such a situation specifically.

  2) When the actor is reckless or negligent in bringing about the situation requiring a choice of evils or in appraising the necessity for his conduct, the justification afforded by this action is unavailable in a prosecution for any offense for which recklessness or negligence, as the case may be, suffices to establish culpability.

d. **Necessity to escape from prison--People v. Unger,** 362 N.E.2d 319 (Ill. 1977).

People v. Unger

  1) **Facts.** Unger (D) was convicted of the crime of escape. D produced evidence that such escape was justified by the affirmative defense of necessity. D had been threatened with homosexual assault, was sexually assaulted, and then threatened with death by his attacker, who thought D had reported the attack. D testified that he was unable to defend himself and that he intended to turn himself in once he had obtained the legal advice of an attorney. D brings this appeal because the trial judge instructed the jury to disregard the reasons given for D's escape and failed to instruct the jury of the affirmative defense of necessity. The appellate court reversed and remanded for a new trial. The People (P) appeal.

  2) **Issue.** May the defense of necessity be used by a convict who escapes prison?

  3) **Held.** Yes. Judgment affirmed.

    a) The introduction of evidence to support the defense of necessity is sufficient to require the giving of an appropriate instruction. D was forced to choose between two admitted evils: an illegal escape or a homosexual assault and fear of reprisal. D was not compelled to escape, but the escape could be considered necessary.

    b) In *People v. Lovercamp*, 118 Cal. Rptr. 110 (1974), the court allowed the defense of necessity in a similar context. The court set forth five conditions to the defense:

      (1) Specific threat of death or serious attack in the immediate future;

      (2) No time for complaint, or a history of futile complaints to authorities;

      (3) No chance to resort to the courts;

(4) No force or violence towards innocent persons during escape; and

(5) Immediate contact with prison officials when prisoner is safe.

c) These factors are relevant to the propriety of the defense but they are not necessary. D was entitled to an appropriate instruction.

4) Dissent.

a) The use of the necessity defense in prison escape cases must be confined within well-defined boundaries such as those in *Lovercamp*. D did not satisfy those conditions here.

b) Unless the necessity defense is specifically confined, it will encourage potential escapees, disrupt prison discipline, and result in injury to prison guards, police, or private citizens.

e. **Necessity defense--United States v. Schoon,** 971 F.2d 193 (1992).

United States
v. Schoon

1) Facts. Schoon (D) was one of 30 people who gained admittance to the Tucson IRS office where they chanted "Keep America's tax dollars out of El Salvador" and splashed simulated blood on counters, walls, and carpeting, obstructing office operations. They refused to disperse when so ordered by a federal police officer. At trial, D attempted to assert a necessity defense, contending they acted to avoid further bloodshed in El Salvador. The trial court precluded the necessity defense, and D was convicted of obstructing the activities of the IRS office and failing to comply with an order of a federal officer. D appeals.

2) Issue. May a defendant who is charged with indirect civil disobedience raise the defense of necessity?

3) Held. No. Convictions affirmed.

a) A necessity defense must show that one: (i) was faced with a choice of evils, and chose the lesser; (ii) acted to prevent imminent harm; and (iii) reasonably anticipated a direct causal relationship between the conduct and the harm to be averted.

b) The trial court held that: (i) there was no immediacy; (ii) the action taken would not abate the evil; and (iii) other legal alternatives existed.

c) Direct civil disobedience involves protesting a law by breaking the law. Indirect civil disobedience involves violating a law or interfering with a government policy that is not, itself, the object of the protest. In addition to agreeing with the trial court's reasoning, we find that D engaged in indirect civil disobedience because the group was not challenging the laws under which they were charged.

d) The necessity defense requires that the commission of a crime avert the occurrence of an even greater harm. For example, prisoners may escape a burning prison. But we assume in such cases that the lawmaker, if confronted with such facts, would have carved out the exception which is subsequently claimed as justified by necessity.

e)   Indirect civil disobedience, however, involves the breaking of a law (other than the one sought to be repealed) as symbolic and to draw attention to a cause. We rule that the necessity defense is inapplicable to acts of indirect civil disobedience because legal alternatives will never be deemed exhausted when the harm can be mitigated by congressional action.

f.   Extreme necessity--Regina v. Dudley and Stephens, 14 Q.B.D. 273 (1884). *See supra.*

Cruzan v. Director, Missouri Department of Health

g.   Euthanasia--Cruzan v. Director, Missouri Department of Health, 497 U.S. 261 (1989).

1)   Facts. Nancy Cruzan suffered severe injuries in a motor vehicle accident, and as a result, was in a vegetative state. Nancy's parents (Ps) sought to have her artificial nutrition and hydration procedures halted. The state court held that Nancy had a constitutional right to refuse or direct the withdrawal of "death prolonged procedures." The state court also held that Nancy's wishes had been expressed during a conversation with a close friend. The Supreme Court of Missouri reversed, finding that Nancy's conversation with her friend was unreliable for the purpose of determining her intent. The Supreme Court granted certiorari.

2)   Issue. Does a person in a vegetative state have a constitutional right to require the hospital to withdraw life-sustaining treatment?

3)   Held. No. Supreme Court of Missouri is affirmed.

a)   We have long held that medical treatment requires the informed consent of a patient, thus indicating that one possesses a constitutionally-protected liberty interest not to consent and to refuse treatment.

b)   We assume for the purposes of this case that the United States Constitution would grant a competent person the right to refuse lifesaving measures.

c)   But Ps argue that an incompetent person should possess the same right, ignoring the fact that an incompetent person is unable to make an informed or voluntary choice.

d)   It is a surrogate who must exercise Nancy's right which Missouri permits in accordance with procedural safeguards. Missouri requires an incompetent person's wishes to be proven by clear and convincing evidence.

e)   Such a procedural requirement is not barred by the Constitution.

4)   Concurrence (Scalia, J.). Federal courts have no business in this field which has been reserved to the states. There is no "right" here which has been historically protected against state interference, and thus, there is no due process violation. While petitioners argue that this would not be suicide, under common law it would be. The notion that refusing treatment is a passive act, rather than an affirmative step to end one's life, does not withstand scrutiny. The distinction should be between various forms of inaction. Otherwise, one may not commit suicide by walking into the sea, but may sit on the beach until the tide comes in and completely submerges him.

h.   **Assisted suicide--People v. Kevorkian,** __ N.W.2d __ (Mich. 1994).

People v.
Kevorkian

1)   **Facts.** Dr. Jack Kevorkian (D) was prosecuted under a Michigan statute for intentionally assisting several persons to commit suicide. D raised several defenses, including the unconstitutionality of the statute under the Due Process Clause. The Michigan Supreme Court upheld the statute in the following opinion.

2)   **Issue.** Does the Due Process Clause encompass the fundamental right to commit suicide and, if so, does it include the right to assistance?

3)   **Held.** No.

a)   Advocates of assisted suicide rely on *Compassion In Dying v. Washington,* 850 F. Supp. 1454 (W.D. Wash. 1994), in which a federal court found that suicide falls within the realm of personal liberty which the government may not enter. They also argue there is no fundamental difference between *Cruzan's* holding, which recognized the right to refuse life-sustaining treatment, and the act of suicide.

b)   This court disagrees, finding merit in the distinction between acts that artificially sustain life and acts that artificially curtail life.

c)   *Cruzan* does not hold that there is a fundamental liberty interest in suicide, nor does *Planned Parenthood of Southeastern Pennsylvania v. Casey,* 112 S. Ct. 2791 (1992), which deals with the issue of abortion.

d)   Historically, the states have not criminalized suicide, but no such concession was made to those who assist in such suicide.

4)   **Dissent.** There is no logic in permitting one to have feeding tubes removed, but preventing him from further actions to end his life, thus condemning him to starve to death.

5)   **Dissent.** The decision to die is so personal in nature that society is not in a position to judge the appropriateness of such a decision. Therefore, a complete ban on physician-assisted suicide represents an undue burden on the rights of the terminally ill.

6)   **Comment.** Is there any logic to the notion that it is a crime to assist in a suicide, where the act of suicide is not a statutory crime? In those states that have not criminalized suicide, how can it be a crime to assist in the commission of a non-criminal act?

D. PRINCIPLES OF EXCUSE

1. **Introduction.** Because punishment for crime is based on the existence of a culpable mental state, some allowance must be made for situations where the mental state is affected to preclude formation of the culpable intent.

2. **Duress and Coercion (Compulsion).**

   a. **Statement of the rule.** Acts done under the immediate threat of death or serious bodily injury, where there is both reasonable cause to believe and actual belief that such harm is threatened, will be excused.

   b. **Model Penal Code.**

      1) It is an affirmative defense that the actor engaged in conduct because he was "coerced" to do so by the use of, or a threat to use unlawful force against his person or the person of another, which a person of reasonable firmness in his situation would have been unable to resist.

      2) The defense is unavailable if the actor recklessly placed himself in the situation in which it was probable that he would be subjected to duress. It is also unavailable if he was negligent in placing himself in such a situation, whenever negligence suffices for culpability.

      3) Note that under the duress sections, if another person threatens to kill you unless you kill two others, and you kill them, you may be excused. Query why the defendant is excused here and not under the section on necessity.

   c. **Application--State v. Toscano,** 378 A.2d 755 (N.J. 1977).

      1) **Facts.** Toscano (D), a chiropractor, was involved in a conspiracy to defraud insurance companies by staging accidents and filing fraudulent claims. D admitted that he made up a medical bill and medical reports, but claimed he did so only because of threats made by the co-conspirators. D did not receive compensation for his participation. The trial court instructed the jury that the peril allegedly faced by D was not imminent, present, and pending such that he could not seek police protection, and therefore D had no defense of duress. D was convicted. The conviction was upheld on appeal and the state supreme court granted certification to consider the issue.

      2) **Issue.** In order to establish a defense of duress, must a defendant have acted in response to a threat of harm that was present, imminent, and impending?

      3) **Held.** No. Judgment reversed and a new trial ordered.

State v.
Toscano

a) The common law rule allowed a defense of duress but only when the alleged coercion involved a use or threat of harm that was present, imminent, and pending, inducing an apprehension of death or serious bodily harm unless the act was done. Such a threat to a close relative would suffice. Some cases vary the seriousness of the threat necessary according to the crime committed. This rule has been criticized for impairing the deterrent value of the criminal law.

b) Some commentators have proposed a duress defense based on the subjective reaction to unlawful demands. The Model Penal Code approach allows consideration of a reasonable person's reaction to the threat faced by the defendant, allowing consideration of age, sex, etc., but not temperament. This is the best approach and is hereby adopted as the standard for a duress defense in all but murder cases.

4) **Comment.** The New Jersey Legislature subsequently adopted a statute along the lines of the Model Penal Code.

3. Intoxication.

a. **General rule.** Voluntary intoxication is no defense to a crime. However, evidence of drunkenness may be introduced to show that the defendant did not have the requisite intent that is required when specific intent is an element of the crime. For example, murder in the first degree requires premeditation and deliberation; intoxication would perhaps negate this. However, where no specific intent is required (such as for involuntary manslaughter), intoxication would be no defense to the crime.

b. **Analysis.**

1) The idea is that the individual has control over drinking; *i.e.,* he can decide whether he will drink in the first place. He knows the dangers from doing so, and therefore if he drinks he must accept the consequences.

2) If A is drunk and kills a person as a result, if A is punished, is it not for drinking that A is being punished? If this is so, and deterrence of drinking is the rationale, should not all drinkers (not just those who commit crimes) be punished? For example, if A voluntarily fires a gun into the middle of a crowd, even if he does not want to injure someone, if B is killed thereby, A may be held for murder (*i.e.,* he intended to fire the gun into the crowd, and objectively speaking the killing of a person was substantially certain to follow).

a) **Proof of general intent.** Intent is inferred by the results that occur. Therefore, general intent may be proved simply by showing that the prohibited result was caused by a voluntary act of D.

b) **Transferred intent.** When a person has the required intent to commit one criminal act, he may be held responsible for results that he did not intend if he inflicts the kind of harm intended and if the injuries sustained do not require a different mens rea.

(1) Usually the intent from the first crime will only be transferred to the second where the first act was "malum in se" For example, where A attempts to hit B and unintentionally hits and injuries C, A is guilty of assault on C.

(2) The transfer generally occurs only where the unintended result involves the same mens rea requirement as the intended act. Therefore, if A shoots at B, misses, and the bullet strikes an oil lamp, igniting a fire, A is not guilty of arson because arson requires that specific intent to start a fire be shown (specific intent is discussed below), and here A can only be held to have had the intent to do personal injury.

Regina v. Kingston

c. **Intoxication--Regina v. Kingston,** 4 All E.R. 373 (1993), *rev'd,* House of Lords, 3 All E.R. 353 (1994).

1) **Facts.** Penn lured a 15-year-old boy to his flat, drugged him, and then invited Kingston (D) to come there to sexually abuse the boy. Penn photographed and audiotaped what took place, for the purpose of blackmailing D. D was subsequently charged with indecent assault and battery, and at trial testified he sometimes drank coffee at Penn's but was not sure if he had on that evening. D's words on the audiotape indicated that he did drink coffee and asked if Penn had put something into the coffee causing D to feel sleepy. The trial court instructed the jury that if it found that D intended to commit the indecent assault, prior to being drugged, then the drug was irrelevant. The jury could acquit only if it found that because of the drug, D did not intend to commit an indecent assault. D was convicted. D appeals.

2) **Issue.** If an intentional act arises out of circumstances for which an accused bears no blame, may he be entitled to a judgment of acquittal?

3) **Held.** Yes. Conviction set aside.

a) The pedophiliac inclinations of D are not illegal; acting upon them is. However, if D crossed the boundary between inclination and action because of a third party's clandestine act, then justice is not served by convicting the person who crossed the line.

b) Involuntary intoxication, by alcohol or drugs, negates the mens rea.

4) **Dissent.** The drug is not alleged to have created D's desire, but rather to have enabled its release. But the reasoning is that where blame is absent, the necessary mens rea must be absent. This is not logical. These factors being used to require a judgment of acquittal would be more appropriately considered for determining D's sentence, not his guilt or innocence.

5) **Comment.** Some would argue that, contrary to the dissent's apparent belief that recognizing involuntary intoxication as an absolute defense would impact upon a vast number of prosecutions, instances of involuntary intoxication are relatively rare. The more common scenario does not

involve a clandestine act by a third party. More often than not, it involves a defendant who suffered unexpected effects from a new medication or an interaction between alcohol and medication of which he had not been forewarned.

d. Culpable intent while intoxicated--Roberts v. People, 19 Mich. 401 (1870).

1) **Facts.** Roberts (D) was convicted of assault with the intent to murder. D testified that he was too drunk at the time of the act to have the required intent. D appeals.

2) **Issue.** May voluntary intoxication be a legitimate defense to a crime requiring intent?

3) **Held.** Yes. Judgment reversed.

   a) Voluntary drunkenness will not excuse the assault part of the offense but, if sufficient, it will excuse the specific intent. If D's drunkenness was so extensive that D's mental faculties were incapable of entertaining the necessary intent, he will be excused.

   b) If D's drunkenness was such that he could not appreciate right and wrong, yet he still formed the necessary intent, he would be guilty. He would, in that case, be treated as having intended the obscuration of his facilities.

   c) As long as D had the intent, he is guilty, even if he would not have had the intent if he had not been intoxicated. These are all questions for the jury upon retrial.

e. Specific and general intent--People v. Hood, 462 P.2d 370 (Cal. 1969).

People v. Hood

1) **Facts.** Hood (D) had been drinking before a police officer attempted to arrest him. D resisted the arrest and, using the police officer's gun, shot the police officer. D was convicted of assault with a deadly weapon and assault with intent to commit murder. The convictions were reversed because of conflicting jury instructions given on the effect of intoxication. The court then gave an extended analysis of the issue.

2) **Issue.** Is assault a specific intent crime to which evidence of intoxication is material?

3) **Held.** No.

   a) The problem of intoxicated offenders caused courts to develop the distinction between specific and general intent crimes. A drunken criminal may be less culpable for his acts than a sober criminal, but he should not entirely escape the consequences of his conduct.

   b) General criminal intent is that intention to do a proscribed act. Specific intent is the intent to do some further act or achieve some additional consequence. A drunken person is usually able to form the intent to strike someone else, to commit an assault. However, he would be unlikely to be able to formulate an intent to commit a battery for the purpose of killing.

    c)   Assault is a general intent crime, and intoxication is no defense.

4)   **Comment.** The court reaffirmed that assault with a deadly weapon was a general intent crime in *People v. Rocha*, 479 P.2d 372 (Cal. 1971). A specific intent crime requires not only that D do the prohibited act, but that he do it with a particular state of mind.

State v.
Stasio

f.   **Elimination of distinction between specific and general intent crimes--State v. Stasio,** 396 A.2d 1129 (N.J. 1979).

1)   **Facts.** After drinking much of the day, Stasio (D) entered a tavern and demanded that the bartender give him money. When the bartender refused, D attempted to knife him. D was charged with assault with intent to rob and assault with a dangerous weapon. At a conference in chambers, D informed the judge that his defense would be intoxication to the point that he could not have formed the intent to rob. The judge responded that he would charge the jury that voluntary intoxication was not a defense. D did not take the stand at the trial and was convicted by a jury on both counts. The appellate division reversed the convictions and ordered a new trial. The State (P) appeals.

2)   **Issue.** Does voluntary intoxication constitute a defense to a specific intent crime?

3)   **Held.** No. But because the trial judge erred in permitting the defense to withhold its evidence of intoxication due to an anticipated jury instruction, we affirm the appellate division's decision and order a new trial.

    a)   Voluntary intoxication will not excuse criminal conduct. The need to protect the public from those who become voluntarily intoxicated is obvious. One who voluntarily becomes intoxicated should not be insulated from criminal responsibility.

    b)   Distinguishing between specific and general intent crimes would give rise to incongruous results by irrationally allowing intoxication to excuse some crimes but not others. Some defendants would be completely acquitted because not every specific intent crime has a lesser included general intent offense. Thus, the offender would be denied exculpation, receive partial exculpation, or be totally exculpated depending upon the nature of the crime with which he is charged.

    c)   Until a stuporous condition is reached, the probability of existence of intent remains. Just because alcohol removes inhibitions does not mean that it vitiates intent.

    d)   This holding does not mean that voluntary intoxication is always irrelevant in criminal proceedings, only that it is not a complete defense.

4)   **Dissent.** The majority departs from precedent. There must be a concurrence of an evil mind and an evildoing hand before D may be convicted.

A person who intentionally commits an act is more culpable than one who engages in the same conduct without an evil design. The majority's opinion will not reduce alcohol-induced crime.

4. Mental Disorder.

   a. **Insanity defense.** An accused may be found not guilty if, at the time of the crime, he was so impaired by mental illness or retardation that he was "insane." There is a general presumption of sanity, however, so that an accused must affirmatively raise the defense. Many states require the prosecution to prove beyond a reasonable doubt that the accused was sane at the time of the offense, while others require the accused to persuade the jury of his insanity by a preponderance of the evidence. Every jurisdiction has procedures for commitment of an accused found not guilty by reason of insanity. There are several different standards for insanity applied by the various jurisdictions.

   b. **Traditional *M'Naghten* approach** [M'Naghten's Case, 8 Eng. Rep. 718 (1843)]. Under the common law, a person who did not know what he was doing due to some mental defect, and who thus lacked an understanding will, could not be convicted. In the mid-1800s, a man named M'Naghten tried to assassinate the Prime Minister of England, who he believed persecuted him. He shot the Prime Minister's secretary by mistake. M'Naghten was tried and found not guilty by reason of insanity. His defense counsel had relied on a recently published book on insanity that repudiated many of the incorrect scientific beliefs on which the traditional common law test was based, including the idea that the human mind is compartmentalized. However, after M'Naghten's acquittal, the Queen directed a study of the law of insanity. Under pressure from the Queen, the judges adopted the traditional test, which came to be known as the *M'Naghten* test.

   1) **Test.** Under *M'Naghten*, an accused must show that as a result of his mental illness he either (i) did not know the nature and quality of his act, or (ii) did not know that the act was wrong.

   2) **Criticism.** The test assumes that a person's understanding or reasoning ability may be separated from other aspects of personality. Most psychiatrists now agree that personality is unitary and interrelated. The test limits admissible evidence to matters concerning the understanding, thereby excluding much relevant information on the accused's mental condition relevant to determining whether he should be held criminally liable.

   c. **Irresistible impulse approach.** Some states permit the acquittal of an accused whose commission of the crime was caused by an insane impulse that controlled his will. This approach is added to *M'Naghten* as an additional grounds for a finding of not guilty.

   d. ***Durham* or product approach.** New Hampshire formulated a test whereby an accused could be acquitted by reason of insanity upon a showing that the crime was the product of a mental illness. The approach was adopted by the Court of Appeals for the District of Columbia in *Durham v. United States*, 214 F.2d 862 (D.C. Cir. 1954), but was later abandoned in *United*

States v. Brawner, 471 F.2d 969 (D.C. Cir. 1972). Many authorities criticize the rule as being far too broad and vague, and it is little followed today.

State v. Crenshaw

e.   Cognitively impaired offender--State v. Crenshaw, 659 P.2d 488 (Wash. 1983).

1)   Facts. Crenshaw (D) and his wife went to Canada on their honeymoon. While there, D got in a fight and was deported. D waited for his wife in Washington but she did not come until two days later. D believed she had been unfaithful. In their motel room, D beat his wife unconscious. He then went to a store, stole a knife, and returned to the motel where he stabbed his wife 24 times. Then D went to a farm, borrowed an ax, returned to the motel, and decapitated his wife. He placed the body in a blanket and put the head in a pillowcase. D then put the body parts in his wife's car and cleaned the room of blood and fingerprints with a bucket and sponge. Before leaving, D paid his bill and visited with the manager over a beer. When he left, D drove to a secluded area where he hid the body parts in brush. He drove about 200 miles before picking up hitch-hikers, to whom he confessed. They reported the crime to the police, who arrested D and obtained a voluntary confession. At trial, D asserted the defense of not guilty by reason of insanity, claiming that under the Moscovite religious faith that he followed, it would be improper for him not to kill his wife if she committed adultery. He also produced evidence of his history of mental problems, for which he had been hospitalized. The court instructed the jury that the defense applies only if they found that D was unable to perceive the nature and quality of the acts with which he was charged or was unable to tell right from wrong with reference to the particular acts. "Right and wrong" was defined as "knowledge of a person at the time of committing an act that he was acting contrary to the law." D was convicted. He appeals, claiming the instruction was improper.

2)   Issue. May an accused's sanity be tested by his knowledge that his acts were legally wrong?

3)   Held. Yes. Judgment affirmed.

a)   The jury instruction relayed the traditional *M'Naghten* test, except for the last paragraph that equated "legal" and "moral" wrong. In *M'Naghten's Case*, the justices opined that a person who acts under a partial insane delusion that he was revenging some supposed grievance is punishable if he knew at the time of committing the crime that he was acting contrary to law. They also stated that an accused is punishable if he was conscious that the act was one that he ought not to do, meaning it was morally wrong, and if the act was also contrary to the law, but that the accused need not have actual knowledge of the law.

b)   In this case, assuming that D acted under a delusion that he was revenging the supposed grievance of his wife's infidelity, it was only a partial delusion because he acted normally to the manager and others at the time of the offense. His attempts to hide his crime showed he knew that he was acting contrary to law. It was not improper to equate moral and legal wrong since D knew that his acts were illegal. Strict application of the *M'Naghten* rule is appropriate because only those who have lost contact with reality so completely that they are beyond any of the influences of the criminal law are to benefit from the insanity defense.

    c)   Another approach is that society's morals, not D's morals, are the standard for judging moral wrong. Even if D thought that, pursuant to his religious beliefs, it was not morally wrong to kill his wife, there is evidence that he knew his act was morally wrong from society's viewpoint as well as illegal. Once moral wrong is equated with society's morals, moral and legal wrong are easily equated, since the law expresses collective morality.

    d)   Finally, D did not prove that his alleged delusions stemmed from a mental defect, and he did not prove that he was legally insane at the time of the crime. His conduct, other than killing his wife, was rational. No one ever kills his wife in a rational way, but not every man who kills his wife is insane.

  4) **Dissent.** While moral and legal may be synonymous in a particular case, they may also be distinguishable. The jury should decide this issue, not the court. In this case, there was evidence that D's perception of right and wrong and his capacity to appreciate the consequences of his behavior were very likely distorted when he committed the crime. (By limiting the jury's consideration to D's knowledge that the act was illegal, D was deprived of his right to be judged as to his knowledge of the difference between moral right and wrong.)

  5) **Comment.** The Washington Supreme Court held that this jury instruction was improperly given in another case in which the accused stated that he knew his crime was illegal, but that he felt it was not particularly wrong in the eyes of God because his victim was "into sorcery." The court distinguished between acting pursuant to religious beliefs, as Crenshaw had allegedly done, and acting in the belief that God was directing the act; this has been labeled the "deific decree" exception to the general rule that legal and moral wrong are the same thing. [*See* State v. Cameron, 674 P.2d 650 (Wash. 1983)]

                                   Rules. to ask - notes

f.   **Broadening of defense beyond *M'Naghten*--United States v. Freeman,** 357   United States
F.2d 606 (2d Cir. 1966).   v. Freeman

  a)   **Facts.** Freeman (D) was tried for selling narcotics. At his trial, D claimed that at the time of the alleged sale of narcotics, he did not possess sufficient capacity and will to be held responsible for the criminality of his acts. D's expert witness testified that D was a narcotics addict and a confirmed alcoholic, and that these conditions, combined with physical trauma, had caused delusions, hallucinations, and amnesia. He testified that D knew that he was selling heroin on the nights in question, but that he was not aware of the social implications of the transactions. The government's expert testified that D could distinguish between right and wrong within the meaning of the *M'Naghten* test despite his use of narcotics and alcohol. He referred to the fact that D had taken precautions against being apprehended when he made the sale. The trial judge determined that the *M'Naghten* requirements were not met and found D guilty. D appeals.

b) **Issue.** Does the insanity defense include states of mind broader than those relevant under the *M'Naghten* test?

c) **Held.** Yes. Judgment reversed.

(1) The *M'Naghten* test is unrealistic and ignores the problem of those who can somewhat tell right from wrong but lack the capacity to control their acts.

(2) Because the *M'Naghten* test unnecessarily restricted psychiatrists' testimony and deprived the fact finders of information needed to make a judgment, other tests arose. Among these was the irresistible impulse test, which was not much more sophisticated because it is too narrow and incorrectly implies that a crime impulsively committed must have been committed in a sudden and explosive fit.

(3) The *Durham* rule holds a defendant not criminally responsible if the unlawful act was the product of mental disease or mental defect. The problem with this approach is that it does not provide any standards to measure the defendant's competency. It is based on labels and classifications that invade the jury's province in rendering independent legal and social judgments.

(4) The American Law Institute ("ALI") formulated a test whereby an accused is not responsible for criminal conduct if at the time of such conduct as a result of mental disease or defect he lacks substantial capacity either to appreciate the wrongfulness of his conduct or to conform his conduct to the requirements of law. This approach reflects the teachings of modern psychiatry and permits full development of relevant information and expert opinion. It is the best available test and should have been applied to D's case.

g. **Model Penal Code approach.** The Model Penal Code permits an acquittal by reason of insanity if, because of a mental disease or defect, the accused either (i) lacked substantial capacity to appreciate the criminality of his conduct, or (ii) lacked substantial capacity to conform his conduct to the requirements of law. This test is broader than *M'Naghten*. The main criticism has been directed at the second part of the test.

United States
v. Lyons

1) **Involuntary drug addiction not sufficient--United States v. Lyons,** 731 F.2d 243, 739 F.2d 994 (5th Cir. 1984).

a) **Facts.** Lyons (D) was tried for knowingly and intentionally securing controlled narcotics by misrepresentation, fraud, deception, and subterfuge. D disclosed that he intended to rely on a defense of insanity, based on the theory that his involuntary drug addition affected his brain both physiologically, and psychologically, so that he lacked substantial capacity to conform his conduct to the requirements of the law. The United States (P) made a motion in limine to exclude any evidence of D's drug addiction. The court granted the motion and D appealed. A panel of the court reversed, and the court agreed to rehear the case en banc.

b) **Issue.** May involuntary drug addiction alone constitute a mental disease or defect depriving an accused of substantial capacity to conform his conduct to the requirements of the law?

c) **Held.** No. Judgment reversed on other grounds.

   (1) Evidence of narcotics addiction, without other physiological or psychological involvement, does not raise an issue of a mental defect or disease that can serve as a basis for the insanity defense. An addict has some reasoned choice when he knowingly acquires and uses drugs. It would be inconsistent to immunize narcotics addicts from criminal sanctions for obtaining drugs when mere possession and sale of narcotics is illegal.

   (2) Drug use may produce actual physical damage to the brain itself that may constitute mental disease or defect. D should be allowed to introduce any evidence that tends to suggest such damage to the extent that it may have resulted in his lacking substantial capacity to appreciate the wrongfulness of his conduct.

   (3) D did seek to introduce the evidence to show that he lacked substantial capacity to conform his conduct to the requirements of the law. This prong of the ALI test does not comport with current medical and scientific knowledge. Most psychiatrists now believe they cannot measure a person's capacity for self-control. The line between an irresistible impulse and an impulse not resisted is not ascertainable, and there is no objective basis for distinguishing between offenders in the two categories. Experts and jurors alike are asked to speculate about volition with no articulated standards. Thus, this prong of the test is no longer recognized.

2) **Proof of capacity to conform one's conduct--State v. Green,** 643 S.W.2d 902   State v. Green
(Tenn. Ct. App. 1982).

a) **Facts.** Green (D) had been treated for psychiatric problems from the age of seven, when he would fight other children for no reason. He attacked his mother with a knife when he was 12, and began the unusual behavior of not talking to others, laughing hysterically, refusing to bathe, and staying in bed all day and outside all night. At times he was treated with medication. D left his parents' home and lived with various relatives for several months. He continued to exhibit his bizarre behavior. D went to the FBI and told them that someone was directing his mind. D claimed someone had invented an "ousiograph" machine that could detect this interference. Some time thereafter, a police officer was murdered. A note on the body was addressed to the FBI agent D had contacted and contained nonsensical references to an "ousiograph." D was apprehended after the police contacted the FBI and learned of D's earlier interview. D was charged with the murder, but was incompetent to stand trial. After over a year of therapy, D was deemed competent to stand trial. Despite D's defense of insanity, the jury convicted D of the murder under the Model Penal Code test. D appeals, claiming the overwhelming proof of insanity could not support the verdict.

b) **Issue.** May a person be convicted of an offense when the evidence of insanity is overwhelming and is not sufficiently rebutted by the prosecution?

c) **Held.** No. Judgment reversed.

(1) The lay testimony regarding D's strange activity was confirmed by several experts who had evaluated and observed D. These experts unanimously testified that D was insane when he killed the police officer, and that D suffered from paranoid schizophrenia. D was unable to communicate the events of the murder for several months, but after treatment D did relate that a voice had told him he would be Adolf Hitler if he killed. The staff who treated him testified that D's condition gradually improved.

(2) The only rebuttal testimony offered by the prosecution was lay testimony to the effect that at certain times shortly after the arrest, D was coherent, polite, and not unusual but dirty and smelly. This testimony is not inconsistent with the conduct of a paranoid schizophrenic, who can act in a seemingly normal way until someone speaks to him or moves in a way that he perceives as threatening.

(3) The evidence of D's insanity spans several years. It is essentially impossible that D could successfully fake the symptoms. In light of this evidence, the prosecution had the burden to prove D's sanity beyond a reasonable doubt. This required proof that (i) at the time of the offense D was not suffering from a mental disease or defect, or (ii) if he was, the disease did not prevent him from knowing the wrongfulness of this conduct and from conforming his conduct to the requirements of law.

(4) The state's evidence was consistent with the absence of a mental disease, but it was not inconsistent with the presence of the disease, inasmuch as a paranoid schizophrenic can act normally. Thus, the state did not prove beyond a reasonable doubt that D was not suffering from a mental disease.

(5) The state also failed to prove that D appreciated the wrongfulness of his conduct, although inferences to that effect could be drawn. But even if D did know that what he did was wrong, the evidence does not demonstrate that D could conform to the legal requirements. The only argument that the state made was that because D did not act violently to other police officers, he could control himself. This argument would preclude the insanity defense in any case in which the defendant did not commit an offense against every person, and furthermore it ignores the fact that a paranoid schizophrenic may act normally.

(6) Because the evidence is insufficient to support the verdict, the conviction must be set aside.

State v. Stras-   **3)**   **Insanity as a constitutional defense to criminality--State v. Strasburg,** 110 P.
burg   1020 (Wash. 1910).

a)   **Facts.** Strasburg (D) was convicted of assault; he pleaded insanity but, adhering to a state statute, the trial court excluded this as a defense. The statute further provided that after conviction the issue of insanity was to go to the issue of the type of punishment D would receive; if found insane, D would go to a mental hospital. D appeals.

b)   **Issue.** Does one have a constitutional right to a defense of insanity?

c)   **Held.** Yes. Reversed.

(1)   The constitutional right to a trial by jury includes the right to plead insanity, because sanity is an element of the crime. If insanity is shown, D cannot be convicted of a crime.

d)   **Comment.** Insanity is not just a factor in determining the type of treatment that a person receives; it is a determinant of status (*i.e.,* whether D will be labeled a "criminal").

4)   **Insanity as an independent defense--State v. Korell,** 690 P.2d 992 (Mont. 1984).

State v. Korell

a)   **Facts.** Korell (D) was a Vietnam veteran who suffered several traumatic experiences during his tour of duty. After returning to the United States, he experienced severe psychological problems. He set fire to at least two structures and, believing that his former job supervisor was trying to kill him, D broke into his home and fired several shots at him. At trial, the jury was instructed that it could consider mental disease or defect only insofar as it negated the mental state required for the offenses charged. D was convicted of attempted murder and sentenced to 35 years in prison. D appeals.

b)   **Issue.** Is insanity allowed as an independent defense to murder?

c)   **Held.** No.

(1)   In 1979, Montana abolished the traditional insanity defense, substituting alternative procedures for considering a defendant's mental condition.

(2)   During trial, mental disease or defect evidence is used if it is relevant to prove that, at the time of the offense charged, an accused did not have the state of mind that is an element of the crime charged, *e.g.,* that the defendant did not act purposely or knowingly.

(3)   Such evidence is also considered at the dispositional stage and may result in the waiver of mandatory minimum sentences.

(4)   But the legislature has made a conscious decision to hold individuals who act with a proven criminal state of mind accountable, regardless of their mental condition.

5)   **Modern federal approach.** After John Hinckley was found not guilty by reason of insanity of attempting to assassinate President Reagan, a widespread movement to abandon the volitional impairment aspect of the insanity defense

culminated in the adoption of 18 U.S.C. section 20. This section recognizes the insanity defense only when the defendant, as a result of a severe mental disease or defect, was unable to appreciate the nature and quality or the wrongfulness of his acts. This eliminated the volitional aspect of the insanity defense. Section 20 also places on the defendant the burden of proving insanity by clear and convincing evidence.

State v.
Guido

h. **Meaning of "disease"--State v. Guido,** 191 A.2d 45 (N.J. 1963).

1) **Facts.** Guido (D) killed her husband by shooting him several times as he slept on the couch in their living room. D had wanted a divorce, but her husband had refused, despite his ongoing extramarital affair. D's husband had physically injured her on a few occasions and had constantly threatened her. D was charged with murder. Two court-appointed psychiatrists examined her, made medical findings, and concluded that she was "legally" sane when she shot her husband. D's defense counsel met with the psychiatrists and persuaded them to change their opinion regarding "legal" insanity. This fact was elicited at the trial, and in his closing argument, the prosecutor asserted that the defense had been concocted between D's attorney and the psychiatrists. D was convicted. D appeals.

2) **Issue.** Is it fraudulent for a defense attorney to change the opinion of psychiatrists as to whether the examinee suffers from a mental "disease"?

3) **Held.** No. Judgment reversed.

   a) The psychiatrists' change in opinion did not relate to their medical findings, but instead reflected a change in their understanding of what a mental "disease" is under the law. Originally, they believed that the *M'Naghten* rule required a disease that is a psychosis, and that a lesser illness would not suffice. D's attorney explained to them that an "anxiety neurosis" such as D suffered may legally qualify as a "disease."

   b) Although the *M'Naghten* rule requires a "disease of the mind," it does not define what a "disease" is, even though the difference between criminal liability and freedom from moral blame hinges on whether the person suffers from a disease. The *M'Naghten* rule focuses on the effect of disease, not on identifying a specific disease that excuses the offense. The distinction is between one who acts with moral depravity or weakness and is thus without excuse, and one who because of a disease either does not know what she is doing, or does not know the act is wrong.

   c) There is no clear definition of "disease," and D should not be penalized because her attorney and the witnesses were groping for an understanding of what the law requires as a "disease."

Jones v.
United States

i. **Commitment of insanity acquittee--Jones v. United States,** 463 U.S. 354 (1983).

1) **Facts.** Jones (P) was arrested for attempted shoplifting. He was arraigned for petit larceny, punishable by up to one year of imprisonment. A court-ordered determination of competency to stand trial resulted in an eventual

plea of not guilty by reason of insanity. P was committed to a mental hospital. In the District of Columbia, a person acquitted on insanity is automatically committed, and has a right to a hearing within 50 days at which he can prove by a preponderance of the evidence that he is no longer mentally ill or dangerous. If he fails, he is entitled to a similar hearing every six months, or the hospital can certify him as recovered at any time. By contrast, the civil commitment procedure requires the government to prove by clear and convincing proof that the person is mentally ill, and the person may demand a jury at the civil commitment proceeding. Once civilly committed, the patient has release opportunities similar to criminal committees. P's first two release hearings were unsuccessful and, because he had already been hospitalized for 17 months, he demanded unconditional release or recommitment under civil-commitment standards. His request was denied. The Supreme Court granted certiorari.

2) **Issue.** May a person committed to a mental hospital after being acquitted by reason of insanity be held for longer than the maximum sentence authorized for the crime he was acquitted of?

3) **Held.** Yes. Judgment affirmed.

   a) Due process imposes minimum procedural protections for civil-commitment proceedings. [Addington v. Texas, 441 U.S. 418 (1979)] A finding of insanity at a criminal trial establishes that the person committed a criminal offense because of a mental illness. Such a finding satisfies the minimum due process requirements for commitment when combined with the statutory inference of continuing mental illness that accompanies an insanity acquittal.

   b) A civil commitment requires proof by clear and convincing evidence because society, not the individual, should bear the risk of an incorrect determination. Proof of insanity at a criminal trial requires only a preponderance of the evidence. But because in the latter class of cases, the acquittee himself proves his mental illness, there is little risk of erroneous commitment. The *Addington* concerns are diminished in cases of insanity acquittees.

   c) The purpose of commitment is treatment. There is no correlation between severity of the offense and the length of time needed for recovery. The otherwise applicable criminal sentence is therefore irrelevant for purposes of the duration of the commitment.

4) **Dissent.** P should be kept beyond the maximum prison term only if civilly committed.

j. Automatism.

1) **Introduction.** Cases have arisen in which the defendant's conduct resulted from a confused or impaired mental condition that was other than insanity; *e.g.,* epileptic seizure, sleep, etc. One approach is to view the condition as legal insanity. The Model Penal Code views this as absence of a volitional act, resulting in acquittal.

2) Application--Regina v. Quick, 3 W.L.R. 26 (1973).

a) **Facts.** Quick (D), a nurse, had diabetes; he had taken insulin earlier in the day, had been drinking, and had eaten little food. He attacked one of his patients. Witnesses said D was glassy-eyed and collapsed on the floor after the attack. D testified that this condition of unconsciousness, coupled by aggression, could be brought on by too high a level of insulin in the blood and that D had been hospitalized on numerous occasions for this condition. There was also testimony that the condition could be "voluntarily" brought on by eating too little or consuming liquor. D was convicted of assault. D appeals.

b) **Issue.** May a diabetic who takes insulin and becomes aggressive offer evidence showing that his disease of the mind is brought on by external factors rather than an internal malady?

c) **Held.** Yes. Judgment reversed.

   (1) Insanity is a defect from an internal condition, a malfunction of the mind caused by disease.

   (2) There are certain conditions similar to insanity caused by external factors, such as drugs, alcohol, hypnosis, etc. This type of transitory effect is not due to disease.

   (3) A defect caused by such factors may be a sufficient defense to a criminal act where the external factor could not reasonably be foreseen by D. If D could have reasonably foreseen the incapacitating result of his act or omission, or if he intentionally self-induced the incapacity, he will not be excused.

   (4) The jury should have been charged with deciding whether a defense existed based on an unforeseen external factor causing involuntary and unconscious automatism.

k. Diminished capacity.

1) Introduction. In some jurisdictions, evidence of mental illness that does not establish insanity may still be admissible to prove that the defendant did not have the specific intent necessary for the crime charged. Even if the defendant may be aware that his act was wrongful and be able to control it, the mental defect may be characterized as diminished capacity and reduce the extent of criminal liability that would otherwise apply.

2) Adoption of ALI test--United States v. Brawner, 471 F.2d 969 (D.C. Cir. 1972).

a) **Facts.** Brawner (D) appealed a conviction of second degree murder and of carrying a dangerous weapon. D's defense was insanity. The D.C. Circuit had previously applied the *Durham* test, discussed *supra*.

b) **Issue.** Should the *Durham* test for insanity be followed?

c)   **Held.** No. Judgment reversed.

   (1)   The *Durham* test was adopted to allow experts to testify in their own terms and not according to legal-moral terms (the right/wrong test). Also, it reflected the notion that results should be reached according to current community standards of culpability. The test has been criticized, however.

   (2)   The use of the term "product" has resulted in expert testimony having undue influence on the jury; in effect, experts giving their medical opinions have dominated the issues. This does not reflect the fact that the defense is based on legal, moral, ethical and other bases, which are represented in the jury.

   (3)   The ALI test provides that a person is not responsible for her unlawful conduct if, at the time the conduct occurred, as a result of mental disease or defect, she lacked the capacity to appreciate the wrongfulness of her conduct, or to conform her conduct to the requirements of the law.

   (4)   A mental disease or defect includes any abnormal condition of mind that substantially affects mental or emotional processes and substantially impairs control.

   (5)   This standard allows expert testimony, but it is in language understood by all those involved with the judicial process and thus leaves the issue ultimately to the jury, where it belongs.

3)   **Rejection of diminished capacity approach--State v. Wilcox,** 436 N.E.2d 523 (Ohio 1982).

State v. Wilcox

   a)   **Facts.** Wilcox (D) suffered from mental diseases. He participated in a burglary during which the victim was shot and killed. At his trial, D attempted to use the psychiatric evidence to show he lacked specific intent to commit aggravated murder or aggravated burglary. The court excluded the psychiatric evidence for any reason other than to support his plea of not guilty by reason of insanity. The jury found D guilty. D appeals.

   b)   **Issue.** Should a court accept psychiatric evidence that an accused has a diminished mental capacity that prevented him from forming specific intent?

   c)   **Held.** No. Judgment affirmed.

   (1)   The diminished capacity defense originated in Scotland as a means to mitigate capital offenses committed by the partially insane to noncapital offenses. It also ameliorates the limitations of the traditional *M'Naghten* test.

   (2)   In jurisdictions such as Ohio that have adopted more enlightened approaches to insanity than the *M'Naghten* test, there is no need of amelioration through the diminished capacity test. Some commentators have noted that the main practical effect of the diminished capacity defense has been to allow mentally ill offenders to receive

shorter and more certain sentences than they would receive if they were adjudged insane and committed.

(3) Mental capacity is a mitigating factor in capital cases under current law, so there is no need for the diminished capacity defense to avoid execution of mentally ill persons.

(4) The remaining reasons advanced for the diminished capacity defense are that it allows for more individualized culpability judgments and is comparable to permitting evidence of voluntary intoxication to be introduced to negate specific intent. The diminished capacity concept requires such subtle distinctions that principled and consistent decision-making in criminal cases would be unlikely. It is entirely different from intoxication; it takes no great expertise for jurors to determine whether an accused was so intoxicated as to be mentally unable to intend anything, or unconscious.

5. **Changing Patterns of Excuse.**

    a. **Introduction.** The opinions of the behavioral scientists have had an effect on court decisions. Despite the assumption that people have free will, increasingly the courts treated people as victims in need of rehabilitation rather than as criminals in need of punishment. Due to the perceived limitations of societal institutions to solve these problems, more recent decisions may be reverting back to those of an earlier time.

Robinson v.
California

    b. **Drug addiction--Robinson v. California,** 370 U.S. 660 (1962).

      1) **Facts.** Robinson (D) was prosecuted for being "addicted to the use of narcotics." The evidence showed that D had scar tissue, needle marks, and discoloration typical of frequent narcotics users. The jury was instructed that D could be convicted if they found that D was either of the "status" or had committed the "act" proscribed by the statute. D was found guilty and appeals.

      2) **Issue.** May a state criminalize mere status as a narcotics addict?

      3) **Held.** No. Judgment reversed.

        a) A state has broad power to regulate narcotics traffic. It can even involuntarily confine addicts for compulsory medical treatment. However, a disease is not a criminal offense. D may have been convicted under the statute without ever having used or possessed narcotics within the state and without ever having done any antisocial act there. Criminal punishment for affliction with a disease is cruel and unusual. A drug addict is a sick person, not a criminal.

      4) **Concurrence.** Drug addiction may be something other than an illness and therefore subject to criminal sanctions, but this statute allows conviction for the bare desire to do a criminal act; *e.g.,* D's compelling propensity to use narcotics.

5) Dissent. The court has made it impossible for the state to deal with defendants who continually use narcotics where the state cannot prove the precise location of use.

c. Alcoholism--Powell v. Texas, 392 U.S. 514 (1968).

1) Facts. Powell (D) was arrested and charged with being found intoxicated in a public place. He was found guilty and fined $20. On appeal, the court ruled that chronic alcoholism, from which D suffered, was not a defense to the charge and fined D $50. D appeals.

2) Issue. May a person be criminally liable for merely being in a public place while suffering from a disease?

3) Held. Yes. Judgment affirmed.

    a) Alcoholism presents a serious public problem. The evidence indicates that there is no known generally effective method for treating alcoholism. Use of the criminal law to incarcerate public drunks affords an opportunity to sober up. Because penal incarceration has stringent time limits, it is probably preferable to an unlimited civil commitment when no treatment is available. The uncertainty of any deterrent effect of the criminal statute does not make the statute unconstitutional.

    b) In *Robinson v. California*, the court held that a statute making it a crime to "be addicted to the use of narcotics" inflicted cruel and unusual punishment because it punished the person's condition. The statute here materially differs because it punishes not chronic alcoholism but public drunkenness. *Robinson* requires some actus reus before criminal penalties may be inflicted. D did commit an illegal act.

4) Concurrence. *Robinson* was limited to situations where no act was involved, where the mental element is not simply one part of the crime, but all of it.

5) Concurrence. If it is not a crime to have an irresistible compulsion to use drugs, it should not be a crime to yield to the compulsion. Here, however, D did not have an irresistible compulsion to be in the public area. He could have taken precautions against being drunk in public.

6) Dissent. The Constitution forbids infliction of criminal penalties upon a person for being in a condition he is powerless to change. D was convicted only because he was in a condition that he had no capacity to change or avoid.

d. Possession of drugs--United States v. Moore, 486 F.2d 1139 (D.C. Cir. 1973).

1) Facts. Moore (D) was convicted of possession of heroin; he appeals the conviction. He contends that he lacked "free will" because he had a long history of drug addiction and he was psychologically and physically dependent. He argues for a distinction between prosecuting for possession and prosecuting for crimes perpetrated to get drugs (robbery, etc.).

2) **Issue.** Is evidence of one's addiction to a drug which results in his loss of control over the use of the drug relevant to his criminal responsibility in unlawfully possessing that drug?

3) **Held.** No Conviction sustained.

    a) The logic of D's argument is unsound; if applied, it would mean that it would have to be applied to all crimes perpetrated by those dependent on drugs.

    b) The argument that loss of self-control is a defense is unsound; all that is needed for conviction is the requisite intent to commit the crime.

4) **Concurrence.** Just because there is a defense in one area where loss of control exists (insanity) does not mean that there must be a defense in other areas where the same argument can be made (drug addiction). There are distinctions in each instance; also, exceptions to liability are based on situations where the legitimacy of the defense is ascertainable and society's interests are manageable when the exception is allowed.

5) **Dissent.** Criminal responsibility is an expression of the moral sense of the community. Our society does not exculpate all persons whose capacity is impaired; the law assumes free will and then recognizes exceptions where there is broad consensus for doing so. Such a consensus exists now for narcotics addiction, at least in the instance of the crime of possession.

IX. THEFT

A. INTRODUCTION

The theft offenses were developed over a period of time as the criminal law expanded to protect property as well as people. The offenses include larceny, embezzlement, extortion, and obtaining another's property by false pretenses. The underlying harm is the unpermitted acquisition of another's property.

B. THE MEANS OF ACQUISITION

1. Trespassory Takings.

a. Larceny.

1) **Common law definition.** Larceny is the unlawful taking and carrying away of the personal property of another with the intent to permanently deprive the owner of it.

2) **Asportation.** This taking or carrying away of the property of another is usually held to mean that some acquisition of control or dominion over the property is necessary.

   a) Possession or control need only be slight; that is, the length of time may be short and the distance moved not far.

   b) Thus, it is sufficient asportation where a thief lifts a person's wallet from his pocket but is detected and drops it before it is removed entirely. All that is required is the entire shifting of the property from the place it has occupied.

3) **Trespass.** Larceny is a crime involving trespass (unlawful taking) from the possession of another. Possession does not necessarily require ownership. This taking can occur by the defendant himself or through an innocent agent (person unaware of the facts—a young child, etc.); but the taking must not be by violence or force from the person of another, or the crime is robbery. In any event, if a person came into possession of property, there was no trespass (and thus no larceny).

   a) **Larceny by trick or device.** In larceny by trick, the person receives goods from another with the latter's consent, but this consent is not valid to impart possession because it is derived by trick, fraud, other unlawful device. This differs from the case of fraud in that the intent to take the goods exists at the time possession is obtained.

      (1) **Example.** A convinces B to let him take B's camera "to show it to my wife," but A has the intent to steal it and does so on obtaining possession; this is larceny by trick or device.

b) **Distinguished from false pretenses.** Distinguishing larceny by trick or device from false pretenses, which is discussed *infra*, can be difficult.

4) **Grand and petit larceny.** When jurisdictions make this distinction, usually petit larceny is only a misdemeanor even though all of the elements for the crime are the same as grand larceny. The difference relates to the fair market value of the goods that are taken (value under a certain amount being petit larceny).

b. **Robbery.**

1) **Definition.** At common law, robbery was the felony of taking and carrying away the personal property of another from his person or immediate presence by violence, force, or fear, with the intent to permanently deprive him thereof.

a) Robbery includes larceny (*i.e.,* has all of the same elements).

b) In addition, robbery includes the elements of a taking without consent, by force or fear.

2) **Elements of robbery.**

a) **Intent.** The defendant must take with the fraudulent intent to permanently deprive the owner of his property. There cannot be robbery, even when force is used, when the defendant honestly believes the property is his, or when he takes the property intending only temporary use.

b) **Property of another.** The property must be the personal property of another (which only means that he has possession thereof).

c) **Taking from the person or his presence.**

(1) There must be a taking and a carrying away. (*See* the discussion under the crime of larceny *supra*.) If the defendant takes a person's wallet and reduces it to his possession by force, but immediately returns it, there is a robbery because he had complete control.

(2) If the property is taken from the immediate presence of the victim, it is considered as having been taken from his person. If A, by fear, causes B to open his safe and A proceeds to take the money therefrom, this is sufficient to constitute a taking from the person.

d) **Taking by force or violence.** The taking must not only be without the consent of the possessor, but must also be accompanied by force or violence or the threat thereof (*i.e.,* the force of fear).

(1) It is not robbery to pick another's pocket when he is unaware it is being done, nor is it robbery to grab a person's purse from her hand and run.

(2) But the use of any force to accomplish the taking (such as grabbing the wallet after struggling with the person who has discovered he is being pickpocketed, or bumping into another to divert her attention while taking her purse) amounts to robbery.

(3) Threat of violence or force which puts another person reasonably in fear of such, when it accompanies the taking, is also sufficient to satisfy this requirement. This fear need not only be fear by the victim for his own person, but may also be fear for injury to property or the person of another.

e) **Consent.** The taking by force must be without the consent of the owner.

3) **Statutory robbery.** Many states have codified robbery. A sample state statutory system follows:

a) **First degree robbery.** Robbery perpetrated by torture or by a person armed with a dangerous or deadly weapon is first degree robbery.

b) **Second degree.** All other robbery is second degree robbery.

c. **Extortion.**

1) **Common law.** At common law, the crime of extortion had a very limited meaning—the obtaining of money or property from another with his consent by the use of one's color of office or official position.

2) **Today.** Statutes have greatly expanded the common law crime. It now includes the obtaining of money or property by any person using force or threat.

a) **Compared with robbery.** Obviously, extortion is very close to the crime of robbery. One difference is that the property need not be taken from the person of the victim (for example, the instance of blackmail).

b) **Consent through force.** Additionally, note that extortion is a taking "with consent"; but since the consent must be induced by force (or the threat of force) or fear, it is difficult to distinguish this "consent" from the "without consent" in robbery.

(1) One difference is that the range of threats that will be sufficient for extortion is greater. All of the force or threats that hold for robbery apply to extortion.

(2) In addition, the threat to accuse the victim or members of his family of a crime, or to expose some secret causing disgrace, etc., is sufficient.

d. **Receiving stolen property.** In most jurisdictions, it is a felony to knowingly receive stolen property. The elements of the crime are as follows:

1) **Control over property.** To be found guilty, the defendant must in some way actually have control over the stolen property; it is not necessary that he actually touch it or have it in his immediate possession.

2) **Stolen property.** The property must still have its "stolen" status when defendant receives it. (It will lose this status if it has been recovered by the police for the owner and then used in an undercover operations).

3) **Intent.** The defendant's intent on receiving the property must be fraudulent (*i.e.*, other than an intent to return the property to the rightful owner).

4) **Knowledge.** The defendant must have knowledge that the property has been stolen.

Common-
wealth v.
Tluchak

e. **Retention after sale--Commonwealth v. Tluchak,** 70 A.2d 657 (Pa. 1950).

1) **Facts.** The Tluchaks (Ds) contracted to sell their farm to the complainant and his wife. The agreement did not include any personal property, but it covered "buildings, plumbing, heating, lighting fixtures, screens, storm sash, blinds, awnings, shrubbery and plants." On taking possession, the complainant found that certain articles that had been on the premises at the time of the agreement were gone (commode, an unattached washstand, hay carriage, electric stove cord, 35 peach trees). Ds were prosecuted for larceny and convicted. The trial court overruled Ds' motion for a new trial and an arrest of judgment. Ds appeal.

2) **Issue.** When sellers retain possession of property that they had agreed to sell, are they guilty of larceny?

3) **Held.** No. Conviction reversed.

　　a) Ds were in lawful possession of the goods; they did not commit larceny by converting the goods to their own use. A criminal trespass is necessary and it cannot be committed by one who has lawful possession.

4) **Comment.** The essential element of trespass was missing. Under some statutes, this result might have been contra. If Ds had been charged with fraudulent conversion or larceny by bailee, they might have been guilty on the theory that a vendor retaining possession of goods he sells is a constructive bailee of the vendor.

Topolewski
v. State

f. **Knowledge and assistance in the taking--Topolewski v. State,** 109 N.W. 1037 (Wis. 1906).

1) **Facts.** Topolewski (D) arranged with a man who owed him money and was an employee of a packing company to place three barrels of meat on the loading platform for D to pick up and take away as though he were a customer. The employee informed the company and it told him to feign cooperation. D took the barrels; he was prosecuted for larceny and convicted. He appeals.

2) Issue. Is there a trespassory taking when the owner knew the goods were going to be taken and he facilitated the taking?

3) Held. No. Conviction reversed.

  a) The element of trespass did not exist. Trespass is lacking when the company allows its property to be taken regardless of the intent of the accused. By telling its employee to place the property on the platform for a man who would come to get it, the company consented to the taking. The company aided the commission of the offense.

2. Misappropriation.

a. Introduction. When there is no trespassory interference with possession because the offender has rightful possession when she forms the intent to take, the crime is not larceny. Instead, it comes within a general class called misappropriation.

b. Conversion after obtaining lawful possession. If possession is unlawfully gained and conversion only occurs afterwards, there is no larceny because there is no trespass. Thus, if a bailee or an agent of the owner has no intent to take the property at the time she receives the goods and only afterward decides to convert them to her use, there is no larceny. If, however, the bailment period has come to an end and then the bailee decides to convert the goods, there is larceny because, at the end of the period, the possession was constructively that of the owner.

  1) Exception. One exception to the rule that lawful possession could not turn into larceny with subsequent conversion was the "breaking the bulk" doctrine, which held that if something was given to a carrier or bailee (*i.e.,* lawful possession) but such person broke open the package and took the goods, this violated the bailment contract, so that the goods returned to the constructive possession of the owner and any taking was a trespass. Also, where express conditions were placed in the bailment contract (or conditions existed on delivery of possession by the owner) and these conditions were broken, some courts held that this terminated the agreement, possession returned to the owner, and any subsequent taking was a trespass.

c. Custody but not possession. In some situations property may be delivered to another in such a way or under such circumstances that the person holding the goods is seen as having only "custody," not possession (possession remaining constructively in the hands of the owner).

  1) Timing of intent. No matter when the intent to take the goods arises, if an employee or a servant takes the goods of her employer or master she is guilty of trespass to possession and thus larceny. For example, if an employer gives her employee money to deposit in the bank and on the way to the bank the employee decides to take the money, there is larceny. If the owner delivers goods to an employee in a bailment capacity, the rules mentioned above for bailees will prevail.

2) Delivery by a third person. If a third person delivered goods to an employee for the master or the employer, and the employee only afterwards formed the intent to convert them, then if the goods never entered into the possession of the master there was no trespass because the servant had lawfully come into possession. However, when the servant first placed the goods where they would ordinarily go (or where instructed to put them), the courts held that the goods then came into the constructive possession of the master and any subsequent taking by the servant was larceny. For example, if the employee delivers goods for her employer and immediately puts the money received into her pocket, there is no larceny; but if the employee takes the money and first puts it in the employer's cash register and then takes it, there is larceny.

3) Bare custody. Bare custody alone can occur in many situations, such as when goods are given to a person merely to look at, or to purchase on approval.

d. Goods delivered by mistake. When a person receives goods that are delivered by mistake (for example, more change is given than intended), and if he is unaware of the mistake at the time it occurs, a subsequent taking will not be larceny; but when the person is aware of the mistake at the time it occurs, the taking of those goods is larceny.

e. Lost property.

1) When a person finds property and has no reasonable means of knowing to whom it belongs, he obtains possession of these goods. A taking of these goods will not be larceny regardless of the taker's intent.

2) If, at the time of finding the goods the person knows or has reasonable means of finding out the owner and he forms the intent to take the goods on finding them, larceny will lie. But where the intent to take the goods only subsequently arises, there is no larceny.

f. Embezzlement. Embezzlement is the statutory offense involving the unlawful and fraudulent appropriation of property by a person to whom it was entrusted.

1) Compared with larceny. Embezzlement came into being to fill in certain gaps in the common law crime of larceny. For example, larceny was a crime against possession, and thus if a bailee obtained possession and only sometime thereafter formed the intent to convert the goods, there was no larceny. Embezzlement, on the other hand, is aimed at the situation where the person lawfully gains possession of the goods of another and thereafter converts it unlawfully to his own use. The rationale is that the breach of trust or confidence is being punished, not trespass to possession.

2) Elements of the crime.

a) Intent. The defendant must have the specific intent to permanently appropriate the property of another to use outside the scope of the trust that placed it in his possession. It is not embezzlement where the defendant takes the property in good faith under a bona fide claim of right, even though in fact the claim of right is untenable. There is no embezzlement where the defendant receives the money pursuant to a bona fide loan.

    b)   **Subject matter of embezzlement.** This is a question of statutory interpretation. Many statutes simply state "the property of another."

    c)   **Relationship of confidence or trust.** The property must have come into the defendant's possession as a result of his fiduciary relationship with the owner. This simply means that the defendant has possession by and for another.

    d)   **Possession.** Some courts have held that because embezzlement was meant to plug gaps in the crime of larceny, embezzlement will not lie unless the defendant has possession of the goods of another, as opposed to mere custody (because in this latter case, conversion will amount to larceny).

        (1)   For example, if goods are delivered by the owner to his employee, there is only custody, and the employee's subsequent conversion can only be larceny.

        (2)   But if a third person delivers money to the employee for the master and the employee does not put it where he is instructed to but immediately converts it, he has possession and is thus guilty of embezzlement.

    e)   **Election.** Normally the prosecution will be required to elect whether it will proceed under the theory of larceny or embezzlement.

g.   **Distinction between larceny and embezzlement--Nolan v. State,** 131 A.2d 851   Nolan v. State (Md. 1957).

  1)   **Facts.** Nolan (D) was the office manager of a finance company; he took money from the company out of the cash drawer at the end of the day after the drawer had been balanced. An accomplice recomputed the report of cash receipts to conceal the theft. D appealed from his conviction for embezzlement.

  2)   **Issue.** When a person misappropriates money paid by customers of his employer and placed in the cash drawer, is the fraudulent conversion embezzlement?

  3)   **Held.** No. Conviction reversed. Case remanded for possible prosecution under larceny.

    a)   D is not guilty of embezzlement because the money had reached its destination and was constructively in the owner's possession.

    b)   Embezzlement statutes are designed to reach offenses outside the reach of common law larceny (which is the taking of goods from the owner's possession).

4) **Concurrence.** The effect of the decision is to reestablish many of the technical differences between larceny and embezzlement. Legislation should provide that indictment of larceny should cover either offense.

h. **Conversion by a bailee--Burns v. State,** 128 N.W. 987 (Wis. 1911).

1) **Facts.** Burns (D), a constable, having taken an insane man into custody after a chase, received from another pursuer money dropped by the insane man in his flight. D converted some of the money to his own use. The trial court instructed the jury that if the accused converted to his own use any of the insane man's money, he did so as a bailee. D appeals his conviction of larceny by bailee.

2) **Issue.** May a person become a bailee for another in the absence of a contract between the parties?

3) **Held.** Yes. Jury instructions were proper.

   a) D was a bailee; he came into lawful possession of the money of another with a duty to account for it for the other. The duty to return the property made D a bailee. A contract is not necessary. The essential mutuality may be created by operation of law as well as by contract.

   b) At common law, a bailee could not be convicted of larceny for misappropriating the bailment because he was given lawful possession of the property. Hence, there was no trespass. To overcome this immunity, the common law distinguished between a breaking into the shipment, which was larceny, and misappropriation of all the bailed property, which was not. The legislature has eliminated that distinction through the creation of the offense of larceny by a bailee.

i. **Embezzlement by an agent--State v. Riggins,** 132 N.E.2d 519 (Ill. 1956).

1) **Facts.** Riggins (D), owner and operator of a collection service, had an oral agreement with the complainant to collect her firm's delinquent accounts. The agreement provided for D to receive a large percentage of the accounts collected and to account only when the fund was completely collected. For two years, D had complete control over the time and manner of collecting the accounts and, with the complainant's knowledge, commingled funds collected for all his clients. D collected several accounts in full without accounting to the complainant. D was convicted under a general embezzlement statute that provided for the punishment of agents and other specified persons receiving money in a fiduciary capacity and fraudulently converting it, irrespective of their interest in the funds. D appeals.

2) **Issue.** May a person be convicted of embezzlement for failing to render an account of business conducted for another?

3) **Held.** Yes. Reversed for prejudicial remarks made by trial court. Remanded for new trial.

a)	The embezzlement statute applies to agents regardless of whether the agent has claim to a commission or an interest in the money.

b)	D acted as an agent for collecting the funds, receiving funds in a fiduciary capacity and having a duty to account, notwithstanding his interest in the funds. He received the money in a fiduciary capacity and is therefore guilty.

**4)	Dissent.** D was not an agent; he was not subject to control of the customer and the customer was not liable for D's acts.

**5)	Comment.** Persons having an interest in the fund they gathered for their principals were considered outside the scope of embezzlement statutes. To reach such persons, new statutes were passed enumerating specific persons, such as brokers and collection agents and making an interest in the fund no defense. D is convicted here under such a statute.

3.	**Fraud.** Various situations arise in which a person acquires the property of another by using fraud to obtain the other's consent.

a.	**False pretenses.** This crime is very similar to that of "larceny by trick or device," mentioned above. The difference is that the owner of the property does not intend just to pass possession but intends to pass ownership or title to the property as well. At common law, there was no crime where title was passed, so this crime was created by statute to remedy the gap in coverage. The elements of the crime are as follows:

1)	**Misrepresentation of a past or existing fact.** There must be some pretense or misrepresentation. This may occur in the form of words or conduct. Mere failure to disclose facts is not usually sufficient.

a)	**Future events.** A statement by the defendant as to future events, as opposed to past or existing facts, is not usually sufficient. Therefore, prediction, promises, dealer's talk or "puffing" do not represent actionable misrepresentations.

b)	**Opinions.** Similarly, mere expression of "opinion" or "belief" is not wrong; but some courts have held that the defendant is guilty of misrepresenting his state of mind or intention (a "fact") when he expresses an intention (as to perform or do something in the future) and does not really have that intention.

2)	**Intent to defraud.** The facts represented must in fact be false ones, and the defendant must have knowledge of this falsity and the specific intent to permanently deprive the owner of his property. The intent to just use the property is not sufficient.

3)	**Reliance.** The misrepresentation must be such that a reasonable person would have relied on it; and, in fact, the owner of the property must have relied on it.

4) **Title.** The owner must intend to part with complete ownership and title to the property, not just possession. This is a fine distinction from the crime of larceny.

5) **Example.** If A promises (with intent to defraud) to sell and deliver goods to B that are not in existence, B pays for them in advance, and A never delivers the goods, false pretenses will lie.

b. **Forgery.**

1) **Definition.** Forgery is the false making of an instrument or document (a writing) or the material altering thereof, which might apparently be of legal efficacy or the foundation of a legal liability, with the intent to defraud.

2) **Elements.**

a) **Intent to defraud.** The defendant must actually have the intent to defraud another, but no one actually need be defrauded (it is enough that one might have been defrauded).

b) **Apparently valid instrument.** The instrument that is the subject of forgery must be a writing or document that, if genuine, would create some legal right or obligation (such as false corporate stock, theater tickets, etc.). A false painting is not the subject of forgery since it is not a writing.

(1) The false writing need only apparently create rights or obligations. In fact, it may not do so.

(2) If an instrument is created with fraudulent intent but clearly does not create any rights or obligation (*i.e.,* a $3 bill), there is no forgery.

c) **Making or alteration.** If an alteration is made, it must be a "material" one so that the instrument has a different effect than it should have.

3) **Examples of forgery.** Signing another person's name on a check or promissory note without authority to do so is forgery; it is not forgery to sign one's own name even when one is without authority to do so (but this may be false pretenses). Another example of forgery is changing the date of a will.

c. **Uttering a forged instrument.** Uttering a forged instrument is the passing or using of a forged instrument with the knowledge that it is false and with the intent to defraud.

1) **Apparent ability to defraud.** The instrument must have the apparent ability to defraud, and it must be used with the intent to defraud; however, it need not in fact defraud anyone.

2) **Uttering.** Some use of a forged instrument must occur; mere possession or awareness that an instrument is forged is not sufficient. To show a

forged receipt to another person in order to obtain credit is a sufficient uttering.

d. **Gaining property by trick--Hufstetler v. State,** 63 So. 2d 730 (Ala. 1953).

1) **Facts.** Hufstetler (D) drove up to a service station operated by the complainant. One of D's companions asked the owner to fill the car with gas; then he asked for a quart of oil; when the owner went to get it, D drove off without paying for the gas. D was convicted in a prosecution for petit larceny; he appeals.

2) **Issue.** Is an actual trespass required for a conviction of larceny when possession is secured by a trick or fraud?

3) **Held.** No. Conviction affirmed.

    a) D, aided and abetted by his companion, committed larceny because the owner had no intention of parting with the ownership of his property until he had received payment therefor.

    b) Although there was no actual trespass, the trick of D vitiated the owner's parting with his goods and the owner retained constructive possession.

4) **Comment.** At common law, the crime of larceny was committed if the owner was induced fraudulently to part only with possession; a similar parting with title and possession constitutes the crime of false pretenses. Here, the owner parted with possession only.

e. **Larceny by trick--Graham v. United States,** 187 F.2d 87 (D.C. Cir. 1950).

1) **Facts.** Graham (D), an attorney, agreed with an immigrant who had been arrested for disorderly conduct to talk to the police so that the arrest might not impede the attainment of citizenship. D charged a $200 legal fee and represented that he needed an additional $2,000 to bribe the police. Instead, D took the $2,000 and used it for his own purposes. D was convicted of grand larceny; he appeals.

2) **Issue.** Is a person who obtains a chattel for a special purpose, intending to convert it to his own use, guilty of larceny?

3) **Held.** Yes. Conviction sustained; jury instructions were proper.

    a) The offense was larceny by trick because D obtained the money from another on a representation that he would perform certain services. Instead, D intended to convert the money to his own use, which he did.

    b) The immigrant never really parted with title to the money (title remained with him until such time as the purpose for which he gave the money to D was accomplished). He never intended that title pass to D.

4) **Comment.** Although a false promise may support larceny by trick, it would be insufficient in a prosecution for false pretenses.

People v.
Ashley

f. **Comprehensive theft statute--People v. Ashley,** 267 P.2d 271 (Cal. 1954).

1) **Facts.** Ashley (D) was the business manager of a corporation chartered for the purpose of introducing people. He obtained loans from two women by promising them certain loan security, which he did not have. He gave them notes of the corporation; the loans were not repaid, and D used the funds for his own purposes. The case was tried under a theft statute that consolidated all theft offenses; an instruction was given to the jury as to both larceny by trick and obtaining money under false pretenses. The jury was told that it would have to agree on the type of theft, if any, that was committed. The jury gave a general verdict of guilty. D appealed from denial of his motion for a new trial.

2) **Issue.** Is a general verdict of guilty under a theft statute lawful?

3) **Held.** Yes. Conviction for obtaining money under false pretenses is affirmed.

a) The statute allows a general verdict of an "unlawful taking"; but the conviction can be sustained only if all the elements of one of the types of theft are present. The statute was meant to eliminate the technicalities that existed in the pleading and proof of these crimes at common law.

b) The crime of obtaining property under false pretenses requires that the specific intent of D not to perform his promise be proved.

c) There was sufficient evidence to sustain the conviction of obtaining property by false pretenses.

Nelson v.
United States

g. **Presumption of intent to defraud--Nelson v. United States,** 227 F.2d 21 (D.C. Cir. 1955).

1) **Facts.** Nelson (D) owed Potomac, a wholesaler, over $1,800 for past purchases of merchandise on credit. His account was more than 30 days in arrears. D attempted to purchase more goods on credit for immediate resale, but Potomac at first refused because of D's outstanding indebtedness. D then represented himself as the owner of a Packard car for which he had paid over $4,000, but failed to mention indebtedness on the car of over $3,000. Instead, he lied to Potomac, stating that he owed only $55 more on the car. D did have $1,000 worth of equity in the car. Relying on these representations, Potomac sold D two television sets for $349 on credit. D left town without paying. The car sustained $1,000 worth of damages in an accident and was repossessed. D was convicted of obtaining goods by false pretenses. D appeals.

2) **Issue.** Can intent to injure or defraud be presumed when an unlawful act, which results in loss or injury, is proved to have been knowingly committed?

3) **Held.** Yes. D's conviction is affirmed.

   a) Wrongful acts intentionally committed cannot be justified on the ground of innocent intent. It is a well-settled rule that intent is presumed and inferred from the result of the action.

   b) It is irrelevant that $349 worth of merchandise was exchanged for a security interest in a car with $1,000 worth of equity. Potomac would not have sold D the goods but for his false representation.

4) **Dissent.** D was guilty of a moral wrong in misrepresenting his equity in the car. But this is not a legal wrong. D's $1,000 equity in the car is three times the amount of his debt to Potomac. A purchaser who makes a false statement in buying on credit has not defrauded the seller if he amply secures the debt.

5) **Comment.** The crime of false pretenses does not occur unless the defendant actually knows of the falsity of his statement, believes it to be false, and it is actually false. The defendant must possess the intent to defraud, but, as this case illustrates, intent may be inferred from the act itself. To require the prosecution to give direct proof of intent to defraud would be an impossible task.

h. **Blackmail--State v. Harrington,** 260 A.2d 692 (Vt. 1969).

State v. Harrington

   1) **Facts.** Harrington (D) was a Vermont attorney retained by Morin to obtain a divorce. D agreed to work on a contingent fee basis (marital assets were approximately $50,000). D and Morin arranged to entice Morin's husband into having sex at a motel with a woman they hired. The woman had a tape recorder and, at the appropriate time, D and his cohorts entered the room and photographed the husband and woman naked in bed. Afterwards, with Morin present, D dictated a proposed divorce settlement in which his client would receive a lump sum of $175,000 and waive her interest in the marital assets. The letter specifically promised that such a settlement would include returning any and all recordings and photographs documenting the motel incident, and a promise that the client would not divulge the incident to anyone. The letter demanded a prompt reply or Morin would commence rather embarrassing divorce proceedings. One of the photographs taken at the motel was included with the letter. D was convicted of extortion. D moves for acquittal.

   2) **Issue.** Does the threat of bringing embarrassing litigation constitute extortion?

   3) **Held.** Yes. Judgment affirmed.

      a) D argues that his letter was not a threat to accuse another of a crime, but merely to bring an embarrassing divorce proceeding in the husband's county of residence.

      b) In *State v. Louanis,* 65 A. 532, the court stated that the threat of any public accusation is as much within the reason of the extortion statute as a threat of a formal complaint.

c) The letter clearly makes an accusation of adultery in support of a demand for a cash settlement.

d) D also argues that he was, by inference, acting merely as an attorney attempting to secure a favorable divorce for his client. But the letter's veiled threats referring to "informer fees" which his client could obtain from the IRS, certainly exceeded the limit of proper representation.

i. **Intent requirement in extortion--People v. Fichtner,** 118 N.Y.S.2d 392, *aff'd,* 114 N.E.2d 212 (1952).

1) **Facts.** Fichtner (D), a store manager, and McGuiness (D), his assistant, caught a customer shoplifting. They threatened to prosecute him unless he paid $75 for goods they claimed he had taken over a long period of time. The customer signed a paper that the money was the correct amount owed, paid part, and Ds put the money in the cash register. The customer later denied that the value of the goods taken was that high. Ds were prosecuted for extortion; the trial court refused an instruction to the jury that if Ds honestly believed the customer owed the full amount they must be acquitted. Ds were convicted and they appeals.

2) **Issue.** Where Ds honestly believe they are entitled to the amount they demanded under a threat of criminal prosecution, but they were in fact wrong, may they be convicted of extortion?

3) **Held.** Yes. Conviction sustained.

a) Good faith is no defense. One of the aims of the extortion statutes was to prevent a creditor from obtaining money owed by a debtor through the threats of prosecution. The validity of the debt is irrelevant. It also does not matter whether the threatened prosecution relates to a crime from which the indebtedness arose, or relates to some other crime.

4) **Dissent.** If Ds acted in good faith, without malice, they had no criminal intent and are not guilty.

5) **Comment.** Other states are contra, especially where Ds' claim arises out of the crime that they accuse the victim of committing.

C. CONSOLIDATION

1. **Consolidation.** The technicality of the various theft offenses has led to some incredible results; for example, a defendant prosecuted for one offense having his conviction reversed on appeal because the elements of the offense charged were not all present (even though he did commit another theft offense for which he was not charged). Also, many of the distinctions between the offenses are more technical than real. For these

and other reasons, many states have passed statutes that deal with the whole theft area as one offense.

2. **Theft.** In order to consolidate some of the above crimes and do away with their highly technical distinctions, the statutory crime of "theft" has been created by many jurisdictions. It includes the common law crimes of (i) larceny, (ii) embezzlement, (iii) larceny by trick or device, and (iv) false pretenses.

   a. **Pleading and proof.** There were formerly great pleading and proof difficulties for the prosecution due to the distinction between the four above-mentioned theft crimes. It is now much easier for the prosecution to bring charges against the defendant.

   b. **Degrees or classifications.**

      1) **Grand theft.** Grand theft applies when the money or labor, property, etc., taken is worth over a certain amount (*e.g.*, $200) or is taken from the person (and is of any value).

      2) **Petty theft.** All other theft is petty theft.

D. PROPERTY SUBJECT TO THEFT

1. **Subject Matter of Larceny.** The crime of larceny is one of trespass to the possession of another's "personal" property. This personal property has modernly been held to be "anything that is capable of appropriation." At common law, the rules as to what was personal property were highly technical (this is probably due to the fact that larceny was punishable by death).

   a. **Household pets.** Pets were not considered "property" because of their "base nature." The rule is contra today.

   b. **Lost and abandoned goods.** Lost goods could be the subject of larceny while abandoned goods could not be.

   c. **Choses in action.** Bills, notes, contracts, bonds, and other evidence of indebtedness were not considered property at common law. The idea was that the piece of paper had no intrinsic value. This result has been changed by modern statutes.

   d. **Real property.** Real property could not be the subject of larceny; thus, fixtures affixed to the land, crops, trees, etc., were not subjects for larceny.

      1) If, however, such items of real property were first severed from the land and then carried away in a distinct transaction, they became the subjects of larceny on the theory that on their severance they came into the constructive possession of the owner as personal property.

      2) A could come onto B's land on one day and cut down his trees; if A returned on another day and carried the trees off, A could

be convicted of larceny; if the cutting and carrying were consummated at one time, there was no larceny.

e. Leased property. Taking of one's own property from one who has a right to its possession (such as a lessee), or taking property that the possessor has stolen or that is illegal to possess (for example, marijuana) all constitute larceny since a trespass to possession is involved.

f. Incorporeal property. Larceny could be committed against a person's right to possess incorporeal property, such as where A taps B's gas line.

g. Anything of value. Modern statutes have extended the law of larceny to include practically everything of value that can be actually taken and carried away. Under some statutes, the crime has even been extended to real property (such as ore or minerals) and to completely intangible items (such as trade secrets).

State v.
Miller

2. Guarantee of Indebtedness--State v. Miller, 233 P.2d 786 (Or. 1951).

a. Facts. Miller (D) induced the Hub Lumber Co. to guarantee his indebtedness to another by falsely representing that he owned a tractor free of encumbrance and by executing a chattel mortgage on the tractor as security. In order for the false pretenses statute to apply, the defendant must have obtained "any money or property whatsoever." D was convicted of the crime of false pretenses and now appeals.

b. Issue. Does a guaranty obtained by false representations constitute property for the purposes of the false pretenses statute?

c. Held. No. D's conviction is reversed and the action is dismissed.

1) English law, the source of false pretenses statutes in this country, has always applied the offense of false pretenses to personal property capable of manual delivery.

2) This court has recognized that property must be capable of being possessed and have title that can be transferred. A guaranty fills neither of these requirements.

3) Obtaining a loan by fraud has been held to constitute the offense of false pretenses. But in the only reported cases on the subject, the victim has lost his money, unlike the present situation.

4) Under some other state false pretenses statutes, D would be guilty. These statutes include the catch-all phrase "any other thing of value," along with the terms "money" and "property" in delineating what may be taken by false pretenses. While D's conduct is morally reprehensible, the legislature has not made it a crime.

d. Comment. The Model Penal Code defines "property" as anything of value. Oregon now defines "property" as "any article, substance, or thing of value . . . ." If decided today, this case would probably come out differently.

3. **Government Records--United States v. Girard**, 601 F.2d 69 (2d Cir. 1969).

a. **Facts.** Lambert (D) was an agent of the Drug Enforcement Administration ("DEA") and Girard (D) was a former agent. Girard offered to secure reports from the DEA for Bond to enable Bond to determine whether any participant in his proposed illegal smuggling venture was a government agent. Bond himself became an informant, and the DEA learned that Lambert was supplying Girard with government reports. Ds were convicted of the unauthorized sale of government property and of conspiring to accomplish the sale. On appeal, Ds contend that they cannot be convicted because the statute only covers tangible property that is a "thing of value" and not the sale of information.

b. **Issue.** Is information a "thing of value" for purposes of theft?

c. **Held.** Yes. Judgment affirmed.

   1) Although the content of writing is intangible, it is a thing of value and thus a protectible property right. Because the Government (P) has a property interest in the records, the misuse of the property by Ds could constitute conversion.

4. **Property Subject to Theft--Regina v. Stewart**, 50 D.L.R. 4th 1 (1988).

a. **Facts.** A union attempting to organize 600 hotel employees was unable to obtain the employees' names, addresses, and telephone numbers, which the hotel classified as confidential. Stewart (D), a self-employed consultant, was hired by someone he assumed to be acting for the union, to obtain said information. D offered a fee to a security guard to obtain the information, but the guard informed his boss, who informed the police. After a long conversation between D and the guard was recorded, D was indicted for "counseling the offense of theft." D was acquitted by a trial judge. The acquittal was reversed on appeal. D appeals.

b. **Issue.** Can the object of theft be a pure intangible?

c. **Held.** No. Acquittal restored.

   1) In order to be the subject of theft, anything, whether animate or inanimate, must be property in the sense that to be stolen, it must belong in some way to someone.

   2) While confidential information may come to be viewed as protected property in civil law, that does not automatically make it property under the criminal code.

   3) Because of the inherent nature of information, treating confidential information as property for purposes of the law of theft would be impractical.

d. **Comment.** The impractical aspect of declaring the employee list as property subject to theft becomes clear when one realizes that the information consisted of names, addresses, and telephone numbers. Clearly, any employee who had her telephone number listed in the telephone book would have already made such information available to the public, so no claim of confidentiality would withstand scrutiny. Presumably, this is also the precise information many individuals have printed on their personal checks and, to some degree, placed in the return address portion of every envelope they mail. However, what if the employee files contained other more personal and less public information such as date of birth, marital status, educational background, and criminal history checks? Would that change the court's reasoning?

5. **Wire Fraud--United States v. Siegel,** 717 F.2d 9 (2d Cir. 1983).

   a. **Facts.** Siegel and Abrams (Ds) were indicted for using the means of wire communication in defrauding a corporation of which they were officers and directors. Ds allegedly committed the fraud by selling merchandise for cash in unreported sales, and then using the proceeds as bribes and as personal funds. Ds were convicted. On appeal, they claimed the evidence was insufficient to prove that they used the money for themselves.

   b. **Issue.** May the breach of a corporate officer's fiduciary duties toward the corporation and its shareholders constitute wire fraud?

   c. **Held.** Yes. Judgment affirmed.

       1) The federal wire fraud statute prohibits the use of wire communications with the intent to defraud to obtain money by means of false pretenses. The scope of this statute is very broad, although a mere breach of fiduciary duty is probably not covered.

       2) In this case, Ds had a duty to disclose the transactions, and their failure to do so could result in harm to the corporation. The jury concluded based on the evidence that Ds used the cash for noncorporate purposes in breach of their fiduciary duties to act in the corporation's best interest and to disclose material information.

       3) Ds claim there was no evidence that they used the funds for their own enrichment. However, of the over $100,000 in cash involved, only $31,000 could be accounted for, thus supporting an inference that Ds used the remainder for their own benefit.

   d. **Dissent.** The court has used the wire fraud statute to create federal fiduciary obligations that subject corporate directors and officers to criminal liability. The government's case is based on inadequate recordkeeping; the corporation had sales of between $30 million and $109 million, while the off-book transactions averaged only about $11,000 per year. This is not realistically material to an investor, especially since there is no evidence that the transactions injured the corporation. The wire fraud statute was not intended to enforce corporate officers' fiduciary duties. The court has created a criminal offense of corporate improprieties.

   e. **Comment.** The *Siegel* case was followed in another situation in which a corporate officer concealed certain transactions by creating false documents in order to create a secret cash fund for the corporation. He was convicted purely on the inference that the funds were diverted for a noncorporate purpose, even though there was no evidence that he used them for personal enrichment.

6. **Mail Fraud--McNally v. United States,** 483 U.S. 350 (1987).

   a. **Facts.** McNally (D), a private citizen, Gray, a public official, and Hunt, a private citizen, were active together in the Democratic Party. Hunt was made chairman of the Kentucky Democratic Party, which gave him de facto power to select insurance companies that the state would use. The Wombwell company had acted as agent for the state and agreed to share certain commissions with agencies specified by Hunt in return for a continued agency relationship. Hunt designated as one of these an agency owned and operated by D but controlled by Hunt and Gray. The agency had been created solely to receive the shared commissions, which totaled about $200,000 over four years. Hunt pleaded guilty to mail and tax fraud. D was charged with mail fraud based on a commission check mailed to Wombwell by an insurance company. The theory was that D was involved in a scheme to defraud the citizens and government of Kentucky of their right to have the state's affairs conducted honestly. D was convicted. The court of appeals affirmed, and the Supreme Court granted certiorari.

   b. **Issue.** Does the violation of an intangible right of the citizenry to good government constitute a basis for criminal liability under the federal mail fraud statute?

   c. **Held.** No. Judgment reversed.

      1) The initial mail fraud statute prohibited the use of the mails in furtherance of "any scheme or artifice to defraud." The Court held that the phrase should be interpreted broadly to protect property rights, and would apply to "everything designed to defraud by representations as to the past or present, or suggestions and promises as to the future."

      2) The statute was later amended to add a prohibition against "obtaining money or property by means of false or fraudulent pretenses." Because this is an added phrase, the courts of appeals have decided that the scheme to defraud language is not limited to property rights, but extends to the deprivation of intangible rights, such as the right to good government. This approach is incorrect, however, because the term "defraud" normally refers to deprivation of property rights, and therefore the amendment to the mail fraud statute was intended to make it clear that the statute applied only to deprivation of money or property. If Congress wants to expand the scope of the statute, it must do so clearly.

      3) The jury was not instructed that they had to find that the Commonwealth was defrauded of any money or property, or that it was deprived of control over the spending of its money. The commissions were paid by the insurer to Wombwell, its agent. The jury was not told that it had to find false representations to Wombwell. The instructions as given do not support a conviction.

d. **Dissent** (Stevens, O'Connor, JJ.). The mail fraud statute has been applied to numerous cases involving intangible rights, including good government cases as well as vote fraud and breach of fiduciary duties. The words of the statute—"any scheme or artifice to defraud"—do not limit its scope to deprivation of money or property. The purpose of the statute is to prevent the use of the mails as instruments of crime, and this purpose is fulfilled by the previously uniform interpretation of the statute that would cover D's activities. The term "defraud" is sufficiently clear that D would be on notice that his actions were covered.

E. MENS REA

1. **Introduction.** Specific intent is required for larceny. The taking had to be done with the specific intent to fraudulently and permanently deprive the possessor of his goods.

   a. **Bona fide claim to possession.** A taking by Λ where Λ has a bona fide claim of right to possession is not larceny, even where A is actually wrong in his claim.

   b. **Intent to take and abandon.** The intent to take property and then to abandon it without returning it to its owner is sufficient.

   c. **Intent to take and use.** If the take intends to just take and use the property and then to return it to the owner, this is not larceny. For example, there is no larceny where a person takes a car for a "joy ride" and then returns it.

   d. **"Continuing trespass" doctrine.** At some point in time, the felonious intent must accompany the trespass to possession. However, it is not always required that there shall be such intent at the time the property was first taken. As long as the taking constitutes a trespass (albeit innocent or in good faith), the trespass "continues" as long as D holds the goods, and if at any time thereafter he forms the intent to steal them, there is then the concurrence of trespass and felonious intent, which constitutes the crime of larceny. For example, D takes the goods of another in the honest, but mistaken, belief that he owns them (innocent trespass). Later he discovers that he does not, but decides to appropriate them anyway. D is guilty of larceny.

People v.
Brown

2. **Permanent Taking--People v. Brown,** 38 P. 518 (Cal. 1894).

   a. **Facts.** Brown (D), age 17, entered the house of a boy with whom he had had an argument, and took a bicycle, intending to return it later. Before he could return it, he was arrested. D was convicted of burglary after a jury instruction that indicated that all that need be shown was an intent to deprive the owner of possession temporarily. D appeals.

   b. **Issue.** Is an intent to deprive the owner of his rightful possession temporarily sufficient to support a theft conviction?

   c. **Held.** No. Conviction reversed.

1) The jury instruction was incorrect. A felonious taking requires that the taking be with the intent to deprive the owner of possession permanently.

d. **Comment.** If the taker abandons the property or recklessly exposes it to loss, he may have had the intent to permanently deprive.

3. **Taking with Intent to Repay--Regina v. Feely,** 2 W.L.R. 201 (1973).

a. **Facts.** Feely (D), branch manager of a bookmaking firm, received a memo from the head office that borrowing from the till was not permitted; nevertheless, he borrowed £30. A few days later he was transferred; his successor found the shortage. D offered the explanation that he had taken the money because he was short of cash but that the employer owed him £70, that he intended to repay the money, and that it could be taken out of the amount owed him. The evidence showed that the employer did owe him this amount. D was convicted of theft. He appealed. At the trial, the jury instruction had been that D was guilty if he intended to take the money; it made no difference that he intended to repay.

b. **Issue.** May an intent to repay property taken negate the necessary intent?

c. **Held.** Yes. Conviction reversed.

1) The Theft Act defines theft as taking with the intent to permanently deprive the owner of the property.

2) The issue is whether D, when he took the money, intended a dishonest act (*i.e.,* not to return it). The trial judge should not have made the determination that the taking was dishonest and given the jury only the question of whether D intended to take the money. The jury should be allowed to determine whether the taking was dishonest.

4. **Use of Force--People v. Reid,** 508 N.E.2d 661 (N.Y. 1987).

a. **Facts.** In separate incidents, Reid (D) and Riddles (D) were trying to recover money owed to them by certain individuals. In the course of so doing, Ds used weapons. Ds were each convicted of armed robbery. Ds appeal.

b. **Issue.** Does a person's good-faith claim of right negate the intent to commit robbery if the person uses force to recover money owed to him?

c. **Held.** No. Judgment affirmed.

1) A good-faith claim of right may negate larcenous intent in theft offenses and constitutes a defense to a charge of larceny. Robbery is the use or threat of use of physical force in the course of committing a larceny. Ds claim that therefore the claim of right defense should apply to robbery, and that Ds could at most be charged with assault or unlawful possession of a weapon.

2) Some jurisdictions have followed the approach advocated by Ds. The approach may be appropriate when the defendant was trying to

recover a specific item owned by the defendant, especially since an element of the offense is taking property "from an owner thereof."

3) In these cases, Ds were trying to recover money that did not actually belong to Ds, even though the victims purportedly owed Ds money. To permit the defense would be inconsistent with the public policy of discouraging self-help. The claim of right defense does not even apply to all forms of larceny, such as extortion, which reflects the public policy against use of force or coercion.

TABLE OF CASES

(Page numbers of briefed cases in bold)

Guminga, State v. - **30**

Hall, Commonwealth v. - 23
Hall v. State - 72
Harmelin v. Michigan - **36**
Harrington, State v. - **155**
Harris v. New York - 9
Hayes, State v. - **92**
Hicks v. United States - **88**
Hillsman, United States v. - **118**
Hilton Hotels Corp., United States v. - **94**
Hood, People v. - **127**
Hufstetler v. State - **153**
Hupf, State v. - **62**

Interstate Circuit, Inc. v. United
  States - **101**

Jackson, United States v. (1977) - **81**
Jackson, United States v. (1987) - **13**
Jacobs v. State - 74
Jaffe, People v. - **83**
Jewell, United States - **26**
Johnson, United States v. - **14**
Jones, People v. - 77
Jones v. State - 23
Jones v. United States (1962) - **21**
Jones v. United States (1983) - **136**

Keeler v. Superior Court - **38**
Kelly, State v. - **112**
Kevorkian, People v. - **123**
King v. Barker - 78
Kingston, Regina v. - **126**
Korell, State v. - **135**
Kotteakos v. United States - **105**, 109
Kraft, People v. - 77
Krulewitch v. United States - **99**

Lambert v. California - **35**
Lauria, People v. - **103**
Lewis, People v. - 73
Liberta, People v. - **45**
Liparota v. United States - 34
Louanis, State v. - 155
Lovercamp, People v. - **120**, 121
Luparello, People v. - **89**
Lyons, United States v. - **132**

M.T.S., State in the Interest of - **43**
MacDonald & Watson Waste Oil Co.,
  United States v. - **98**
Maher v. People - **56**
Malone, Commonwealth v. - **61**, 75

Marrero, People v. - **32**
Martin v. State - **19**
McClesky v. Kemp - **68**
McFadden, State v. - **74**
McGee, People v. - 101
McNally v. United States - **161**
McQuirter v. State - **80**
McVay, State v. - **90**
Milenkovic v. State - **48**
Miller, State v. - **158**
M'Naghten's Case - 129, 130, 131,
  132, 136, 139
Moore, United States v. - **141**
Morano, People v. - **77**
Morgan, Regina v. - **41**
Morissette v. United States - **28**
Murdock, United States v. - 34

Nash v. United States - **39**
Nelson v. United States - **154**
Newton, People v. - **19**
New York Central & Hudson River Rail-
  road Co. v. United States - **94**
Nix v. Whiteside - **8**
Nolan v. State - **149**
Norman, State v. - **113**

Olsen, People v. - **27**
Oviedo, United States v. - **85**

Papachristou v. City of Jacksonville - **40**
Park, United States v. - **97**, 98
Patterson v. New York - **5**
Peaslee, Commonwealth v. - **78**
People v. ___ (see opposing party)
Peterson, United States v. - **114**
Phillips, People v. - **64**
Pinkerton v. United States - **101**
Planned Parenthood of Southeastern
  Pennsylvania v. Casey - **123**
Pope v. State - **20**
Pope, State ex rel. v. Superior
  Court - **47**
Powell v. Texas - **141**
Prince, Regina v. - **27**

Quick, Regina v. - **138**

R. v. Eagleton - 78
Regina v. ___ (see opposing party)
Reid, People v. - **163**
Riggins, State v. - **150**
Roberts v. People - **127**
Roberts, People v. - 72

Robinson v. California - **140**, 141
Rocha, People v. - 128
Root, Commonwealth v. - **74**
Rusk, State v. - **42**

Santillanes v. New Mexico - **25**
Satchell, People v. - 64
Schoon, United States v. - **121**
Serné, Regina v. - **63**
Shane, State v. - 56
Shaw v. Director of Public Pros-
  ecutions - **38**
Sherry, Commonwealth v. - **41**
Siegel, United States v. - **160**
Smith, People v. - **65**
Solem v. Helm - 37
Stamp, People v. - 64
Staples, United States v. - **29**
Stasio, State v. - **128**
State v. ___ (see opposing party)
Stephenson v. State - **73**
Stewart, Regina v. - **159**
Strasburg, State v. - **134**

Taylor v. Superior Court - **66**
Tennessee v. Garner - **117**
Thornton, State v. - **55**
Tluchak, Commonwealth v. - **146**
Topolewski v. State - **146**
Toscano, State v. - **124**

Unger, People v. - **120**
United States v. ___ (see opposing party)

Warner-Lambert Co., People v. - 71
Welansky, Commonwealth v. - **59**
Weniger v. United States - 103
Wilcox v. Jeffery - **91**
Wilcox, State v. - **139**
Wiley, United States v.- 46
Williams v. Florida - 7
Williams, State v. - **60**
Williams v. United States - 103

Young, State v. - **79**

Zackowitz, People v. - **4**

Notes

Publications Catalog

Features:
Gilbert Law Summaries
Legalines
Gilbert Interactive Software
CaseBriefs Interactive Software
Law School Legends Audio Tapes
Employment Guides
& Much More!

Prices Subject To Change Without Notice

For more information visit our World Wide Web site at http://www.gilbertlaw.com or write for a free 32 page catalog: Harcourt Brace Legal and Professional Publications, 176 West Adams, Ste. 2100, Chicago, Illinois 60603

Gilbert Law Summaries are the best selling outlines in the country, and have set the standard for excellence since they were first introduced more than twenty-five years ago. It's Gilbert's unique combination of features that makes it the one study aid you'll turn to for all your study needs!

Administrative Law
By Professor Michael R. Asimow, U.C.L.A.

Separation of Powers and Controls Over Agencies; (including Delegation of Power) Constitutional Right to Hearing (including Liberty and Property Interests Protected by Due Process, and Rulemaking-Adjudication Distinction); Adjudication Under Administrative Procedure Act (APA); Formal Adjudication (including Notice, Discovery, Burden of Proof, Finders of Facts and Reasons); Adjudicatory Decision Makers (including Administrative Law Judges (ALJs), Bias, Improper Influences, Ex Parte Communications, Familiarity with Record, Res Judicata); Rulemaking Procedures (including Notice, Public Participation, Publication, Impartiality of Rulemakers, Rulemaking Record); Obtaining Information (including Subpoena Power, Privilege Against Self-incrimination, Freedom of Information Act, Government in Sunshine Act, Attorneys' Fees); Scope of Judicial Review; Reviewability of Agency Decisions (including Mandamus, Injunction, Sovereign Immunity, Federal Tort Claims Act); Standing to Seek Judicial Review and Timing.
ISBN: 0-15-900000-9 Pages: 300 $19.95

Agency and Partnership
By Professor Richard J. Conviser, Chicago Kent

Agency: Rights and Liabilities Between Principal and Agent (including Agent's Fiduciary Duty, Principal's Right to Indemnification); Contractual Rights Between Principal (or Agent) and Third Persons (including Creation of Agency Relationship, Authority of Agent, Scope of Authority, Termination of Authority, Ratification, Liability on Agents, Contracts); Tort Liability (including Respondeat Superior, Master-Servant Relationship, Scope of Employment). Partnership: Property Rights of Partner; Formation of Partnership; Relations Between Partners (including Fiduciary Duty); Authority of Partner to Bind Partnership; Dissolution and Winding up of Partnership; Limited Partnerships.
ISBN: 0-15-900001-7 Pages: 142 $16.95

Antitrust
By Professor Thomas M. Jorde, U.C. Berkeley, Mark A. Lemley, University of Texas, and Professor Robert H. Mnookin, Harvard University

Common Law Restraints of Trade; Federal Antitrust Laws (including Sherman Act, Clayton Act, Federal Trade Commission Act, Interstate Commerce Requirement, Antitrust Remedies); Monopolization (including Relevant Market, Purposeful Act Requirement, Attempts and Conspiracy to Monopolize); Collaboration Among Competitors (including Horizontal Restraints, Rule of Reason vs. Per Se Violations, Price Fixing, Division of Markets, Group Boycotts); Vertical Restraints (including Tying Arrangements); Mergers and Acquisitions (including Horizontal Mergers, Brown Shoe Analysis, Vertical Mergers, Conglomerate Mergers); Price Discrimination — Robinson-Patman Act; Unfair Methods of Competition; Patent Laws and Their Antitrust Implications; Exemptions From Antitrust Laws (including Motor, Rail, and Interstate Water Carriers, Bank Mergers, Labor Unions, Professional Baseball).
ISBN: 0-15-900328-8   Pages: 193 $16.95

All titles available at your law school bookstore
or call to order: 1-800-787-8717

Bankruptcy

By Professor Ned W. Waxman, College of William and Mary

Participants in the Bankruptcy Case; Jurisdiction and Procedure; Commencement and Administration of the Case (including Eligibility, Voluntary Case, Involuntary Case, Meeting of Creditors, Debtor's Duties); Officers of the Estate (including Trustee, Examiner, United States Trustee); Bankruptcy Estate; Creditor's Right of Setoff; Trustee's Avoiding Powers; Claims of Creditors (including Priority Claims and Tax Claims); Debtor's Exemptions; Nondischargeable Debts; Effects of Discharge; Reaffirmation Agreements; Administrative Powers (including Automatic Stay, Use, Sale, or Lease of Property); Chapter 7- Liquidation; Chapter 11- Reorganization; Chapter 13-Individual With Regular Income; Chapter 12- Family Farmer With Regular Annual Income.
ISBN: 0-15-900164-1   Pages: 356 $19.95

Basic Accounting for Lawyers

By Professor David H. Barber

Basic Accounting Principles; Definitions of Accounting Terms; Balance Sheet; Income Statement; Statement of Changes in Financial Position; Consolidated Financial Statements; Accumulation of Financial Data; Financial Statement Analysis.
ISBN: 0-15-900004-1   Pages: 136 $16.95

Business Law

By Professor Robert D. Upp, Los Angeles City College

Torts and Crimes in Business; Law of Contracts (including Contract Formation, Consideration, Statute of Frauds, Contract Remedies, Third Parties); Sales (including Transfer of Title and Risk of Loss, Performance and Remedies, Products Liability, Personal Property Security Interest); Property (including Personal Property, Bailments, Real Property, Landlord and Tenant); Agency; Business Organizations (including Partnerships, Corporations); Commercial Paper; Government Regulation of Business (including Taxation, Antitrust, Environmental Protection, and Bankruptcy).
ISBN: 0-15-900005-X   Pages: 295 $16.95

California Bar Performance Test Skills

By Professor Peter J. Honigsberg, University of San Francisco

Hints to Improve Writing; How to Approach the Performance Test; Legal Analysis Documents (including Writing a Memorandum of Law, Writing a Client Letter, Writing Briefs); Fact Gathering and Fact Analysis Documents; Tactical and Ethical Considerations; Sample Interrogatories, Performance Tests, and Memoranda.
ISBN: 0-15-900152-8   Pages: 216 $17.95

Civil Procedure

By Professor Thomas D. Rowe, Jr., Duke University, and Professor Richard L. Marcus, U.C. Hastings

Territorial (personal) Jurisdiction, including Venue and Forum Non Conveniens; Subject Matter Jurisdiction, covering Diversity Jurisdiction, Federal Question Jurisdiction; Erie Doctrine and Federal Common Law; Pleadings including Counterclaims, Cross-Claims, Supplemental Pleadings; Parties, including Joinder and Class Actions; Discovery, including Devices, Scope, Sanctions and Discovery Conference; Summary Judgment; Pretrial Conference and Settlements; Trial, including Right to Jury Trial, Motions, Jury Instruction and Arguments, and Post-Verdict Motions; Appeals; Claim Preclusion (Res Judicata) and Issue Preclusion (Collateral Estoppel).
ISBN: 0-15-900272-9   Pages: 447 $19.95

Commercial Paper and Payment Law

By Professor Douglas J. Whaley, Ohio State University

Types of Commercial Paper; Negotiability; Negotiation; Holders in Due Course; Claims and Defenses on Negotiable Instruments (including Real Defenses and Personal Defenses); Liability of the Parties (including Merger Rule, Suits on the Instrument, Warranty Suits, Conversion); Bank Deposits and Collections; Forgery or Alteration of Negotiable Instruments; Electronic Banking.
ISBN: 0-15-900009-2   Pages: 222 $17.95

Community Property

By Professor William A. Reppy, Jr., Duke University

Classifying Property as Community or Separate; Management and Control of Property; Liability for Debts; Division of Property at Divorce; Devolution of Property at Death; Relationships Short of Valid Marriage; Conflict of Laws Problems; Constitutional Law Issues (including Equal Protection Standards, Due Process Issues).
ISBN: 0-15-900235-4   Pages: 188 $17.95

Conflict of Laws

By Dean Herma Hill Kay, U.C. Berkeley

Domicile; Jurisdiction (including Notice and Opportunity to be Heard, Minimum Contacts, Types of Jurisdiction); Choice of Law (including Vested Rights Approach, Most Significant Relationship Approach, Governmental Interest Analysis); Choice of Law in Specific Substantive Areas; Traditional Defenses Against Application of Foreign Law; Constitutional Limitations and Overriding Federal Law (including Due Process Clause, Full Faith and Credit Clause, Conflict Between State and Federal Law); Recognition and Enforcement of Foreign Judgments.
ISBN: 0-15-900011-4   Pages: 260 $18.95

Constitutional Law

By Professor Jesse H. Choper, U.C. Berkeley

Powers of Federal Government (including Judicial Power, Powers of Congress, Presidential Power, Foreign Affairs Power); Intergovernmental Immunities, Separation of Powers; Regulation of Foreign Commerce; Regulation of Interstate Commerce; Taxation of Interstate and Foreign Commerce; Due Process, Equal Protection; "State Action" Requirements; Freedoms of Speech, Press, and Association; Freedom of Religion.
ISBN: 0-15-900265-6   Pages: 335 $19.95

Contracts

By Professor Melvin A. Eisenberg, U.C. Berkeley

Consideration (including Promissory Estoppel, Moral or Past Consideration); Mutual Assent; Defenses (including Mistake, Fraud, Duress, Unconscionability, Statute of Frauds, Illegality); Third-Party Beneficiaries; Assignment of Rights and Delegation of Duties; Conditions; Substantial Performance; Material vs. Minor Breach; Anticipatory Breach; Impossibility; Discharge; Remedies (including Damages, Specific Performance, Liquidated Damages).
ISBN: 0-15-900014-9   Pages: 326 $19.95

Corporations

By Professor Jesse H. Choper, U.C. Berkeley, and Professor Melvin A. Eisenberg, U.C. Berkeley

Formalities; "De Jure" vs. "De Facto"; Promoters; Corporate Powers; Ultra Vires Transactions; Powers, Duties, and Liabilities of Officers and Directors; Allocation of Power Between Directors and Shareholders; Conflicts of Interest in Corporate Transactions; Close Corporations; Insider Trading; Rule 10b-5 and Section 16(b); Shareholders' Voting Rights; Shareholders' Right to Inspect Records; Shareholders' Suits; Capitalization (including Classes of Shares, Preemptive Rights, Consideration for Shares); Dividends; Redemption of Shares; Fundamental Changes in Corporate Structure; Applicable Conflict of Laws Principles.
ISBN: 0-15-900342-3   Pages: 308 $19.95

Criminal Law

By Professor George E. Dix, University of Texas

Elements of Crimes (including Actus Reus, Mens Rea, Causation); Vicarious Liability; Complicity in Crime; Criminal Liability of Corporations; Defenses (including Insanity, Diminished Capacity, Intoxication, Ignorance, Self-Defense); Inchoate Crimes; Homicide; Other Crimes Against the Person; Crimes Against Habitation (including Burglary, Arson); Crimes Against Property; Offenses Against Government; Offenses Against Administration of Justice.
ISBN: 0-15-900016-5   Pages: 271 $18.95

Criminal Procedure

By Professor Paul Marcus, College of William and Mary, and Professor Charles H. Whitebread, U.S.C.

Exclusionary Rule; Arrests and Other Detentions; Search and Seizure; Privilege Against Self-Incrimination; Confessions; Preliminary Hearing; Bail; Indictment; Speedy Trial; Competency to Stand Trial; Government's Obligation to Disclose Information; Right to Jury Trial; Right to Counsel; Right to Confront Witnesses; Burden of Proof; Insanity; Entrapment; Guilty Pleas; Sentencing; Death Penalty; Ex Post Facto Issues; Appeal; Habeas Corpus; Juvenile Offenders; Prisoners' Rights; Double Jeopardy.
ISBN: 0-15-900347-4   Pages: 271 $18.95

Dictionary of Legal Terms

Gilbert Staff

Contains Over 3,500 Legal Terms and Phrases; Law School Shorthand; Common Abbreviations; Latin and French Legal Terms; Periodical Abbreviations; Governmental Abbreviations.
ISBN: 0-15-900018-1   Pages: 163 $14.95

Estate and Gift Tax

By Professor John H. McCord, University of Illinois

Gross Estate Allowable Deductions Under Estate Tax (including Expenses, Indebtedness, and Taxes, Deductions for Losses, Charitable Deduction, Marital Deduction); Taxable Gifts; Deductions; Valuation; Computation of Tax; Returns and Payment of Tax; Tax on Generation-Skipping Transfers.
ISBN: 0-15-900019-X   Pages: 283 $18.95

Evidence

By Professor Jon R. Waltz, Northwestern University, and Roger C. Park, University of Minnesota

Direct Evidence; Circumstantial Evidence; Rulings on Admissibility; Relevancy; Materiality; Character Evidence; Hearsay and the Hearsay Exceptions; Privileges; Competency to Testify; Opinion Evidence and Expert Witnesses; Direct Examination; Cross-Examination; Impeachment; Real, Demonstrative, and Scientific Evidence; Judicial Notice; Burdens of Proof; Parol Evidence Rule.
ISBN: 0-15-900020-3   Pages: 359 $19.95

Federal Courts

By Professor William A. Fletcher, U.C. Berkeley

Article III Courts; "Case or Controversy" Requirement; Justiciability; Advisory Opinions; Political Questions; Ripeness; Mootness; Standing; Congressional Power Over Federal Court Jurisdiction; Supreme Court Jurisdiction; District Court Subject Matter Jurisdiction (including Federal Question Jurisdiction, Diversity Jurisdiction); Pendent and Ancillary Jurisdiction; Removal Jurisdiction; Venue; Forum Non Conveniens; Law Applied in the Federal Courts (including Erie Doctrine); Federal Law in the State Courts; Abstention; Habeas Corpus for State Prisoners; Federal Injunctions Against State Court Proceedings; Eleventh Amendment.
ISBN: 0-15-900021-1   Pages: 310 $19.95

Future Interests

By Professor Jesse Dukeminier, U.C.L.A.

Reversions; Possibilities of Reverter; Rights of Entry; Remainders; Executory Interest; Rules Restricting Remainders and Executory Interest; Rights of Owners of Future Interests; Construction of Instruments; Powers of Appointment; Rule Against Perpetuities (including Reforms of the Rule).
ISBN: 0-15-900022-X   Pages: 219 $17.95

Income Tax I - Individual

By Professor Michael R. Asimow, U.C.L.A.

Gross Income; Exclusions; Income Splitting by Gifts, Personal Service Income, Income Earned by Children, Income of Husbands and Wives, Below-Market Interest on Loans, Taxation of Trusts; Business and Investment Deductions; Personal Deductions; Tax Rates; Credits; Computation of Basis, Gain, or Loss; Realization; Nonrecognition of Gain or Loss; Capital Gains and Losses; Alternative Minimum Tax; Tax Accounting Problems.
ISBN: 0-15-900266-4   Pages: 312 $19.95

For more information visit our World Wide Web site at http://www.gilbertlaw.com or write for a free 32 page catalog:
Harcourt Brace Legal and Professional Publications, 176 West Adams, Ste. 2100, Chicago, Illinois 60603

LAW SCHOOL LEGENDS SERIES

America's Greatest Law Professors on Audio Cassette

Wouldn't it be great if all of your law professors were law school legends? You know — the kind of professors whose classes everyone fights to get into. The professors whose classes you'd take, no matter what subject they're teaching. The kind of professors who make a subject sing. You may never get an opportunity to take a class with a truly brilliant professor, but with the Law School Legends Series, you can now get all the benefits of the country's greatest law professors…on audio cassette!

Administrative Law
Professor To Be Announced
Call For Release Date

TOPICS COVERED (Subject to Change): Classification Of Agencies; Adjudicative And Investigative Action; Rule Making Power; Delegation Doctrine; Control By Executive; Appointment And Removal; Freedom Of Information Act; Rule Making Procedure; Adjudicative Procedure; Trial Type Hearings; Administrative Law Judge; Power To Stay Proceedings; Subpoena Power; Physical Inspection; Self Incrimination; Judicial Review Issues; Declaratory Judgment; Sovereign Immunity; Eleventh Amendment; Statutory Limitations; Standing; Exhaustion Of Administrative Remedies; Scope Of Judicial Review.
3 Audio Cassettes
ISBN 0-15-900189-7 $39.95

Agency & Partnership
Professor Richard J. Conviser
Chicago Kent College of Law

TOPICS COVERED: Agency: Creation; Rights And Duties Of Principal And Agent; Sub-Agents; Contract Liability–Actual Authority: Express And Implied; Apparent Authority; Ratification; Liabilities Of Parties; Tort Liability–Respondeat Superior; Frolic And Detour; Intentional Torts. *Partnership:* Nature Of Partnership; Formation; Partnership By Estoppel; In Partnership Property; Relations Between Partners To Third Parties; Authority of Partners; Dissolution And Termination; Limited Partnerships.
3 Audio Cassettes
ISBN: 0-15-900351-2 $39.95

Antitrust Law
Professor To Be Announced
Call For Release Date

TOPICS COVERED (Subject to Change): How U.S. Antitrust Lawyers And Economists Think And Solve Problems: Antitrust Law's First Principle — Consumer Welfare Opposes Market Power; Methods Of Analysis — Rule Of Reason, Per Se, Quick Look; Sherman Act Section 1 — Civil And Criminal Conspiracies In Unreasonable Restraint Of Trade; Sherman Act Section 2 — Illegal Monopolization And Attempts To Monopolize; Robinson Patman Act Price Discrimination And Related Distribution Problems; Clayton Act Section Section 7 — Mergers And Joint

Ventures; Antitrust And Intellectual Property; U.S. Antitrust And International Competitive Relationships — Extraterritoriality, Comity, And Convergence; Exemptions And Regulated Industries; Enforcement By The Department Of Justice, Federal Trade Commission, National Association Of State Attorneys General, And By Private Litigation; Price And Non-Price Restraints.
2 Audio Cassettes
ISBN: 0-15-900341-5 $39.95

Bankruptcy
Professor Elizabeth Warren
Harvard Law School

TOPICS COVERED: The Debtor/Creditor Relationship; The Commencement, Conversion, Dismissal and Reopening Of Bankruptcy Proceedings; Property Included In The Bankruptcy Estate; Secured, Priority And Unsecured Claims; The Automatic Stay; Powers Of Avoidance; The Assumption And Rejection Of Executory Contracts; The Protection Of Exempt Property; The Bankruptcy Discharge; Chapter 13 Proceedings; Chapter 11 Proceedings; Bankruptcy Jurisdiction And Procedure.
4 Audio Cassettes
ISBN: 0-15-900273-7 $45.95

Civil Procedure
By Professor Richard D. Freer
Emory University Law School

TOPICS COVERED: Subject Matter Jurisdiction; Personal Jurisdiction; Long-Arm Statutes; Constitutional Limitations; In Rem And Quasi In Rem Jurisdiction; Service Of Process; Venue; Transfer; Forum Non Conveniens; Removal; Waiver; Governing Law; Pleadings; Joinder Of Claims; Permissive And Compulsory Joinder Of Parties; Counter-Claims And Cross-Claims; Ancillary Jurisdiction; Impleader; Class Actions; Discovery; Pretrial Adjudication; Summary Judgment; Trial; Post Trial Motions; Appeals; Res Judicata; Collateral Estoppel.
5 Audio Cassettes
ISBN: 0-15-900322-9 $59.95

Commercial Paper
By Professor Michael I. Spak
Chicago Kent College Of Law

TOPICS COVERED: Introduction; Types Of Negotiable Instruments; Elements Of Negotiability; Statute Of Limitations; Payment-In-

Full Checks; Negotiations Of The Instrument; Becoming A Holder-In-Due Course; Rights Of A Holder In Due Course; Real And Personal Defenses; Jus Teril; Effect Of Instrument On Underlying Obligations; Contracts Of Maker And Indorser; Suretyship; Liability Of Drawer And Drawee; Check Certification; Warranty Liability; Conversion Of Liability; Banks And Their Customers; Properly Payable Rule; Wrongful Dishonor; Stopping Payment; Death Of Customer; Bank Statement; Check Collection; Expedited Funds Availability; Forgery Of Drawer's Name; Alterations; Imposter Rule; Wire Transfers; Electronic Fund Transfers Act .
3 Audio Cassettes
ISBN: 0-15-900275-3 $39.95

Conflict Of Laws
Professor Richard J. Conviser
Chicago Kent College of Law

TOPICS COVERED: Domicile; Jurisdiction; In Personam, In Rem, Quasi In Rem; Court Competence; Forum Non Conveniens; Choice Of Law; Foreign Causes Of Action; Territorial Approach To Choice/Tort And Contract; "Escape Devices"; Most Significant Relationship; Governmental Interest Analysis; Recognition Of Judgments; Foreign Country Judgments; Domestic Judgments/Full Faith And Credit; Review Of Judgments; Modifiable Judgments; Defenses To Recognition And Enforcement; Federal/State (Erie) Problems; Constitutional Limits On Choice Of Law.
3 Audio Cassettes
ISBN: 0-15-900352-0 $39.95

Constitutional Law
By Professor John C. Jeffries, Jr.
University of Virginia School of Law

TOPICS COVERED: Introduction; Exam Tactics; Legislative Power; Supremacy; Commerce; State Regulation; Privileges And Immunities; Federal Court Jurisdiction; Separation Of Powers; Civil Liberties; Due Process; Equal Protection; Privacy; Race; Alienage; Gender; Speech And Association; Prior Restraints; Religion—Free Exercise; Establishment Clause.
5 Audio Cassettes
ISBN: 0-15-900319-9 $45.95

Contracts
By Professor Michael I. Spak
Chicago Kent College Of Law

TOPICS COVERED: Offer; Revocation; Acceptance; Consideration; Defenses To Formation; Third Party Beneficiaries; Assignment; Delegation; Conditions; Excuses; Anticipatory Repudiation; Discharge Of Duty; Modifications; Rescission; Accord & Satisfaction; Novation; Breach; Damages; Remedies; UCC Remedies; Parol Evidence Rule.
4 Audio Cassettes
ISBN: 0-15-900318-0 $45.95

Copyright Law
Professor Roger E. Schechter
George Washington University Law School

TOPICS COVERED: Constitution; Patents And Property Ownership Distinguished; Subject Matter Copyright; Duration And Renewal; Ownership And Transfer; Formalities; Introduction; Notice, Registration And Deposit; Infringement; Overview; Reproduction And Derivative Works; Public Distribution; Public Performance And Display; Exemptions; Fair Use; Photocopying; Remedies; Preemption Of State Law.
3 Audio Cassettes
ISBN: 0-15-900295-8 $39.95

Corporations
By Professor Therese H. Maynard
Loyola Marymount School of Law

TOPICS COVERED: Ultra Vires Act; Corporate Formation; Piercing The Corporate Veil; Corporate Financial Structure; Stocks; Bonds; Subscription Agreements; Watered Stock; Stock Transactions; Insider Trading; 16(b) & 10b-5 Violations; Promoters; Fiduciary Duties; Shareholder Rights; Meetings; Cumulative Voting; Voting Trusts; Close Corporations; Dividends; Preemptive Rights; Shareholder Derivative Suits; Directors; Duty Of Loyalty; Corporate Opportunity Doctrine; Officers; Amendments; Mergers; Dissolution.
4 Audio Cassettes
ISBN: 0-15-900320-2 $45.95

Criminal Law
By Professor Charles H. Whitebread
USC School of Law

TOPICS COVERED: Exam Tactics; Volitional Acts; Mental States; Specific Intent; Malice; General Intent; Strict Liability; Accomplice Liability; Inchoate Crimes; Impossibility; Defenses;

Insanity; Voluntary And Involuntary Intoxication; Infancy; Self-Defense; Defense Of A Dwelling; Duress; Necessity; Mistake Of Fact Or Law; Entrapment; Battery; Assault; Homicide; Common Law Murder; Voluntary And Involuntary Manslaughter; First Degree Murder; Felony Murder; Rape; Larceny; Embezzlement; False Pretenses; Robbery; Extortion; Burglary; Arson.
4 Audio Cassettes
ISBN: 0-15-900279-6 $39.95

Criminal Procedure
By Professor Charles H. Whitebread
USC School of Law

TOPICS COVERED: Incorporation Of The Bill Of Rights; Exclusionary Rule; Fruit Of The Poisonous Tree; Arrest; Search & Seizure; Exceptions To Warrant Requirement; Wire Tapping & Eavesdropping; Confessions (Miranda); Pretrial Identification; Bail; Preliminary Hearings; Grand Juries; Speedy Trial; Fair Trial; Jury Trials; Right To Counsel; Guilty Pleas; Sentencing; Death Penalty; Habeas Corpus; Double Jeopardy; Privilege Against Compelled Testimony.
3 Audio Cassettes
ISBN: 0-15-900281-8 $39.95

Evidence
By Professor Faust F. Rossi
Cornell Law School

TOPICS COVERED: Relevance; Insurance; Remedial Measures; Settlement Offers; Causation; State Of Mind; Rebuttal; Habit; Character Evidence; "MIMIC" Rule; Documentary Evidence; Authentication; Best Evidence Rule; Parol Evidence; Competency; Dead Man Statutes; Examination Of Witnesses; Present Recollection Revived; Past Recollection Recorded; Opinion Testimony; Lay And Expert Witness; Learned Treatises; Impeachment; Collateral Matters; Bias, Interest Or Motive; Rehabilitation; Privileges; Hearsay And Exceptions.
5 Audio Cassettes
ISBN: 0-15-900282-6 $45.95

Family Law
Professor To Be Announced

TOPICS COVERED (Subject to change): National Scope Of Family Law; Marital Relationship; Consequences Of Marriage; Formalities And Solemnization; Common Law Marriage; Impediments; Marriage And Conflict Of Laws; Non-Marital Relationship; Law Of Names; Void And Voidable Marriages; Marital Breakdown; Annulment And Defenses; Divorce — Fault And No-Fault; Separation; Jurisdiction For Divorce; Migratory Divorce; Full Faith And Credit; Temporary Orders; Economic Aspects Of Marital Breakdown; Property Division; Community Property Principles; Equitable Distribution; Marital And Separate Property; Types Of Property Interests; Equitable Reimbursement; Alimony; Modification And Termination Of Alimony; Child Support; Health Insurance; Enforcement Of Orders; Antenuptial And Postnuptial Agreements; Separation And Settlement Agreements; Custody Jurisdiction And Awards; Modification Of Custody; Visitation Rights; Termination Of Parental Rights; Adoption; Illegitimacy; Paternity Actions.
3 Audio Cassettes
ISBN: 0-15-900283-4 $39.95

Federal Courts
Professor To Be Announced

TOPICS COVERED (Subject to change): History Of The Federal Court System; "Court Or Controversy" And Justiciability; Congressional

Power Over Federal Court Jurisdiction; Supreme Court Jurisdiction; District Court Subject Matter Jurisdiction—Federal Question Jurisdiction, Diversity Jurisdiction And Admiralty Jurisdiction; Pendent And Ancillary Jurisdiction; Removal Jurisdiction; Venue; Forum Non Conveniens; Law Applied In The Federal Courts; Federal Law In The State Courts; Collateral Relations Between Federal And State Courts; The Eleventh Amendment And State Sovereign Immunity.
3 Audio Cassettes
ISBN: 0-15-900296-6 $39.95

Federal Income Tax
By Professor Cheryl D. Block
George Washington University Law School

TOPICS COVERED: Administrative Reviews; Tax Formula; Gross Income; Exclusions For Gifts; Inheritances; Personal Injuries; Tax Basis Rules; Divorce Tax Rules; Assignment Of Income; Business Deductions; Investment Deductions; Passive Loss And Interest Limitation Rules; Capital Gains & Losses; Section 1031, 1034, and 121 Deferred/Non Taxable Transactions.
4 Audio Cassettes
ISBN: 0-15-900284-2 $45.95

Future Interests
By Dean Catherine L. Carpenter
Southwestern University Law School

TOPICS COVERED: Rule Against Perpetuities; Class Gifts; Estates In Land; Rule In Shelley's Case; Future Interests In Transferor and Transferee; Life Estates; Defeasible Fees; Doctrine Of Worthier Title; Doctrine Of Merger; Fee Simple Estates; Restraints On Alienation; Power Of Appointment; Rules Of Construction.
2 Audio Cassettes
ISBN: 0-15-900285-0 $24.95

Law School ABC's
By Professor Jennifer S. Kamita
Loyola Marymount Law School, and
Professor Rodney O. Fong
Golden Gate University School of Law

TOPICS COVERED: Introduction; Casebooks; Hornbooks; Selecting Commercial Materials; Briefing; Review; ABC's Of A Lecture; Taking Notes; Lectures & Notes Examples; Study Groups; ABC's Of Outlining; Rules; Outlining Hypothetical; Outlining Assignment And Review; Introduction To Essay Writing; "IRAC"; Call Of The Question Exercise; Issue Spotting Exercise; IRAC Defining & Writing Exercise; Form Tips; ABC's Of Exam Writing; Exam Writing Hypothetical; Practice Exam And Review; Preparation Hints; Exam Diagnostics & Writing Problems.
4 Audio Cassettes
ISBN: 0-15-900286-9 $45.95

Law School Exam Writing
By Professor Charles H. Whitebread
USC School of Law

TOPICS COVERED: With "Law School Exam Writing," you'll learn the secrets of law school test taking. In this fascinating lecture, Professor Whitebread leads you step-by-step through his innovative system, so that you know exactly how to tackle your essay exams without making point draining mistakes. You'll learn how to read questions so you don't miss important issues; how to organize your answer; how to use limited exam time to your maximum advantage; and even how to study for exams.
1 Audio Cassette
ISBN: 0-15-900287-7 $19.95

Professional Responsibility
By Professor Erwin Chemerinsky
USC School of Law

TOPICS COVERED: Regulation of Attorneys; Bar Admission; Unauthorized Practice; Competency; Discipline; Judgment; Lawyer-Client Relationship; Representation; Withdrawal; Conflicts; Disqualification; Clients; Client Interests; Successive And Effective Representation; Integrity; Candor; Confidences; Secrets; Past And Future Crimes; Perjury; Communications; Witnesses; Jurors; The Court; The Press; Trial Tactics; Prosecutors; Market; Solicitation; Advertising; Law Firms; Fees; Client Property; Conduct; Political Activity.
3 Audio Cassettes
ISBN: 0-15-900288-5 $39.95

Real Property
By Professor Paula A. Franzese
Seton Hall Law School

TOPICS COVERED: Estates—Fee Simple; Fee Tail; Life Estate; Co-Tenancy—Joint Tenancy; Tenancy In Common; Tenancy By The Entirety; Landlord-Tenant Relationship; Liability For Condition Of Premises; Assignment & Sublease; Easements; Restrictive Covenants; Adverse Possession; Recording Acts; Conveyancing; Personal Property—Finders; Bailments; Gifts; Future Interests.
4 Audio Cassettes
ISBN: 0-15-900289-3 $45.95

Remedies
By Professor William A. Fletcher
University of California at Berkeley, Boalt Hall School of Law

TOPICS COVERED: Damages; Restitution; Equitable Remedies (including Constructive Trust, Equitable Lien, Injunction, and Specific Performance); Tracing; Rescission and Reformation; Specific topics include Injury and Destruction of Personal Property; Conversion; Injury to Real Property; Trespass; Ouster; Nuisance; Defamation; Trade Libel; Inducing Breach of Contract; Contracts to Purchase Personal Property; Contracts to Purchase Real Property (including Equitable Conversion); Construction Contracts; and Personal Service Contracts.
3 Audio Cassettes
ISBN: 0-15-900353-9 $45.95

Sales & Lease of Goods
By Professor Michael I. Spak
Chicago Kent College of Law

TOPICS COVERED: Goods; Contract Formation; Firm Offers; Statute Of Frauds; Modification; Parol Evidence; Code Methodology; Tender; Payment; Identification; Risk Of Loss; Warranties; Merchantability; Fitness; Disclaimers; Consumer Protection; Remedies; Anticipatory Repudiation; Third Party Rights.
3 Audio Cassettes
ISBN: 0-15-900291-5 $39.95

Secured Transactions
By Professor Michael I. Spak
Chicago Kent College of Law

TOPICS COVERED: Collateral; Inventory; Intangibles; Proceeds; Security Agreements; Attachment; After-Acquired Property; Perfection; Filing; Priorities; Purchase Money Security Interests; Fixtures; Rights Upon Default; Self-Help; Sale; Constitutional Issues.
3 Audio Cassettes
ISBN: 0-15-900292-3 $39.95

Torts
By Professor Richard J. Conviser
Chicago Kent College of Law

TOPICS COVERED: Essay Exam Techniques; Intentional Torts—Assault; Battery; False Imprisonment; Intentional Infliction Of Emotional Distress; Trespass To Land; Trespass To Chattels; Conversion; Defenses; Defamation—Libel; Slander; Defenses; First Amendment Concerns; Invasion Of Right Of Privacy; Misrepresentation; Negligence—Duty; Breach; Actual And Proximate Causation; Damages; Defenses; Strict Liability, Products Liability; Nuisance; General Tort Considerations.
4 Audio Cassettes
ISBN: 0-15-900185-4 $45.95

Wills & Trusts
By Professor Stanley M. Johanson
University of Texas School of Law

TOPICS COVERED: Attested Wills; Holographic Wills; Negligence; Revocation; Changes On Face Of Will; Lapsed Gifts; Negative Bequest Rule; Nonprobate Assets; Intestate Succession; Advancements; Elective Share; Will Contests; Capacity; Undue Influence; Creditors' Rights; Creation Of Trust; Revocable Trusts; Pourover Gifts; Charitable Trusts; Resulting Trusts; Constructive Trusts; Spendthrift Trusts; Self-Dealing; Prudent Investments; Trust Accounting; Termination; Powers Of Appointment.
4 Audio Cassettes
ISBN: 0-15-900294-X $45.95

All titles available at your law school bookstore
or call to order: 1-800-787-8717

Current & Upcoming Titles

   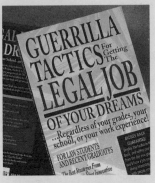

Gilbert's Pocket Size Law Dictionary
Gilbert

A dictionary is useless if you don't have it when you need it. If the only law dictionary you own is a thick, bulky one, you'll probably leave it at home most of the time — and if you need to know a definition while you're at school, you're out of luck!

With Gilbert's Pocket Size Law Dictionary, you'll have any definition you need, when you need it. Just pop Gilbert's dictionary into your pocket or purse, and you'll have over 3,500 legal terms and phrases at your fingertips. Gilbert's dictionary also includes a section on law school shorthand, common abbreviations, Latin and French legal terms, periodical abbreviations, and governmental abbreviations.

With Gilbert's Pocket Size Law Dictionary, you'll never be caught at a loss for words!

Available in your choice of 4 colors, $7.95 each:

- Black ISBN: 0-15-900255-9
- Blue   ISBN: 0-15-900257-5
- Burgundy ISBN: 0-15-900256-7
- Green ISBN: 0-15-900258-3

Limited Edition: Simulated Alligator Skin Cover
- Black ISBN: 0-15-900316-4 $7.95

What Lawyers Earn: Getting Paid What You're Worth
NALP

"What Lawyers Earn" provides up-to-date salary information from lawyers in many different positions, all over the country. Whether you're negotiating your own salary — or you're just curious! — "What Lawyers Earn" tells you how much lawyers really make.
ISBN: 0-15-900183-8 $17.95

The 100 Best Law Firms To Work For In America
Kimm Alayne Walton, J.D.

An insider's guide to the 100 best places to practice law, with anecdotes and a wealth of useful hiring information. Also included are special sections on the top law firms for women and the best public interest legal employers.
ISBN: 0-15-900180-3 $19.95

The 1996-1997 National Directory Of Legal Employers
NALP

The National Association for Law Placement has joined forces with Harcourt Brace to bring you everything you need to know about 1,000 of the nation's top legal employers, fully indexed for quick reference.
It includes:
- Over 22,000 job openings.
- The names, addresses and phone numbers of hiring partners.
- Listings of firms by state, size, kind and practice area.
- What starting salaries are for full time, part time, and summer associates, plus a detailed description of firm benefits.
- The number of employees by gender and race, as well as the number of employees with disabilities.
- A detailed narrative of each firm, plus much more!

The National Directory Of Legal Employers has been published for the past twenty years, but until now has only been available to law school career services directors, and hiring partners at large law firms. Through a joint venture between NALP (The National Association For Law Placement) and Harcourt Brace, this highly regarded, exciting title is now available for students.
ISBN: 0-15-900179-X $49.95

Proceed With Caution: A Diary Of The First Year At One Of America's Largest, Most Prestigious Law Firms
William Formon

In "Proceed With Caution" the author chronicles the trials and tribulations of being a new associate in a widely coveted dream job. He offers insights that only someone who has lived through the experience can offer. The unique diary format makes Proceed With Caution a highly readable and enjoyable journey.
ISBN: 0-15-900181-1 $17.95

The Eight Secrets Of Top Exam Performance In Law School
Charles Whitebread

Wouldn't it be great to know exactly what your professor's looking for on your exam? To find out everything that's expected of you, so that you don't waste your time doing anything other than maximizing your grades?

In his easy-to-read, refreshing style, nationally-recognized exam expert Professor Charles Whitebread will teach you the eight secrets that will add precious points to every exam answer you write. You'll learn the three keys to handling any essay exam question, and how to add points to your score by making time work for you, not against you. You'll learn flawless issue spotting, and discover how to organize your answer for maximum possible points. You'll find out how the hidden traps in "IRAC" trip up most students… but not you! You'll learn the techniques for digging up the exam questions your professor will ask, before your exam. You'll put your newly-learned skills to the test with sample exam questions, and you can measure your performance against model answers. And there's even a special section that helps you master the skills necessary to crush any exam, not just a typical essay exam — unusual exams like open book, take home, multiple choice, short answer, and policy questions.

"The Eight Secrets of Top Exam Performance in Law School" gives you all the tools you need to maximize your grades — quickly and easily!
ISBN: 0-15-900323-7 $9.95

Guerrilla Tactics for Getting the Legal Job of Your Dreams
Kimm Alayne Walton, J.D.

Whether you're looking for a summer clerkship or your first permanent job after school, this revolutionary new book is the key to getting the job of your dreams!

"Guerrilla Tactics for Getting the Legal Job of Your Dreams" leads you step-by-step through everything you need to do to nail down that perfect job! You'll learn hundreds of simple-to-use strategies that will get you exactly where you want to go.

"Guerrilla Tactics" features the best strategies from the country's most innovative law school career advisors. The strategies in "Guerrilla Tactics" are so powerful that it even comes with a guarantee: Follow the advice in the book, and within one year of graduation you'll have the job of your dreams… or your money back!

Pick up a copy of "Guerrilla Tactics" today…and you'll be on your way to the job of your dreams!
ISBN: 0-15-900317-2 $24.95

Checkerboard Careers: How Surprisingly Successful Attorneys Got To The Top, And How You Can Too!
NALP

Fast paced and easy to read, "Checkerboard Careers" is an inspirational guide, packed with profiles and monologues of how successful attorneys got to the top and how you can, too.
ISBN: 0-15-900182-X $17.95

FREE! Gilbert Law Summaries 1st Year Survival Manual

Available from your BAR/BRI Bar Review Representative or write:

Gilbert Law Summaries
176 West Adams, Ste. 2100
Chicago, Illinois 60603

Also available on our World Wide Web site at
http://www.gilbertlaw.com

To Order Any Of The Items In This Publications Catalog, Call Or Write:
Harcourt Brace Legal and Professional Publications, 176 West Adams, Ste. 2100, Chicago, Illinois 60603
1-800-787-8717